THE BEDFORD SERIES IN HISTORY AND CULTURE

Charles de Gaulle

A Brief Biography with Documents

Charles G. Cogan

Harvard University

BEDFORD BOOKS *of* ST. MARTIN'S PRESS

Boston   New York

For my wife, Susie, and my brother, Jack

For Bedford Books
President and Publisher: Charles H. Christensen
General Manager and Associate Publisher: Joan E. Feinberg
History Editor: Niels Aaboe
Developmental Editor: Jane Betz
Editorial Assistant: Richard Keaveny
Managing Editor: Elizabeth M. Schaaf
Production Editor: Anne Benaquist
Copyeditor: Susanna Brougham
Indexer: L. Pilar Wyman
Text Design: Claire Seng-Niemoeller
Cover Design: Richard Emery Design, Inc.
Cover Art: General Charles de Gaulle. © Dominique Berretty/Rapho.

Manufactured in the United States of America.

0 9 8 7 6

f e d c b a

For information, write: St. Martin's Press, Inc., 175 Fifth Avenue, New York, NY 10010
Editorial Offices: Bedford Books *of* St. Martin's Press, 75 Arlington Street, Boston, MA 02116

ISBN: 0–312–10790–0 (paperback)
      0–312–12804–5 (hardcover)

Acknowledgments

Pages 31, 52: Rights reserved, Charles de Gaulle Foundation.
Page 128: UPI/Bettman.

Foreword

The Bedford Series in History and Culture is designed so that readers can study the past as historians do.

The historian's first task is finding the evidence. Documents, letters, memoirs, interviews, pictures, movies, novels, or poems can provide facts and clues. Then the historian questions and compares the sources. There is more to do than in a courtroom, for hearsay evidence is welcome, and the historian is usually looking for answers beyond act and motive. Different views of an event may be as important as a single verdict. How a story is told may yield as much information as what it says.

Along the way the historian seeks help from other historians and perhaps from specialists in other disciplines. Finally, it is time to write, to decide on an interpretation and how to arrange the evidence for readers.

Each book in this series contains an important historical document or group of documents, each document a witness from the past and open to interpretation in different ways. The documents are combined with some element of historical narrative—an introduction or a biographical essay, for example—that provides students with an analysis of the primary source material and important background information about the world in which it was produced.

Each book in the series focuses on a specific topic within a specific historical period. Each provides a basis for lively thought and discussion about several aspects of the topic and the historian's role. Each is short enough (and inexpensive enough) to be a reasonable one-week assignment in a college course. Whether as classroom or personal reading, each book in the series provides firsthand experience of the challenge—and fun—of discovering, recreating, and interpreting the past.

Natalie Zemon Davis
Ernest R. May

Preface

I became steeped in the subject of Charles de Gaulle, that mythic figure often puzzling to Americans, during my long residence in France in the 1980s, when Jean Lacouture's prodigious and lyrical three-volume biography of the General was published. My interest continued into the 1990s at Harvard University under the other great authority on de Gaulle, Stanley Hoffmann, and in conferences and occasional presentations in France under the auspices of the Charles de Gaulle Foundation.

More than a quarter of a century has passed since General de Gaulle died, and perhaps it is an indication of how enduring his legacy has been that in Jacques Chirac we now have the first mainstream Gaullist president of France since de Gaulle's death. Georges Pompidou, who succeeded de Gaulle, was more business-oriented than the typical Gaullist; also he had had a falling out with de Gaulle toward the end of the latter's presidency. Pompidou had not been in the Resistance; he was not a Gaullist baron; and he had no sympathy for and little understanding of the General's social doctrine — participation.

Although Jacques Chirac is a political weathervane — a *girouette,* as the French would say — he does represent the mainstream of the Gaullist party, the Rally for the Republic (RPR), and the elections proved that. He also has in him a strain of Gaullist populism, mixed with the traditions of the Radical party in Corrèze, thus enabling him to develop a mass appeal that his rival, Edouard Balladur, could not match.

Although Chirac and Edouard Balladur were both brought up the ladder by Pompidou, Balladur inherited the "Pompidolien" mantle. And it was Chirac, exuding a sort of animal power, whom the French people chose to end the sepulchral presidency that François Mitterrand's second term had become.

We are faced today, to a degree greater than at any time since the early 1970s, with the Gaullist legacy. In structure and constitution, the French state and the French presidency as we know them today are made in de Gaulle's image; and however much some contest the monarchical quality of the present French state or, to use a more modern term, its democratic deficit, the French people like this system. De Gaulle's Fifth Republic represented a sharp break with the previous French tradition of parliamentary supremacy and its consequent weak governments. Although the power of Parliament may be adjusted slightly upward, there seems very little urge to go back to the previous system, precisely because it is synonymous with a weak France.

I have divided this work into two main parts and describe its plan in the Introduction. Since this is a biography with documents, the citations are heavily but by no means exclusively drawn from the corpus of de Gaulle's writings. These primary sources have included mainly *War Memoirs; Memoirs of Hope; Lettres, notes, et carnets (Letters, Notes, and Notebooks)*; and *Discours et messages (Speeches and Messages)* (which contain, among other things, de Gaulle's seminal press conferences). *War Memoirs* and *Memoirs of Hope* as well as de Gaulle's press conferences and major statements in the periods 1940–42 and May 1958–December 1964 have already been translated into English, and I have made use of these translations. All the other original materials that appear here have been translated by me. I considered *Lettres, notes, et carnets* to be particularly important, partly because they have not been translated into English and partly because most of the themes in de Gaulle's books are in these volumes. Part Two is a compilation of documents or extracts of documents, most of which were authored by de Gaulle.

As de Gaulle himself said, in reference to his *War Memoirs* (compiled on the basis of some three thousand documents selected for him by his secretary), "My major concern, throughout my long work, was to rely on this mass of supporting documents. I positively stuck to this (*Lettres, notes, et carnets,* vol. 7 [Paris: Plan, 1985], 221)."

In the appendices are suggestions for further reading (in English), including the two-volume translation of Lacouture's three-volume work. For those who read French, there are two invaluable new works: the proceedings of the de Gaulle conference in Paris of November 19–24, 1990 (*De Gaulle en son siècle* [Paris: Documentation Française/Plon, 1992]); and Alain Peyrefitte's *C'était de Gaulle* (Paris: Fayard, 1994), the first of three volumes containing Peyrefitte's edited notes on cabinet meetings and side conversations with de Gaulle beginning in 1962.

ACKNOWLEDGMENTS

First of all, I would like to express my appreciation to Professor Ernest May, co-advisory editor of the Bedford Series in History and Culture, for having suggested that I undertake this work; to Charles Christensen for having seconded the suggestion; and to the able and exigent editor assigned to develop the book, Jane Betz. I would also like to recognize and thank the meticulous and patient production editor Anne Benaquist, managing editor Elizabeth Schaaf, editorial assistant Richard Keaveny, and copyeditor Susanna Brougham.

Secondly, I would like to thank Professor Stanley Hoffmann for the generous attention and valuable advice he gave to me throughout. Without having benefited from his pedagogy over the last five years, I would not have been able to write this book. I would also like to thank those who have assisted me in the conception of this book, in particular Professor May and Professors Maurice Vaïsse and Georges-Henri Soutou.

Finally, I would like to thank Professor Samuel P. Huntington, who graciously accepted me as a visiting scholar at the John M. Olin Institute for Strategic Studies, Center for International Affairs, Harvard University. I have benefited greatly from association with him and his colleagues as well as with the brilliant dozen or so younger scholars whom he brings to the Institute each year.

Charles G. Cogan

Contents

PART ONE

A Short History of Gaullism

1

Introduction:
The Meaning of Gaullism

AN ASSESSMENT OF GAULLISM

The life of Charles de Gaulle (1890–1970) encompassed eighty years, which happened to include a considerable slice of French history; indeed, it was probably the most critical time span in that country's long existence. De Gaulle played a role in France's military and political life beginning in World War I, though he did not emerge as a world figure until World War II. Once he arrived on the public stage, de Gaulle was to far outlast those he regarded as his World War II "counterparts," Franklin D. Roosevelt and Winston Churchill,[1] as well as Adolf Hitler and Joseph Stalin. By the 1960s, when de Gaulle's influence in international affairs was at its peak, none of the figures from the wartime period was still exerting influence. Only China's Mao Tse-tung could come near to matching de Gaulle's seniority in the world arena.

Charles de Gaulle has now been dead for twenty-five years, and for this reason alone it is an apt moment for an assessment of de Gaulle and the loosely defined concept associated with him: "Gaullism." Also, the cold war and the uncertainty surrounding that struggle are gone, and the *nation,* so central in de Gaulle's thinking, has triumphed over ideology in central and eastern Europe, and indeed in Russia, as de Gaulle long ago predicted it would.

Though the future of Europe, which involves essentially the relationship between the major nations of Europe, is far from clear, it is possible now to arrive at an assessment of Gaullism: what it has meant to France, to Europe, and to the world at large. The structure of this assessment is denoted by the chapter titles, which are as follows:

The Meaning of Gaullism
De Gaulle and the Saving of the French Nation
De Gaulle and the Reordering of the French State
De Gaulle, Man of the Traditional European Concert
The Legacy

3

The chapter plan also follows a time line, though not a rigid one. Chapter 2 takes de Gaulle from his early youth through World War II and the "saving" of France. Since Gaullism would not have existed without the uniqueness of the individual himself, this first chapter discusses de Gaulle's personality, his background, and the influences upon him.

Chapter 3 deals with de Gaulle's reordering of the French state—he spelled out its main thrust in his Bayeux speech of June 1946—though the reforms that accomplished this goal had to wait until he returned to power in 1958 and carried out the constitutional referendums of that year and of 1962, setting in place the institutions of the Fifth Republic—a system that the historian François Furet has referred to as a "Monarchy of the Republic."[2]

Chapter 4, which discusses de Gaulle's foreign and security policy, focuses on the period 1962–69, which saw the throwing off of the Algerian incubus; the call for a strategic directory of the United States, Britain, and France; the attempt to place a state structure over the Common Market; the Franco-German alliance; the attempted détente with the Soviet Union; the recognition of China; and the withdrawal from the military structure of NATO (North Atlantic Treaty Organization). I describe de Gaulle as the man of the traditional European concert to denote his attachment to the system called by that name in the century preceding World War I. Gaullism is a focus on the primacy of Europe, existing within a system of sovereign states that maintain an equilibrium with one another while striving for closer cooperation. In this system, France would be at the center and, according to Gaullist hopes, in the lead.

In these chapters, the dynamic in de Gaulle's thought and action is emphasized: why and when he changed his views on colonialism and the Third World, on Germany, on the United States, on Russia, and so on. In general, de Gaulle's views evolved as a matter of his own reflection and his interaction with the events unfolding around him, in which he often played a major part. He both forced history and was forced by it.

Though de Gaulle's thinking about the polity of France and the relationship of nations evolved over time, it maintained a certain constancy and continuity; de Gaulle is one of the few statesmen of the postwar period whose thinking formed a strategic ensemble although, because ruse was very much a part of his statecraft, his intended policy was not always readily discernible. American policymakers especially found this to be true.

The administration of Franklin Roosevelt appeared to believe that de Gaulle's Free French movement represented little more than an exhibition of French cantankerousness after France's humiliating defeat of 1940. And Roosevelt was not alone in his distemper toward the General, as Max Ascoli, in his introduction to the papers of one of Roosevelt's key advisers, Adolph A. Berle, Jr., pointed out: "In their antagonism toward the Free French movement and Charles de Gaulle personally, the President, Berle, and most of official Washington went to the extreme. It took time for many authoritative people to get rid of the notion: there was no France."[3]

Had there not been a Franklin Roosevelt, and had the Roosevelt administration not been able to run an elitist foreign policy largely closed to the public, de Gaulle might later have had a different view of the United States and NATO. Indeed, the whole history of Franco-American relations from World War II to the present might have lost some of its contentiousness. Clearly, it is important to understand de Gaulle in order to plumb the foundations of French-American misunderstandings, which stem mainly from the complexes that arose during World War II.

It was de Gaulle's self-appointed mission to prove that there *was* a France. He could not be dismissed as easily as Franklin Roosevelt wanted ("It is the proper time to . . . eliminate the Jeanne d'Arc complex and return to realism," wrote Roosevelt to Churchill in December 1943.)[4] And to make his point stick, de Gaulle would insist that no one who was a part of the collapsed and surrendering France of 1940 would be associated with *his* France. Whether he did this to save the nation's honor, to live up to his own self-image as a risk-taker, or, as he once tossed off to the journalist Roger Stephane,[5] out of a sense of political ambition, we will never know fully.

Quite apart from de Gaulle's prodigious effort, initially employing only a handful of followers, to lift France from the abyss of defeat in 1940 to a place at the table of the conquerors in 1945, there is the issue of whether his assertion of the interests and traditions of the nation-state (shown in his insistence on not calling Russia anything but that name)[6] helped speed the end of the era of ideology by his very example. One may even ask how much his defiant nationalism and his challenge to the superpowers has influenced the behavior of the "new authoritarians" of the post–cold war era—leaders like Slobodan Milosevic, Serbia's nationalistic president, who have sprung up from the remains of the Soviet empire.

Even if Gaullism was an epiphenomenon, sublimating France's shocking and sudden defeat of 1940, there is no denying the phenomenon of the man himself. Indeed, as a charismatic and mystical leader, de Gaulle has no equivalent in his time other than Adolf Hitler, described, from an opposite pole of Christian morality, in the General's *War Memoirs:*

For Moloch, all things are justified. Moreover, if Hitler was strong, he was no less cunning. He knew how to entice, and how to caress. Germany, profoundly seduced, followed her Fuehrer ecstatically. Until the very end she was to serve him slavishly, with greater exertions than any people has ever furnished any leader.[7]

But Hitler, of course, had his weaknesses as a leader, as de Gaulle also pointed out:

Hitler was to encounter the human obstacle, the one that cannot be surmounted. He based his colossal plan on the strength he attributed to man's baseness. Yet men are made of souls as much as of clay. To behave as if everyone else will never have any courage is to venture too far.[8]

The following view of de Gaulle by a defeated Germany would seem like nothing so much as a prescient call for a postwar Franco-German entente had it not come from the pen of Heinrich Himmler, Hitler's Gestapo chief, in an unofficial memorandum to de Gaulle transmitted through Swedish Red Cross channels as the war was ending:

Agreed! You have won. Considering where you started from, one bows low indeed to you, General de Gaulle. . . . But now what will you do? Rely on Americans and the British? They will deal with you as a satellite, and you will lose all the honor you have won. Ally yourself with the Soviets? They will restore France to their laws and liquidate you. . . . Actually the only road that can lead your people to greatness and to independence is that of an entente with a defeated Germany. Proclaim it at once![9]

Considering where de Gaulle had started from — alone in England as the French surrendered in 1940 — and where he ended — as the incarnation of a new and unbowed France suddenly appearing as one of the five veto-wielding powers on the United Nations Security Council in 1945, we can indeed ask where else could be found such a genius of representation or, as Henry Kissinger put it, such an "illusionist":

For the greater part of his career [de Gaulle] has had to be an illusionist. In the face of all evidence to the contrary, he has striven to restore France's greatness by his passionate belief in it.[10]

And where else could be found a man for whom history was so palpable it was not only to be experienced but to be recreated?

THE GAULLIST AGENDA

According to de Gaulle, the history of France was one of oscillation between periods of dissension, which had brought on national tragedies, and periods of unity, when the state was strong and French *grandeur* was manifest: "All our history is the alternation between the immense sorrows of a disorganized people and the rich grandeurs of a free nation rallied under the aegis of a strong state."[11]

De Gaulle believed, as had others before him, that this tendency toward disunity was in the contentious and unstable nature of the people themselves. France, said de Gaulle, was "a country which, since the Gauls, has been periodically the stage for those 'sudden and unexpected upheavals' which astonished Caesar."[12] The systemic focus of this disunity was the French parliamentary system. De Gaulle had grown up under this system, created by the formation of the Third Republic in 1875. The Third Republic represented the apotheosis of French parliamentary supremacy in modern times. The chief of state was a largely ceremonial position. Not only was there no authority in the executive to dismiss the National Assembly,[13] the assembly could turn out the government in a vote of no confidence. This meant, as de Gaulle put it, a "perpetually unstable regime [with] successive ministerial crises."[14]

Unity

To de Gaulle, the system of the Third Republic was a prescription for parliamentary jockeying among special interests and executive inaction and weakness. At only one period in de Gaulle's early life had "unity" been miraculously imposed in France, and this was in the crucible of World War I: It was the silent pact of the "sacred union," which was associated with Raymond Poincaré (who had become president of France in 1913) and which began, in symbolic and real terms, on Mobilization Day, August 2, 1914. It was a day de Gaulle described as "animated . . . with the common certainty that France was in the greatest possible danger and with the unanimous will to save her forever."[15]

Under this impulse of unity and at critical moments during the war, key individuals intervened to save France from military disaster: Marshal Joseph Joffre in 1914, Marshal Ferdinand Foch in 1917, and Prime Minister Georges Clemenceau in 1917–19. Fifty years after the Battle of Verdun (1915–16), de Gaulle was to declare the ossuary at Douaumont a "monument of national union"; the battle had proved that the French, when they submitted themselves to the "laws of cohesion," were capable of exemplary tenacity.[16]

However, in 1919, with the war over, Clemenceau was turned out by the Parliament. A period of weak regimes followed, as twenty-seven cabinets succeeded one another in the space of twenty years and while, as de Gaulle put it, "disaster was lurking on the horizon without anyone doing anything to prevent it." This he described as the "regime of the parties," which meant that "naturally we were beaten, crushed in 1940. Nothing had been prepared, we were divided by the parties, we didn't have the necessary arms."[17]

Though out of political prudence de Gaulle rarely said so outright, the "regime of the parties" was synonymous with the Parliament: "I considered it necessary for the government not to derive from the parliament, *in other words the parties,* but over and above them, from a leader directly mandated by the nation as a whole and empowered to choose, to decide, and to act"[18] (italics added).

When he faced France's military disaster in 1940, de Gaulle, whether consciously or not, sought to replicate the World War I scenario in which a leader rose from the crowd and invoked French unity. It was the only response to such a challenge that he had known of or heard about at close hand. And yet, though they imposed themselves with great verve and energy, the leaders in World War I already held a large measure of authority; de Gaulle did not. That made de Gaulle unique, adventurous, and, most pertinent, rebellious. Jean Lacouture entitled the first volume of his biography of de Gaulle *The Rebel.*[19]

To emerge as a leader, de Gaulle took on the seemingly impossible task of delegitimizing the Vichy government. It was not, however, a parliamentary government: During the period 1940–45, the French Parliament was absent from the fray. It had, in effect, been disbanded by the Pétain regime to whom it had turned over power in July 1940. Said de Gaulle: "In fact, during five years, the greatest drama of our history took place without the regime [of the parties] having taken the least part in it!"[20]

By November 1943, de Gaulle had emerged as the leader of France. As he saw the war entering its climactic year,[21] he inaugurated at Algiers the Consultative Assembly of the Resistance in order that political elements not tainted by association with Vichy could find expression in anticipation of the end of hostilities. But this body was strictly consultative, as de Gaulle made bluntly clear: "Until the future general elections, I am responsible for the nation's fate to the nation and only to the nation."[22]

The wartime situation was indeed unique and ephemeral, as de Gaulle himself observed in his *War Memoirs*, with a touch of nostalgia for France's monarchical past:

> I had every apparent justification for prolonging the sort of monarchy which I had recently assumed and which the general consent had subsequently confirmed. But the French people was itself and not any other; if it did not desire such a regime, nothing could impose it. To what upheavals would I condemn France by claiming to impose my absolute authority. . . . I had no desire to maintain the momentary dictatorship which I had exercised in the course of the storm.[23]

At the war's end in 1945, the return of the political parties and the election of a new National Assembly became inevitable. Many delegates to the Consultative Assembly envisioned a postwar system in which the chief of state would be a figurehead, the upper house (the Senate) would be abolished, and all powers would be invested in what had been the lower house, the Chamber of Deputies. De Gaulle, however, saw this model of a "single and sovereign assembly" as an avatar of the Convention of the French Revolution. Such an assembly, though it would "spare itself the guillotine," would find "no obstacle to its energies" because all public power would be concentrated in it.[24]

In practice, parliamentary supremacy was, in de Gaulle's view, a prescription for the inconsistency and confusion that had brought disaster to France. "The fundamental principle of the French parliamentary regime," said de Gaulle, was this: "Let no head show above the trenches of democracy."[25] Churchill later was to capture the saliency of this system when he used the phrase "tyrannical weakness" to describe the French Parliament.[26]

De Gaulle saw his contrasting approach as a formula for effective government, in which the latter would not be at the mercy of Parliament. Above the whole system would be a national arbiter who would bring order to the ensemble:

> As I saw it, it was essential that the powers be separated so that there would be, respectively and effectively, a government, a Parliament, and a judiciary. It was essential that the chief of state, by the method of his election, by his rank, his powers, be in a position to fulfill the function of national arbiter. It was essential that the people be able to associate themselves directly, by means of a referendum, with the crucial decisions that would determine its destiny.[27]

Not only the Convention, which had brought on the Terror (1792–94), but the French Revolution itself can be considered a symbol of French dis-

unity. As the historian Fabrice Bouthillon[28] has pointed out, the third
estate, in declaring itself a constituent assembly, deprived the leading
elements of the ancien régime—the clergy, the nobility, and the monarchy, bound in a sort of mystical union with the French people—of their
special status in French society. Moreover, this exercise in starting
anew—the so-called tabula rasa—in effect repudiated fourteen centuries
of French history. This approach was utterly unacceptable to de Gaulle,
for whom French history appears to have begun with Clovis, the first
Merovingian king (471–511), at the moment of his conversion to Christianity with his baptism at Reims. In a revealing passage on the refusal of the
legitimist (Bourbon) heir to return to the throne of France in 1873 because
of a quarrel over the use of the revolutionary or royalist flag, de Gaulle
wrote:

> With much clarity and talent, *The Great Refusal of the Count of Cham-
> bord* recounts and comments upon a capital and sad event in our history.
> Capital because it wrote an end to everything our country had in terms of
> institutions. Sad, like everything signifying that that which was will never
> be again.[29]

Unity and Aggrandizement

This does not mean that de Gaulle viewed the French Revolution with a
wholly negative eye, though he does seem to associate it with the general
decline of French grandeur that began in the eighteenth century. After he
had returned in the late 1950s to head the French state again, he noted this
decline with some mitigated satisfaction: "In spite of all she had lost over
the past two centuries in terms of relative power and wealth, [France had]
a leading international role which suited her genius."[30]

The past two centuries referred to by de Gaulle began around the time
of the Treaty of Paris in 1763. This treaty had ended the Seven Years' War
(known in the United States as the French and Indian War), which turned
out poorly for France vis-à-vis both Prussia and Britain. Other references in
de Gaulle's work, as Fabrice Bouthillon has pointed out,[31] date France's
period of troubles from the French Revolution itself. At Lille in 1947,
de Gaulle spoke of the "one hundred and fifty years of terrible wars and fierce
internal struggles [which] had gravely weakened [France]."[32] In Paris in 1951,
he spoke of France's "one hundred and fifty years of ordeals."[33]

But the concept of revolution appealed to de Gaulle because it connoted
a will to break up a frozen society. On more than one occasion during
World War II, de Gaulle referred to the Gaullist movement as "revolutionary." In a memorable speech in London on April 1, 1942, de Gaulle

declared that one should not fail "to recognize one thing which dominates the whole French question today—the fact of revolution. For France, betrayed by her ruling and privileged classes, has embarked on the greatest revolution in all her history."[34]

Furthermore, de Gaulle felt that some periods during the French Revolution were positive: That is, they produced unity and, as a consequence, the enhancement or aggrandizement of France. In the same speech in London referred to previously, de Gaulle contrasted unfavorably the generalship of the ancien régime with that of the Revolution: "A revolutionary France still preferred to win the war with General Hoche rather than lose it with Marshal de Soubise."[35] This remark pointed up the fact that few figures from the French establishment had joined the Free French movement in London. "People . . . are surprised," said de Gaulle, "at not finding among us outworn politicians, sleepy academicians, intrigue-hardened businessmen, and promotion-weary generals."[36]

De Gaulle also measured the Napoleonic period along the same scale of France's position in the world. Napoléon, before his demented ambition brought him down, reached the second great apogee of French aggrandizement. Referring to the time when it was "[France's] turn to be a world giant,"[37] de Gaulle also made specific mention of "the nation-giant [which France] was at the time of Louis XIV and Napoléon."[38] But after the final defeat of Napoléon in 1815, France began to enter a period of sharp decline: "Our old ambitions of European hegemony and natural frontiers were countered by the treaties of 1815 and, after 1870, by the unity and strength of a threatening Germany."[39]

France's inability to keep its "natural frontiers" was not only a source of historical regret for de Gaulle but also a matter of continued dissatisfaction. He described France as "mutilated of the territories nature intended her to have" and "separated from a third of the population springing from her stock."[40]

The abyss, of course, was reached in June 1940. "This nation," said de Gaulle, "which had figured among the first for so many centuries . . . had collapsed in an incredible disaster."[41] Toward the end of World War II, de Gaulle addressed the Consultative Assembly of the Resistance in the following terms:

> Perhaps France is now confronting one of those moments in history when a people is offered a destiny great in proportion to the gravity of its ordeal. But we cannot uphold our rights nor accomplish our duties if we forgo power itself. . . . We must reinstate the power of France. This, henceforth, is our great cause.[42]

And indeed it was. If there was one continuous thread in de Gaulle's actions after he reached the political and decision-making level, it was the aggrandizement of France. Most of the time he did this aggrandizing with a measured and often masked consistency. Sometimes he overreached himself, perhaps reacting to the emotions of the moment, as in his cry "Long live Rhineland France" in a speech at Strasbourg on October 5, 1945,[43] and as in his more famous "Long live free Quebec" speech on July 24, 1967, from the balcony of the town hall in Montreal.[44]

The theme of the aggrandizement of France was combined in the Gaullist context with a larger theme—that of the concert of European nations. De Gaulle spoke with genuine feeling of the "higher rationality of Europe" in arguing against the destruction of Germany after World War II.[45] Indeed, touring that war-ravaged country, he found that the sight of towns virtually bereft of adult males tugged at his heart as a European.[46] Had he been allowed to attend the wartime conferences, he recorded, "I would have defended the equilibrium of Europe."[47] Yalta was unacceptable to de Gaulle in the following sense: "Indeed I could not accept that the fate of Europe was in fact decided without Europe."[48] For de Gaulle, Europe essentially meant continental Western Europe, a point that will be explored further in Chapter 4.

But within this higher purpose of a strengthened European concert of nations was always the notion, sometimes hidden, that France, in balancing within this European equilibrium, should increase its power vis-à-vis the others. This aim is understandable, considering that France started out from a position of extreme weakness with its European counterparts: crushed by Germany in 1940, at times mercilessly harassed by Britain in the reaches of the French Empire during World War II, and facing at the end of the war the troops of its former ally Russia—the new threat to Western European civilization and "the most terribly imperialist and colonialist power ever known"[49]—at a distance of only three hundred miles from the French border.[50]

The work of aggrandizement can be seen, in this light, as the restoration of some of the former grandeur of France. De Gaulle's view of history was not merely better schooled than others', it was rooted in a way that Americans might find difficult to appreciate; in contrast to them, the French had been living on the same soil for fourteen centuries. That de Gaulle would take exception to the fact that Woodrow Wilson, in seeking a compromise peace in 1916, did not demand the return of Alsace-Lorraine to France[51] is indicative of de Gaulle's long historical reach, which left his interlocutors baffled but also at a disadvantage. For de Gaulle, the warning flag raised at Sadowa, when the Prussians defeated the Austrians in 1866, seemed equally as present in his mind as Hitler's takeover of the Rhineland seventy years later—both events elicited abject French inaction. Wrote de Gaulle: "With how much blood and tears did we pay for the error of the Second Empire in letting Sadowa happen without moving the army to the Rhine?"[52]

Just as de Gaulle would say, concerning his departure from government in 1946, that "with the General vanished something primordial, permanent, and necessary which he incarnated in history,"[53] so one can say that there was something primordial about the whole de Gaulle experience, as though he had suddenly arisen on June 18, 1940, from the back pages of history, representing ancient Gaul ("I, General de Gaulle, now in London, call on all French officers and men . . .")[54], although his name, suggests Jean Lacouture, comes from the Flemish and means "wall" or "rampart."[55]

NOTES

[1] And it was as counterparts that de Gaulle indeed regarded them: He exercised the same powers, he noted, as "Roosevelt, Churchill, and Stalin exercised, in proportion, of course, to the relative importance of their means and ours." Charles de Gaulle, *The Complete War Memoirs of Charles de Gaulle,* vol. 2, *Unity, 1942–1944,* trans. Richard Howard (New York: Simon and Schuster, 1964), 601 (all volumes hereafter cited as *WM*).

[2] Except as otherwise noted, the statements of Prof. Furet cited in this book are from two lectures (on Jan. 24 and 31, 1989), which were part of a seminar entitled The Revolution of 1789 and Us, organized by the Fondation Saint-Simon in Paris, Jan. 17–Mar. 21, 1989.

[3] B. B. Berle and T. B. Jacobs, eds., *Navigating the Rapids, 1918–1971* (New York: Harcourt Brace Jovanovich, 1973), xxvi (from the papers of Adolph A. Berle).

[4] Roosevelt was reacting negatively to the arrest by the French National Committee of several high-ranking Vichyite officers in North Africa. Roosevelt to Churchill, Dec. 22, 1943; *From War to Freedom,* No. 5457, Franklin D. Roosevelt Presidential Library.

[5] "I was politically ambitious, and there was a meeting of circumstance and ambition." Roger Stéphane, *Tout est bien* (Paris: Quai Voltaire, 1989), 37.

[6] In the first visit of a Soviet chief of state to France, that of Nikita Khrushchev in March 1960, de Gaulle addressed a toast to him that included the following words: ". . . in the situation in which the world finds itself today, Russia and France need to see each other. I said Russia and France. It is really the two of them we are talking about." Charles de Gaulle, *Discours et messages,* vol. 3, *Avec le renouveau, Mai 1958–Juillet 1962* (Paris: Plon, 1970), 173 (all volumes hereafter cited as *DM*).

After the visit, de Gaulle was left with the impression that "something of profound importance had occurred in the time-honored relationship between Russia and France." Charles de Gaulle, "Renewal, 1958–1962," pt. 1 of *Memoirs of Hope: Renewal and Endeavor,* trans. Terence Kilmartin (New York: Simon and Schuster, 1971), 234 (hereafter cited as *MH*).

[7] Moloch, a Semitic god to whom children were sacrificed, is a biblical characterization of evil. *WM,* vol. 3, *Salvation, 1944–1946,* 866.

[8] Ibid., 866.

[9] Ibid., 868.

[10] Henry A. Kissinger, *The Troubled Partnership* (New York: McGraw-Hill, 1965), 44.

[11] From the speech at Bayeux, June 16, 1946. The text of this speech, with minor excisions, is in Part Two, The Documents. *DM*, vol. 2, *Dans l'attente, Février 1946–Avril 1958* (Paris: Omnibus/Plon, 1993), 314. (In this study, the abbreviation *DM-OP* will indicate when the Omnibus/Plon edition is used. Alone, *DM* signifies the earlier Plon edition.)

[12] "Endeavor, 1962–   ," pt. 2 of *MH*, 305.

[13] "I am convinced that one of the weaknesses of the Third Republic . . . was that in fact, in the Constitution of 1875, the right of dissolution did not exist." *DM-OP*, vol. 2, 430.

[14] Ibid.

[15] *DM-OP*, vol. 4, *Pour l'effort, Août 1962–Décembre 1965*, 894.

[16] *DM-OP*, vol. 5, *Vers le terme, Janvier 1966–Avril 1969*, 1008.

[17] *DM-OP*, vol. 4, 974–75.

[18] *MH*, pt. 1, 6.

[19] Jean Lacouture, *De Gaulle*, vol. 1, *Le rebelle* (Paris: Seuil, 1984) (all volumes hereafter cited as *JLDG*).

[20] *DM-OP*, vol. 2, 484.

[21] *WM*, vol. 2, 471.

[22] *WM*, vol. 3, *Salvation, 1944–1946*, 788.

[23] Ibid., 938–39.

[24] Ibid., 480.

[25] Ibid., 962.

[26] Churchill to Eisenhower, Dec. 7, 1954; *Documents of DDE-President*, Dwight D. Eisenhower Presidential Library.

[27] *WM*, vol. 3, 480.

[28] "Les schèmes qu'on abat," *Commentaire*, no. 64 (Winter 1993–94): 781–87. (Second in a two-part article, the first of which was in *Commentaire*, no. 63 [Fall, 1993]).

[29] Charles de Gaulle, *Lettres, notes, et carnets*, vol. 12 (Paris: Plon, 1987), 145 (all volumes hereafter cited as *LNC*) (letter to the book's author, René de la Croix, duc de Castries, July 7, 1970). The count, a descendant of the Bourbon monarchs of the ancien régime and therefore a so-called legitimist, insisted on the use of the white flag, symbol of France's "divine right" monarchy rather than the revolutionary tricolor. His demand was rejected by the rival monarchical faction, the Orléanists, who as a result became the main pretenders to the throne of France.

[30] *MH*, pt. 1, 166.

[31] See note 28.

[32] *DM-OP*, vol. 2, 359.

[33] Speech of Sept. 12, 1951. *DM*, vol. 2, 461.

[34] Sheila Mathieu and W. G. Corp, trans., *The Speeches of General de Gaulle*, vol. 2 (London: Oxford University Press, 1943), 20 (all volumes hereafter cited as *SCDG*). For large extracts from this speech, see Part Two, The Documents.

[35] Ibid. Charles de Rohan, prince de Soubise, was an incompetent French general beaten by the Prussians at the Battle of Rossbach in 1757. Lazare Hoche, son of a groom in the king's stables, was one of the great generals of the revolutionary period, carrying on successful campaigns against the Prussians and the Austrians. He was also, with his "columns of death," the man largely responsible for suppressing the revolt of the Catholic nobility and peasants in the Vendée (1793–95).

[36] Ibid.

[37] *DM-OP*, vol. 4, 843.

[38] Ibid., 934.

[39] *Major Addresses, Statements, and Press Conferences of General Charles de Gaulle, May 19, 1958–January 31, 1964* (New York: French Embassy Press and Information Division, 1964), 116.

[40] Since de Gaulle was describing the situation at the end of World War II, presumably he was referring to Belgian Wallonia, the French-speaking part of Switzerland, and a few francophone pockets inside the Italian frontier. The "natural frontiers" refer primarily to the Rhine River. *WM,* vol. 3, 936.

[41] Ibid., 716.

[42] Ibid., 731–32.

[43] *DM,* vol. 1, *Pendant la guerre, Juin 1940–Janvier 1946,* 623.

[44] *DM-OP,* vol. 5, 1051–52.

[45] *WM,* vol. 3, 847.

[46] Ibid., 903.

[47] Ibid., 898.

[48] *DM-OP,* vol. 5, 1110.

[49] Address to the nation, Nov. 4, 1960. *DM-OP,* vol. 3, 707.

[50] As a general point of reference, the distance between Strasbourg and Berlin is 570 kilometers (356 miles).

[51] *WM,* vol. 3, 762.

[52] *WM,* vol. 1, *The Call to Honour, 1940–1942,* trans. Jonathan Griffin, 10. Sadowa was the decisive battle of the Austro-Prussian War, a war the French had not expected the Austrians to lose. The Rhineland was demilitarized by the Treaty of Versailles in 1919; and Hitler, in sending troops into it in Mar. 1936, was violating the treaty.

[53] *WM,* vol. 3, 995.

[54] *SCDG,* vol. 1, *June 18, 1940–December 31, 1941,* 1. For the full text of the June 18, 1940, broadcast, which was heard by few people and of which no recording was made, see Part Two, The Documents.

The famous couplet "France has lost a battle! But France has not lost the war!" was not part of this speech. De Gaulle had it posted on the walls of London in July 1940 as part of a proclamation. *DM,* vol. 1, 19.

[55] *JLDG,* vol. 1, 10. Fabrice Bouthillon has speculated on the impact that would have come from a similar appeal from another senior French officer of the period, Col. Revers, whose name means "defeat." See note 28.

2

De Gaulle and the Saving
of the French Nation,
1890–1946

*For all the satisfaction of its [World War II's] denouement, it had
left—and forever!—a secret grief in the depths of the national con-
science.*[1]   —*Charles de Gaulle*

EARLY LIFE

Charles de Gaulle was a child of the revanchist (revenge) period in France.
As he was to write himself in 1913, "Chauvinism, if it is an excess, is [still]
worth a hundred, a thousand times more than a patriotism that reasons too
often."[2] De Gaulle was born in Paris in 1890, twenty years after the shock
of the Franco-Prussian War. Unlike in 1815, when the "mastodon of
Europe"[3] was brought down by a coalition of virtually all the major European nations, France in 1870 was humbled by the sole power of Prussia.
Worse, France's provinces of Alsace and Lorraine, whose various parts
had been either under French control or subject to French influence for
more than two hundred years, were taken from it. In 1879 they were
declared an integral part of Germany. France's "lost provinces" were
colored in black on French maps, and the city of Strasbourg in Alsace
became a particular symbol of French determination to right the perceived
wrong. (Strasbourg was to retain its potency years afterwards. On March
1, 1941, Colonel Leclerc,[4] who had just led the first significant Free
French engagement of the war, the capture of Koufra, Libya, from the
Italians, vowed not to lay down his arms until the French flag flew again
over the cathedral of Strasbourg. Later during World War II, arguing
Strasbourg's significance for the French nation, Charles de Gaulle with
great difficulty persuaded the Allied Command not to evacuate the city
during the Battle of the Bulge.)
     By the end of the nineteenth century, France's desire for revenge had

only grown stronger. Its drive into North and West Africa, to match the British thrust for empire on the continent, was still not enough compensation for the loss of the two provinces. The only means for revenge had to be through the French army. And so the young Charles de Gaulle thought more and more of a military career. In 1904, at the age of fourteen, he announced his intentions to his parents at the dinner table: "My mind is made up—I am going to prepare for St. Cyr. I want to be an officer."[5]

The second brother in a family of four brothers and one sister, Charles was the tallest of all, at six feet five inches. In games as a child, Charles had been the most pugnacious of the brothers, always demanding to play the role of king of France.[6]

In 1905, as a fifteen-year-old student at the College (junior high school) of the Immaculate Conception in Paris, de Gaulle wrote a fictional work entitled "The German Campaign." In this extremely detailed scenario, General de Gaulle, at the head of one of two French armies, successfully repels a German invasion of France in 1930.[7] The opening sentence, as if placing France back into its true Napoleonic grandeur, reads: "In 1930, Europe, irritated with the government's ill will and insolent actions, declared war on France."[8] As with everything that de Gaulle was to write subsequently on military subjects, this precocious effort revealed an impressive knowledge of history, terrain, and tactics.

The de Gaulle family had a tradition of service to the French state. In the eighteenth century, the family had acceded to the position of *noblesse de robe*—that is, they were considered a sort of nobility by virtue of posts occupied in service to the monarchy, but not by heredity. Charles de Gaulle's great-grandfather, Jean-Baptiste Philippe de Gaulle, was a king's prosecutor who was jailed during the French Revolution and released on the day the Terror ended (July 27, 1794). However, despite the *de* in de Gaulle's name, his was not a French noble family by blood.

At the age of twenty-two, Charles de Gaulle's father, Henri, was headed for studies at the prestigious École Polytechnique but had to renounce this possibility because of the sudden death of his father. This tragedy left the family with meager financial resources, and Henri was needed to help in the care of his paralyzed second brother. He became a secondary school history teacher. Charles de Gaulle said he had learned history at his father's knee. The biographer Pierre Galante describes de Gaulle as having inherited his ardent nature from his mother (one-half Irish from an Australian mother) and his mental conditioning from his father.[9]

De Gaulle's father was a sort of hybrid, and this is reflected in de Gaulle's later political positions. A closet if not an outright monarchist, Henri de Gaulle nevertheless fell on the other side of the great divide represented by the Dreyfus affair at the turn of the century. Henri de Gaulle was a supporter of Alfred Dreyfus, the Alsatian Jew unjustly (as it gradually became known) accused of spying for Germany against France. Though a strong Catholic, Henri did not go along with the prevailing Catholic, monarchist, and military sentiment against Dreyfus.

The hybrid image is also revealed in the following event: When a Jesuit lycée (high school) in Paris was inspected as a result of an anticlerical ordinance passed in 1905, the authorities were surprised to find a lay assistant principal on its premises—Henri de Gaulle. (To circumvent this wave of republican anticlericalism, Charles de Gaulle was sent to continue his Jesuit education for one year in Belgium.)

As a young man, Henri de Gaulle had seen military service during the Franco-Prussian War and was wounded during the Germans' siege of Paris.[10] Charles, in a letter to his father in the summer of 1918, wrote of "the never-forgotten example that you gave in advance to your sons at the beginning of your life, fighting with honor the same enemy whom today they are fighting."[11] Finally, in 1919, the aspirations of the de Gaulle family were fulfilled. De Gaulle wrote, "The song of the Gallic rooster has finally made the sun of revenge burst forth."[12]

Charles de Gaulle's ascension, fueled by an extraordinary ambition, appears not to have been undertaken out of disappointment with his father, to whom he always referred in terms of respect. It seemed rather to be a compensation to his father, who had taught him a great deal yet had not risen to a position of distinction. In this, Charles de Gaulle undertook to transcend his own origins. In the French tradition, he sought to create his own elite; later he described the Gaullist movement as "an elite begun from nothing."[13] It was a sort of sudden transcendence, a rather rare phenomenon in France's hierarchical society, in which a new elite springs up when an old one has failed. Napoléon had done it. Charles de Gaulle would do it too.

MILITARY CAREER

At the French military academy of St. Cyr, which he entered at the age of nineteen, de Gaulle was regarded as an aloof loner with an air of superiority.[14] De Gaulle was nourished on ambitions and dreams: "For he who is a dreamer, the hours are gray," he would write later.[15]

De Gaulle would also write later on the practice of leadership: "It is necessary for a great leader to have less virtue than grandeur."[16] Another way of putting it, as de Gaulle did with his usual excessive solemnity, was that

> in the prestige that a leader should inspire, he should impart some degree of fear. For the subordinates, a leader should not be a man like them. . . . The best advice one can give is to be cold in the exercise of authority. The prestige of the leader, the fear he inspires, are powerfully increased by an impassive attitude, precisely because it gives the impression naturally of an impassivity in the heart, which is the privilege of the gods.[17]

In a similar vein, de Gaulle characterized "the error of certain officers (especially younger officers), who think they have to sacrifice everything to 'persuasion,' through reasoning and discussion, while they should persuade by authority."[18]

Charles de Gaulle wrote of the revolutionary general Lazare Hoche in words he might as well have used to describe himself: "Matured ahead of his age by the habit of command, his impetuous spirit and his brilliant sense of words gave way to a cold dignity and laconic language."[19] In his book *The Edge of the Sword* (1932), de Gaulle wrote that "certain men have, one might almost say from birth, the quality of exuding authority, as though it were a liquid, though it is impossible to say precisely of what it consists. Even those who come under its influence feel surprised by their own reactions to it."[20]

Charles de Gaulle entered World War I as a captain. His courage seems never to have been called into question. His chagrin was so great at being captured, a year and a half into the war, that one tends to forget that he had seen extensive combat action until that moment. From the engagement that resulted in his capture, de Gaulle was decorated with the Legion of Honor; on July 23, 1919, Marshal Philippe Pétain signed the following citation, written by de Gaulle's regimental commander, Colonel Emile Boud'hors:

> On March 2, 1916, at Douaumont, under an incredible bombardment, as the enemy broke through the line and attacked his company from all sides, [he] organized, after a ferocious hand-to-hand combat, a core of resistance where all fought until their ammunition was gone, their rifles broken, and the unarmed defenders fell. Although gravely wounded by a bayonet thrust, [he] continued to be the soul of the defense, until he fell unconscious under the effect of gas. Two earlier wounds, two citations.[21]

Without elaborating, de Gaulle admitted that there was some exaggeration in the citation (gas was not used in the engagement, and the bayonet wound was not critical). But, de Gaulle added in a letter to Colonel Boud'hors, "It is nevertheless precious to me, because I see in it above all a testimony of your esteem toward me."[22] De Gaulle's own description of the moment of his capture, when he and a party of four or five came across a group of Germans, was as follows:

> One [of the Boches] made a bayonet thrust at me that went through my card-holder and wounded me in the thigh. . . . Several seconds later, a grenade that literally exploded under my nose stunned me. I was on the ground for a moment. The Boches, seeing I was wounded, made me go back to the place I had come from and where they were [now] installed.[23]

Forced to sit out the war from March 1916 on, de Gaulle immediately set about planning to escape. The account of his seven escapes, all of which ended in falling again into the hands of the Germans, as though the physical act of the escape was the main point of the exercise, is related in a lengthy citation he wrote himself as a preliminary to his being awarded the Medal of the Escaped Prisoners.[24]

During his time in prison, de Gaulle perfected his German (as a child of the revanchist period, his second language naturally was German) and gave lectures on history and strategy to his fellow prisoners. In 1924, de Gaulle published his first book. Entitled *La discorde chez l'ennemi (The Enemy's Dissensions)*, it was a work he had largely pondered while in German captivity. The book analyzes why Germany lost World War I.

The searing experience of World War I did not destroy in de Gaulle, as it did in some others, the tendency toward the glorification of war. Before the war, in 1913, he had written, "Certainly war is an evil, and I am the first to agree, but it is a necessary evil."[25] In 1917, while in German captivity, de Gaulle reflected that the war and its "crushing character" made "many now want to refuse to war the somber beauty that was habitually accorded to it. They are wrong. Does this war demand less than other wars? . . . In any event, this war is thus; one must take it as it is and conquer it."[26] In 1927 he would write, "The test of war imposes on those who undertake it a degree of personal sacrifice that is beyond expression."[27]

After the war, de Gaulle was assigned to Poland, where he helped train officers of the Polish army. He was eager for action and wrote his mother from prison on September 1, 1918: "To return to France and be holed up in some office is absolutely revolting to me."[28] In Poland, he displayed an astonishing knowledge of Polish history in lectures before his French military colleagues. The texts of these lectures are preserved in a collection of his works, *Lettres, notes, et carnets*.

In Poland, he also came in contact with representatives of other Allied nations and did not always like what he saw. In June 1919, in a letter to his father, he wrote:

> While 1,500 French officers fight, or prepare to do so, among the Polish troops, Americans, Britons and Italians come running to Warsaw to display their insolence and uselessness. They are part of vague[ly conceived] commissions, the main task of which, though not admitted, is to make business deals of all kinds. . . . Like most of my compatriots, I am ending this war overflowing with a general feeling of xenophobia and convinced that, in order to make ourselves respected, the reasoned use of our military force, the first in the world today, will be required.[29]

De Gaulle had sought the Polish tour as a means of making up the ground he had lost to other officers who had served actively in the French army throughout World War I. At the end of his Polish service, in the spring of 1920, he wrote to his father that he had received in Poland "quite exceptional [performance] reports, which have completely restored the military situation that odious captivity had taken away from me."[30]

Charles de Gaulle returned from his Polish tour in 1921. (Later, during the interwar period, in the years 1929–31, he was again posted abroad, to the Levant.) In 1922, he married Yvonne Vendroux, whose family had long been established in Lille as textile merchants. Yvonne was in the mold of a traditional, northern French wife: loyal, sturdy, and not particularly loquacious. The marriage produced three children, Geneviève, Anne, and Philippe. (Anne, born with Down's syndrome, received loving and protective care from her parents but died in 1948.)

From 1925 to 1927 Charles de Gaulle was assigned to the staff of Marshal Philippe Pétain, then vice president of the Supreme Defense Council, the highest position in the French military. Few in the military could match de Gaulle's powers of expression and his prodigious memory. One could perhaps sense that something strange was afoot in France's hierarchical society one morning in 1927, when a marshal of France, Philippe Pétain, sat in the audience while the young Captain de Gaulle delivered a lecture on military doctrine at the French War College. "The sharks who swam around the ship waiting for me to fall overboard so as to devour me were kept at a good distance," wrote de Gaulle to his father.[31]

In 1927, de Gaulle began a book on the French army under the direction of Marshal Pétain. The manuscript, originally entitled *The Soldier*, was finished the next year but not published until ten years later as *France and Its Army*. Pétain, who had kept his copy of the manuscript holed up in his desk, claimed it was a joint staff study and, apparently hoping it would come out under his own name, sat on it for nearly ten years.[32] De Gaulle ultimately faced down Pétain on this matter; at least one other officer had helped de Gaulle in the preparation, but it was unquestionably de Gaulle's work. De Gaulle's startling chutzpah can be only partly explained by the fact that Pétain, though still retaining the lifetime title of marshal, had been replaced in 1931 by General Maxime Weygand as vice president of the Supreme Defense Council. In a letter to Pétain on August 18, 1938, de Gaulle recalled the elapsed time in the following terms:

> Without going into detail on the reasons that caused you to end our collaboration eleven years ago, it certainly has not escaped you that in the course of these eleven years, the elements of this affair have changed as far as I am concerned. Morally, I have received some wounds—even from you, Marshal—lost some illusions, discarded some ambitions. From the point of view of ideas and style, I was unknown; this is no longer the case. In brief I am now lacking both the malleability and the [anonymity] that would be necessary for me to allow others to take the credit, in matters of letters and history, for which I may have some talent.[33]

In the end, Pétain only grudgingly allowed de Gaulle to publish a foreword acknowledging Pétain's direction in the matter. And Pétain sought (without ultimate success) to eliminate flattering references to himself in the foreword, possibly with the aim of dispelling an impression of harmony between the two men.[34] The affair of the book foreshadowed the cataclysmic dispute that was to erupt between the two in June 1940. Later, during World War II, de Gaulle described Pétain, in one of his notes to himself, as "a very great man who died around 1925."[35]

In the 1930s, de Gaulle carried on an extensive correspondence with Paul Reynaud, a leader of the Radical (middle class) party, in which he advised Reynaud on military matters. Reynaud was several times a minister during the 1930s, and in March 1940 he succeeded Edouard Daladier as prime minister. The correspondence was not without flattery: "There is no doubt that the near future is conserving for your policy and your personality a triumph proportional to their value and their courage."[36] Neither did de Gaulle refuse Reynaud's offers of help, as in December 1935, when it was a question of de Gaulle's being placed on the promotion list. In his letter accepting this offer, de Gaulle observed, "It cannot have escaped you, less than anyone, that the interest you have publicly displayed with regard to certain ideas of military reform has drawn the attention of certain people, and even a little discontentment (which is human) vis-à-vis my modest personage."[37]

At the time Reynaud was president of the Supreme Defense Council, and de Gaulle, who had met him a year earlier, was seeking to impose on Reynaud his theories on armored warfare and in particular his proposal for a self-contained armored strike force for France. De Gaulle's theories found little favor with the French general staff, which was both fixated on the efficacy of defense, as demonstrated in World War I, and disinclined, as victors of that war, toward making aggressive or adventurous moves. His call for a professional army in his 1937 book *Toward a Professional Army* met with disapproval within and outside the army. A professional force instead of a conscript force was seen by the left as "antirepublican" and a possible coup instrument.

As de Gaulle put it, the French army, "following a common tendency among the victors, estimated that a future conflict would be like the last one."[38] To de Gaulle, the official French military doctrine of the period was, quite simply, defeatist.[39] De Gaulle's reasoning behind his call for an armored strike force, which earned him the sobriquet "Colonel Motor,"[40] was that France could no longer rely on superior population resources. At the end of the eighteenth century, when the rifle and the bayonet were the essential weapons and France had a population approximately two and a half times that of England, the strategy of "big battalions" was an excellent one. But France no longer had the factor of mass at its disposal. Its population in the twentieth century was well under that of Germany. "In the present struggle of arms," wrote de Gaulle, "mechanized force is the card of France."[41]

De Gaulle began proposing this armored strategy for France in 1933. To his dismay, and through the prism of his own ego, he began to see what he called his "plan of salvation" for France being applied in its entirety in Germany.[42] Later de Gaulle would write to Reynaud, "France is still lacking this instrument of maneuver and shock that your servant has been proposing for five years toward and against all the conformists of all parties and all professions."[43]

In December 1936, de Gaulle, whose manic-depressive tendencies led him at times into moments of black pessimism,[44] made the following end-of-year prediction in a startlingly premonitory letter to his mother:

> We are headed rapidly into a war with Germany, and since it will not take much for things to turn badly for us, Italy will not fail to take advantage of the situation and give us a kick in the rear. It is a question of survival. All the rest is literature. Now, I ask you, who can we count on for armed assistance? Poland is nothing, and besides she is playing a double game.

England has a fleet but not an army, and an air force that at the moment is far behind. We don't have the means to refuse the help of the Russians, whatever horror we may have for their regime. It's the history of François I allied with the Muslims against Charles V.[45]

Four months later, in a letter to Reynaud in April 1937, de Gaulle recalled a parliamentary statement in March 1935 by the then minister of war, General Louis Maurin. Maurin's statement included the following:

How can one believe that we are still thinking of the offensive when we have spent billions to establish a fortified barrier [the Maginot line]? Are we crazy enough to go beyond that barrier, into I don't know what kind of adventure?

That alone, gentlemen, shows you what is the thinking of the government. Because the government, at least in my person, knows full well the plan of war.[46]

De Gaulle commented: "Hitler, having read these declarations, was fixed in his mind. He would be able, a year later, to cross the Rhine with the certainty that we would not move (March 7, 1936)."[47] The German move into the Rhineland—the area demilitarized by the Treaty of Versailles and lying between the Rhine River and the part of France's border with Germany fortified by the Maginot line—was the key event in the test of wills between the two countries in the 1930s. France, unsupported by the British, remained immobile. As de Gaulle wrote to a friend in the spring of 1939, "If we French had done our duty on March 7, 1936, peace would have been ensured."[48] Later, in July 1939, de Gaulle mused on "what might have happened to Hitler if, on March 7, 1936, at the news of the violation of the Rhineland by the Reichswehr, such a [mobile mechanized] French force [as de Gaulle had been advocating] had moved to the Rhine in one bound, as the treaties authorized it to do?"[49]

But what might have been was not. The Munich crisis of 1938 ended with Hitler's taking over the German-speaking portion of Czechoslovakia, the Sudetenland. France was swept into war in September 1939 on the guarantee given by its ally, Britain, to Poland in March of that year, in reaction to Hitler's having completed the dismemberment of Czechoslovakia—thus proving that he was not pursuing only German-speaking lands.

After the war had begun and Poland had fallen, de Gaulle wrote the following prediction on October 22, 1939:

In my opinion, the enemy will not attack us for a long time. His interest is to let our army, mobilized and passive, "stew in its own juices," while in the meantime acting elsewhere. Then, when he judges that we are tired, disoriented, and discontented with our own inertia, he will, in the final analysis, take the offensive against us with, from the moral and material point of view, a set of cards completely different from what he has today.[50]

The prediction had an eerily prophetic ring to it; the period of the *drôle de guerre* ("phony war") was setting in.

In publishing his several works on military strategy in the interwar period, de Gaulle had earned a reputation in military circles as a maverick with a tinge of insubordination. His interventionism reached its zenith in a memorandum entitled "The Coming of the Mechanized Force,"[51] which he addressed to eighty senior civilian and military personnel in France on January 21, 1940, when he was still a colonel.

In carrying on his lengthy correspondence with Paul Reynaud, de Gaulle was implicitly defying his military superiors. If de Gaulle did not see himself as *the* key player, he saw himself as *one* of the key players in the momentous events to come. Even before disaster struck France, he was elucidating the concept of "two wars," an initial one and a later one. On February 21, 1940, in the midst of the "phony war," de Gaulle wrote Reynaud in the following terms:

> If it is true that we took up arms to prevent Germany from establishing her hegemony . . . we have not succeeded. Indeed . . . [we have not] even tried. This hegemony is, as of now, virtually achieved. . . . It leaves for the modern conquerôrs only a few formalities to fulfill: to finish obtaining by fear the necessary resignations, [and] to complete various political and economic agreements.
>
> One can therefore say that the war is lost. But there is still time to win another. This other war could undo what the enemy has achieved in the first one.[52]

On March 21, 1940, a month after de Gaulle wrote this letter, Reynaud replaced Edouard Daladier as prime minister. Reynaud planned to make de Gaulle the secretary of a new war committee he was creating, but Daladier, who became minister of national defense and war in the new cabinet, opposed de Gaulle's nomination, and Reynaud had to abandon the idea.[53]

De Gaulle could also see that the French Empire was vital to the prosecution of the "other," or "second," war. In 1939, de Gaulle had written, "Considering the range, the speed, and the power of modern mechanized weapons, national defense is no longer on the scale of territory. Everyone must have a strategic 'vital space': bases abroad, faraway strong points, lines of observation, communications."[54]

Perhaps de Gaulle had already visualized that this "second war," a war waged from the "vital space" of the French Empire, would be conducted by a group other than the one presently in power in Paris. In one of his lectures to his fellow officers in captivity during World War I, he had struck such a premonitory note:

> It is extremely rare in the life of a people, especially in the case of France, that a war has been conducted to the end by the same organization envisaged before the war and presiding over the start of it. When a people enters into the immense and multifaceted ordeal that war most often represents, even in the case when this ordeal was long foreseen and prepared for, it always seems the case that one is taken by surprise, [and] that the organization created before the war with the objective of ensuring its conduct is defective or insufficient.[55]

THE SURRENDER

Suddenly, the "phony war" was over. Without warning, the Germans moved into Norway and Denmark on April 9, 1940, and again without warning, launched a blitzkrieg attack on France, Belgium, and the Netherlands on May 10, 1940. On May 18, Marshal Philippe Pétain was brought in by Prime Minister Reynaud as vice president of the Council of Ministers. On May 19, Reynaud, who himself took over the additional charge of the Ministry of National Defense and War from Edouard Daladier, replaced Maurice Gamelin with Maxime Weygand as commander in chief of the French army. On May 24, 1940, Colonel Charles de Gaulle was made a temporary brigadier general as of June 1, a promotion that in part recognized his exceptional record as commander of the Fourth Armored Division, particularly in the Battle of Montcornet, for which he was cited in an order of the army by General Weygand.[56] However, as de Gaulle himself indicated, the promotion appears to have been in some part due to the influence of Reynaud, who now held the portfolio of National Defense and War in addition to being prime minister.[57]

Whether by grand design or not, de Gaulle, flushed with his unique success as an armored commander in the field ("Things are going *very well* for me," he wrote to his wife on May 21),[58] used his promotion to general as a springboard to get himself elevated to the political level; he positioned himself to become a player in the "second war." On June 3, 1940, his moment of truth came in a letter to Reynaud, in which de Gaulle's urge to dominate the prime minister is only barely controlled by a few courteous and flattering expressions. Key portions of the letter follow:

We are at the edge of the abyss and you are carrying France on your shoulders. . . .

Our initial defeat stemmed from the enemy's application of my ideas. . . .

After this terrible lesson, you who alone followed me are now the master, partly because you followed me, and this is known.

But once having become master, you are abandoning us to men of the past. I do not question their past glory. . . . But I say that these men of the past, if they are given their way, will lose this new war.

These men of the past fear me because they know I am right and have the necessary dynamism to force their hand. . . .

The country feels urgently that now is the time for renewal. It would hail with hope the arrival of a new man, of a man of the new war.

Get away from conformism, from past experience, from school solutions. . . .

[Should I] be attached to you as someone without responsibility—a cabinet chief, a chief of a study office? No! I mean to act with you but by myself. Otherwise it is useless. And I prefer to command.

If you give up the idea of taking me as under secretary of state, at least make me the chief not just of one of your four armored divisions but of the armored corps encompassing all of them. . . . I am the only one capable of commanding this corps.[59]

Two days later de Gaulle's power play paid off. On June 5, he was named by Reynaud as under secretary of state (which in France means a junior minister) in the Ministry of National Defense and War. Reynaud, as his minister and the prime minister, immediately charged de Gaulle with the preparation of a fallback plan whereby the government would retreat to a place where it could continue to resist if France became largely occupied by the Germans. Brittany (the Breton Redoubt plan) was an initial option, and then North Africa.

There was, however, a notable lack of enthusiasm for the fallback plan at senior levels of the French government. Maxime Weygand, the French army's commander in chief and de Gaulle's military superior by five stars to two (and even those two represented only those of a temporary brigadier general), thought the Breton Redoubt plan was impractical and was incensed that Reynaud had consulted de Gaulle about it before informing him.[60] De Gaulle was, however, a member of the government and therefore part of the political authority, belonging in principle, at least, to the "robe" rather than the "sword." In fact, from the outset of his appointment to the government, de Gaulle sensed Weygand's disposition not to continue the war and sought unsuccessfully to have him replaced.[61]

Weygand, who had been de Gaulle's commander in Poland after World War I and later was commander in chief of the army (1931–35), had been brought back into the army in 1939 from the Suez Canal Company. In May 1940, he again became commander in chief, replacing Maurice Gamelin. De Gaulle was later to describe Weygand, who was to push actively for an armistice in the face of the German invasion, in the following terms: "Capitulation is an abyss from which a chief never returns."[62] Clearly Weygand, seventy-three, and Pétain, eighty-four, were the "men of the past" whom Reynaud was coming to rely on, as de Gaulle noted in his letter to the prime minister on June 3. "Old age is a shipwreck," de Gaulle would later write, adding, "That we might be spared nothing, the old age of Marshal Pétain was to identify itself with the shipwreck of France."[63]

In connection with the fallback option, de Gaulle was charged by Reynaud with carrying out a liaison with the British government. On June 9, 1940, de Gaulle went to London, where he met Winston Churchill for the first time. They met again on June 11 south of Paris at Briare, where the retreating French general staff had set up temporary headquarters because of the dissolving military situation. On that evening and the following morning, the Supreme French-British Council met under the presidency of Churchill and Reynaud, and de Gaulle was in on the meeting. After the June 11–12 meeting, Churchill wired to Franklin Roosevelt: "Reynaud . . . [in contrast to Pétain] is for fighting on and he has a young General de Gaulle who believes much can be done."[64]

De Gaulle and Churchill met yet again on June 13 at Tours Prefecture, where the heads of the two governments held another session that de Gaulle, informed late of the meeting, attended only briefly.[65] In the course of the June 13 meeting, it became apparent that the French government was near to giving up. Weygand was pushing for an armistice, and Reynaud, at the insistence of his ministers, announced to the British that he would have to ask them to release France from the pact Reynaud himself had signed on March 28, promising that France would not make a separate peace. Churchill refused his consent and urged that the issue be held in abeyance, pending an appeal by Reynaud to U.S. president Franklin D. Roosevelt. Reynaud indicated that unless the United States declared war on Germany, France was not going to continue the fight.[66]

De Gaulle reacted to the June 13 meeting at Tours with a note to Reynaud on the following day; a portion of it follows:

> The statement that you made yesterday to Messrs. Churchill and Halifax indicates that you consider France's continuation of the war to be conditional.
>
> I am convinced that this new position will lead us to an attempt at

negotiation with the enemy powers. Now, to make such an attempt will be the equivalent, in my opinion, of denouncing in the heat of the fighting our commitments with England and of renouncing subsequent assistance by the United States. I estimate that the consequence could be the physical, moral, and economic dismemberment of France and its empire.[67]

The letter, in which de Gaulle asked to be relieved of his post in the government, was not sent. De Gaulle was dissuaded from doing so by George Mandel, the minister of labor, whom de Gaulle saw that same evening in Tours.[68]

De Gaulle, still consulting with the British on the fallback option, now focused on North Africa. He arrived in London again on the morning of June 16, after visiting Brittany to help organize defense efforts there and then crossing the Channel aboard the destroyer *Milan*.[69] Upon arriving in London, de Gaulle learned that the French government, which had moved on to Bordeaux on June 14, 1940, had confirmed Reynaud's oral request to be relieved of the French-British agreement of March 28. The British government's answer, then in preparation, was not communicated to the French government because a new idea suddenly arose: an instant union between Britain and France, concocted by Lord Halifax, the British foreign minister, and by Jean Monnet, who was in London as French delegate to the French-British armaments mission.

Though there were many practical difficulties in the union proposal, de Gaulle saw it as a fillip to Reynaud to continue the struggle in North Africa. He convinced Churchill, who in turn persuaded the British cabinet to accept it. On the afternoon of June 16, de Gaulle telephoned Reynaud to inform him of the idea and the British cabinet's acceptance of it. It was decided that Reynaud would meet Churchill at Concarneau, Brittany, on the following morning to discuss British shipping assistance for the move to North Africa.[70]

De Gaulle prepared to leave for Bordeaux, and Churchill arranged a plane for him that would remain at his disposal "in case of events which might lead me to return."[71] Upon arriving in Bordeaux at 9:30 P.M. on June 16, he found that Reynaud had failed to persuade the cabinet to continue the struggle and had resigned. Unable to stand up to Weygand and influenced by his mistress, Countess Hélène de Portes, who had brought other members of the peace faction into his entourage,[72] Reynaud was on the point of a nervous breakdown that he could assuage only by resigning.[73]

Not only had the cabinet rejected the French-British union proposal, it had endorsed an idea presented the day before by Camille Chautemps, who, with Pétain, was a vice president of the council. Chautemps had suggested that the Germans be approached concerning their conditions for an armistice; if their terms were unsatisfactory, they could still be rejected.[74]

Later on the same evening of June 16, President Albert Lebrun asked Marshal Pétain to form a government. He did this without making any political soundings or reference to Parliament. Lebrun appears to have been like flotsam, borne by events. De Gaulle later observed, "The President of the Republic abstained from raising his voice, even within the cabinet."[75]

Pétain, the revered figure, the "hero of Verdun" in World War I, was seen as the man who could handle this most difficult of all transitions. But to de Gaulle, Pétain's appointment meant "certain capitulation" for France, and he decided at once to return to London the following morning.[76] As de Gaulle explained it,

> I thought, in fact, that it would be the end of honor, unity, and independence if it were to be admitted that, in this world war, only France had capitulated and that she had let the matter rest there. For in that case, whatever might be the issue of the conflict . . . [the country's] self-disgust and the disgust it would inspire in others would poison its soul and its life for many generations.[77]

De Gaulle, who observed in his *War Memoirs*, "The future lasts a long time,"[78] somehow could sense that France would be finished as a great military power if nothing further were done at that point. It was as though France would be reduced militarily for generations to the level of Italy. And yet, as de Gaulle noted in his *War Memoirs*, "For fourteen centuries, military power had been second nature to France. If our country had on many occasions neglected her defense, misprized her soldiers, lost her battles, she had nonetheless appeared at all times eminently capable of the greatest military actions."[79]

On the following morning, June 17, de Gaulle left for London from the airport at Bordeaux. It was a "leap into the unknown" of tremendous risk. He had left his family behind (by this time they had arrived in Brittany) but was able to arrange for them to get to London.

On June 18, 1940, the next day, Charles de Gaulle, announcing himself as *"Moi, le général de Gaulle,"* broadcast over the BBC that France would remain in the war and called on the French people in England to rally to him.[80] In this startling display of authority, two facts were capital and were due in part to his unorthodox and carefully nurtured relationship with Paul

General de Gaulle, pictured here shortly after his arrival in London in June 1940, was extolled by the British press as the "hero of Abbéville." This was the last in a series of engagements in which de Gaulle's Fourth Armored Division acquitted itself creditably before superior German forces.

Reynaud: He had acceded to the rank of general (albeit brigadier general, and of temporary grade only), which raised him above the level of a putschist colonel; and he had been a minister in Reynaud's government. As de Gaulle put it in a letter to Winston Churchill on June 23, 1940, "I was a member of the last independent French government."[81] (He was also the only member of that government who was still wholly free from German control.)

There was a third, intangible factor in de Gaulle's seizing of authority, unknown to the outside world. He had clicked with Churchill: Their futures were thenceforth intertwined. De Gaulle had the support of a great power behind him.

His reputation in the upper reaches of the French military hierarchy as at best a maverick and at worst an insubordinate did not seem to bother de Gaulle. He had long established a viewpoint on such matters. In a history lecture at St. Cyr in 1921, he had stated, in another of those premonitory phrases often found in his work, that a leader should not be hampered by excessive obedience. This was the problem of Marshal Patrice de Mac-Mahon in the Franco-Prussian War: "Mac-Mahon, the soul of loyalty, saw with [the] good sense of an experienced soldier what should be done, but [was] too ingrained with obedience to resist successfully the empress [Eugénie] and the government."[82]

In his second published work, *The Edge of the Sword*, de Gaulle had written:

> After the battle of Jutland and the English failure to take the opportunity offered them of destroying the German fleet, Admiral Fisher, then First Sea Lord, exclaimed in a fury after reading [Admiral] Jellicoe's dispatch: "He has all [Admiral] Nelson's qualities but one: he doesn't know how to disobey!"[83]

On July 10, 1940, at the small spa town of Vichy to which the French government had repaired, the National Assembly,[84] by a vote of 569–80, with eighteen registered abstentions,[85] turned over full powers to Marshal Philippe Pétain and in effect endorsed the armistice he had concluded with the Germans on June 22, 1940. Pétain was given the authority to draw up a new constitution for France, which would then be ratified by the assemblies it created.[86]

But the Pétain government never created a new constitution. Instead, Vichy closed off republican government by instituting on July 11, 1940, Constitutional Act No. 3, which stated that neither of the two chambers could meet except by convocation of the chief of state.[87]

De Gaulle, with his view "from the outside" (he had made two trips to

London in the critical month of June), and with his insight into the peace faction—what he called the "party of surrender" from his ministerial vantage point—considered that the French government had done something terribly wrong, which would have consequences far into the future. As de Gaulle argued the case, the armistice placed the Vichy government "under the complete dependence of enemy powers" and also was in "contradiction with the existing commitments between France, Great Britain, and their allies."[88]

This was the British view as well. In the days leading up to the resignation of Paul Reynaud, the British and the French had not worked out any satisfactory terms for a separate peace by the French. The British held that this peace would be permissible only if the French fleet were to sail immediately for British ports.[89] On June 23, the day after the armistice was signed, the British government issued a communiqué stating that the terms violated the French-British accord and that the Pétain government could not be considered that of an independent country.[90]

Pétain's paternal image beclouded the situation, and de Gaulle was aware of this. He described Pétain in the following terms, in a letter to a British acquaintance on February 18, 1942:

> The affair of Uncle Béno [Pétain] is . . . unpleasant and dishonest. . . . He is the flag that covers this adulterated merchandise. What is bad in his case is that he knows it. But he accepted that from the beginning because he has a sort of fatal attraction for unfortunate things and at the same time a desire, inexcusable at his age, to maintain a brilliant position, at least in appearance.[91]

Indeed, from the point of view of the "party of surrender," to use de Gaulle's phrase, the installation of Pétain was ingenious. The marshal's prestige was not to be underestimated. Witness this testimony by de Gaulle himself, albeit in 1966 at the fifty-year anniversary of the Battle of Verdun, with Pétain dead and de Gaulle having long since triumphed over him:

> Military art has four essential characteristics: prediction, method, organization, then, when the action is unleashed with its flood of alarms and pretenses, a silent serenity, which neither shocks nor mirages can shake and to which, from the depths of their anguish, subordinates respond by their own abnegation.
> Pétain possessed par excellence these gifts of a chief. . . . If by misfortune, at other times, in the deep winter of his life, the attrition of age led Marshal Pétain into condemnable failings, the glory that he had acquired twenty-five years earlier at Verdun, then retained in sub-

sequently leading the French army to victory, cannot be contested nor underrated by the nation.[92]

But the year was now 1940, and when this providential figure, his prestige still intact, told the French people he had achieved peace with honor, they tended by and large to believe him. Somehow, the victor of Verdun was spreading a balm of honor over what had been a humiliating rout. Said Pétain, in a speech to the French people from Bordeaux on June 25, 1940:

> The armistice has been concluded. The fighting is over. The conditions to which we had to subscribe are severe. A large part of our territory is going to be occupied temporarily. . . . Our armies will have to be demobilized, our matériel turned over to the adversary, our fleet disarmed in port. In the Mediterranean the naval bases will be demilitarized.
>
> At least honor has been saved. No one will make use of our airplanes and our fleet. We will keep the land and naval forces necessary for the maintenance of order in the Métropole and in our colonies. The government remains free. France will be administered only by Frenchmen.[93]

In truth, the Pétain regime had taken the easy way out. De Gaulle, who had always had a contempt for easy solutions (what he called "solutions of facility")[94] issued a ringing denunciation. "This armistice is dishonorable," the General stated in an open message to Pétain on June 26, 1940, replying to the marshal's speech from Bordeaux the day before.[95] Later, in a similar vein during a speech on July 27, 1940, de Gaulle stated: "In an abominable panic the capitulation was signed."[96]

Historically speaking, what had taken place was unprecedented: "We the French," wrote de Gaulle, "had in the course of time endured many disasters, lost provinces, paid indemnities, but the state had never accepted the domination of a foreign power."[97] What would have been justified, in de Gaulle's opinion, was a military cease-fire between the Alps and the Atlantic, carried out by a military commander under the orders of the government—which would repair to Algiers, "taking with it the treasure of French sovereignty, which for fourteen centuries had never been surrendered, continuing the battle, keeping its word to the Allies."[98] What was condemnable on Vichy's part was

> to have retired from the war with the empire intact, the fleet untouched, the air force largely undamaged; to have withdrawn our African and Levantine troops without a single soldier lost; to have abandoned all those forces which, in France itself, could be transported elsewhere; to

have broken our alliances; above all, to have submitted the state to the Reich's discretion.[99]

Instead, the French government at Bordeaux, indeed virtually the entire French establishment, gave way to panic. There seemed to be no way to stop Hitler's juggernaut. The French-British union idea was belittled by the French cabinet at Bordeaux during the evening of June 16, which saw Reynaud's resignation. Weygand had been insisting that the British would be quickly defeated by the Germans.[100] Churchill was later to remark, "When I warned them [France] that Britain would fight on whatever they did, their generals told their Prime Minister and his divided Cabinet, 'In three weeks England will have her neck wrung like a chicken.' Some chicken! Some neck!"[101]

THE GAULLIST COMPORTMENT

Starting from nothing except what he saw as the necessity of representing an unbowed France, de Gaulle adopted a certain unbending comportment that was not foreign to his own temperament. Having to embody the hopes of the French people and the image of a "France indomitable in the midst of her trials" made de Gaulle constantly aware of the effect he should try to create. "[It] was to dictate my bearing and to impose upon my personality an attitude I could never again change. For me this meant, without respite, a stubborn self-supervision as well as an extremely heavy yoke."[102] In June 1942, as heavy clouds were developing in Free French–British relations over British actions in French zones of influence in Africa and the Middle East,[103] de Gaulle told Churchill, "I am too poor to be able to bow."[104] De Gaulle by his own admission "deliberately adopted [a] tough, rigid attitude"[105] in the face of the Allies' political behavior, which he described as "a kind of consecrated egoism."[106] Since France was excluded from Allied discussions, wrote de Gaulle, "I felt myself justified, whenever it was necessary, to act in her own behalf and independently of the others."[107]

But de Gaulle went still further. In a press interview on February 23, 1942, referring to his quarrels with the Allies in various parts of the French Empire, the General said, "We have, in the common interest, the right and the duty to show ourselves intransigent."[108] On another occasion, in the summer of 1941 and in the midst of serious disputes with the British over who was to have political control in the Levant, de Gaulle sent a message to the Free French delegation in London, which included the following words: "Our greatness and our strength consist solely in intransigence concerning the rights of France. We shall have need of this intransigence up to the Rhine, inclusive."[109]

In a history lecture at St. Cyr in 1921, de Gaulle had spoken about the Franco-Prussian War in terms that, as if foreordained, were later to apply to himself after the fall of France: "It was necessary, in those disastrous days, that France be carried away by that irresistible national movement that had saved it so many times in its history."[110] In World War I, two such men who were able to call forth this kind of movement were inspirational figures for de Gaulle: Marshal Foch, whose motto was "One is only conquered when one admits to being conquered,"[111] and Georges Clemenceau, who assumed the premiership of a faltering France in 1917 under the slogan "The single thought of a total war."[112] "The French nation had responded as one to the appeal of Clemenceau," de Gaulle wrote.[113] Clemenceau had taken charge of the country after the disastrously costly French offensive in the Chemin des Dames in April 1917 had led to widespread morale problems and mutinies in a number of units, accompanied by troubles on the labor front. Together with Foch, who oversaw the military campaign that ended the war, he presented an image of an aggressive and uncompromising France, which could not have failed to make an impression on de Gaulle as he emerged from captivity in Germany.

For de Gaulle, this kind of "irresistible national movement" could be represented by one man. His most recent role model in French history was Clemenceau, the fiercely republican Jacobin from one of the most conservative regions in France, the Vendée, and the man who had said, "The [French] Revolution is a bloc" (in other words, it cannot be separated into good and bad phases). Wrote de Gaulle: ". . . the great, the irresistible force of Clemenceau in [19]17–18–19. He was France."[114]

In a conversation with de Gaulle on September 29, 1942, Winston Churchill remarked that de Gaulle always spoke as if he were France. He, Churchill, had never been willing to accept this point of view. He saw in the General a very honorable part of France but not France per se. Other parts of France might be called upon, as a result of events, to play a more important role than they did at that time.

The General replied that if Churchill were not convinced that de Gaulle represented all of France, why would the prime minister discuss any important question with him? As de Gaulle explained, his "person," in contrast to what he represented, was negligible.[115]

De Gaulle explained on a number of occasions that identifying himself with France itself was a way of constituting a new legitimacy for his weakened and demoralized people. This legitimacy, which de Gaulle claimed to represent, was based on honor, duty, and greatness *(grandeur)*, and not on legal norms, which at the time were deficient and had to be changed. This line of reasoning, very difficult to accept in the stable and prudential democracies of the United States and Great Britain, was not wholly unfamiliar in France. Though France was not a land of pronunciamentos, as de Gaulle contemptuously referred to the actions of the Algiers putschists in April 1961,[116] it was a land of changing and contested constitutions, and hence it was frequently questioned who had the legitimate right to govern.

This rationale concerning his legitimacy, which de Gaulle referred to continually, made him yearn for a "utopia of unanimity" concerning his leadership; the referendum became his chosen instrument for confirming his claim to legitimacy throughout his public career, and it ultimately became wearisome to the French people.[117] Even a loyal follower such as Michel Debré, de Gaulle's first prime minister under the Fifth Republic, would write, "The General was a difficult man because he continually mixed up his image with the future of France. I was always preoccupied with the future of the country more than the personal image of the General. He sometimes tended to reverse these priorities."[118]

De Gaulle's concept of honor, with its spiritual and abstract qualities, was also at a remove from the pragmatic Anglo-American mentality. In an interview with a Mexican journalist in February 1942, he identified his concept of honor with the Latin mentality. He spoke of the "instinctive links that unite everything that is Latin," while recognizing the fact that tyrannical regimes had been imposed on certain Latin states. Said de Gaulle: "In what we think, in what we desire, in our conception of honor, of right, and of duty, there is a community [of outlook] that makes it incumbent upon us Latins to become one of the powers of the world."[119]

Though in the cultural, linguistic, and religious sense, de Gaulle identified himself and France with the Latin world, he saw the historical roots of the French people as different from those of their Latin neighbors. In one passage in his *War Memoirs,* he evoked a vision of a peaceful Europe that could be achieved "only by an association among Slavs, Germans, Gauls and Latins."[120] Again—and this is a point that will be developed later— Europe for de Gaulle meant essentially continental Europe.

In a sense, de Gaulle had been preparing all his life for what happened to him in June 1940, when he broke from the French government and started his resistance movement (*La France Libre*—"Free France"). De Gaulle's second book, *The Edge of the Sword,* is a compilation of moral precepts for leadership, both military and political; it starts with the premise that "in the last resort, the nature of . . . decision is a moral one."[121] It is almost as though de Gaulle, in establishing these precepts (conveyed in chapter titles like "Action," "Character," and "Prestige"), was laying out for himself the standards that would be required for him to assume the leadership of France.

This constant invocation of the myth of de Gaulle as France made it difficult to sort out the degree of his personal ambition in these undertakings. The lack of intimacy in de Gaulle's approach served only to deepen the mystery. Even his own entourage, "paralyzed by the historic stature of the person and often disconcerted by his style,"[122] dared not contradict him.

Stanley Hoffmann has noted in de Gaulle's thinking "an element of mysticism that Americans did not appreciate."[123] De Gaulle's use of elevated language fell curiously on American ears. It was not merely a question of referring to himself in the third person, as he did, for example, when he described himself after he had "assumed" France in 1940:[124] ". . . de Gaulle, that almost legendary character who incarnated this prodigious liberation in all eyes . . ."[125] His use of Old World, Catholic-derived imagery seemed bizarre to most Americans and ridiculous to some. Recalling in his *War Memoirs* a speech he had made at Tunis on June 27, 1943, de Gaulle wrote:

> "To France," I cried, "to our lady France we have only one thing to say, that nothing matters to us except to serve her. We must liberate her, conquer her enemy, punish the traitors, preserve her friends, tear the gag from her mouth and the chains from her limbs so that she can make her voice heard and resume her march toward her destiny. We have nothing to ask of her except, perhaps, that on the day of liberty she will open her motherly arms to us so that we may weep for joy within them, and that on the day death comes to take us she will bury us gently in her good and sacred soil."[126]

This mélange of religious and nationalist imagery ("The church is eternal, and France will not die")[127] has been analyzed by Fabrice Bouthillon,[128] including the parallel between the Gaullist image of occupied France, fighting France, and victorious France on the one hand; and the image of the church suffering in purgatory, the church militant on earth, and the church triumphant in glory, on the other.[129]

In part this imagery stemmed from the fact that Vichy, while ending republican government in France, had wisely retained the trappings of the French Revolution which had produced the Republic: the tricolor flag and

"The Marseillaise." This forced the Gaullists to dig back further into the traditions of the French nation and come up with symbols of their own. The myth formation centered on the figure of Joan of Arc, who had saved France in an earlier era from another foreign invader, the English. Early on, de Gaulle invoked the memory of Joan of Arc, as in this evocative (and provocative) statement on May 10, 1941, at Brazzaville:

> A country three-quarters conquered. Most of the men in public positions collaborating with the enemy. Paris, Bordeaux, Orléans, Reims transformed into foreign garrisons. A representative of the invader dictating law in the capital. Treason on all sides . . . the French people hiding their fury. Such was the outward aspect of France five hundred and twelve years ago [in 1429], when Joan of Arc came forward to fulfill her mission. Such is the outward aspect of France today.
>
> . . . It was because of the same secret faith and hope that from Joan of Arc's sword sprang the great movement that drove the foe from France. Tomorrow, the weapons of those who are fighting for our country will drive the enemy from our land. . . .
>
> Joan of Arc, true, pure and saintly daughter of France, tomorrow, the National Festival of May 11th—*your* feast day—will see the whole French nation united in the will to liberation.[130]

With the symbolic figure of Joan of Arc came the Gaullist flag, the Cross of Lorraine; Joan of Arc was born in Lorraine, at Domrémy, circa 1412. The quasi-religious symbolism also found its way into Gaullist decorations. On November 15, 1940, the General created the Order of the Liberation, which had as its decoration the Cross of the Liberation. Holders of the decoration were to carry the title Crusaders of the Liberation.[131]

De Gaulle did not, however, abandon the traditional French symbols, the tricolor flag and "The Marseillaise." Instead, he supplemented them while incorporating them.

De Gaulle sought to capture for his countrymen the ancient French spirit of fury against the foreign foe—the image of *la furia française*[132]— as he did in this passage from a broadcast on the eve of Bastille Day, 1942, evoking the wrathful and bloodthirsty message of "The Marseillaise":

> . . . These flags, these processions, this *Marseillaise* [on Bastille Day] will signify that France is making ready . . . for the day of wrath when . . . the whole nation will rise to drive out and punish the enemy. . . . The flags are for pride; the processions are for hope; the *Marseillaise* for wrath. We need, and we still have, pride, hope, and wrath.[133]

For an "irresistible national movement" to succeed, it had to be unified under one chief. Here, de Gaulle's ideals and ambitions came together. He had stated at the beginning of 1941, "General de Gaulle declares that he does not recognize nor support organizations other than Free France or organizations duly attached to it."[134] A year and a half later, de Gaulle placed the issue in more pointed and personal terms: "I consider that those who are my collaborators and, better still, my companions, should follow me and help me, after they have made me understand their reasoning. Otherwise, Fighting France would become the Tower of Babel."[135]

De Gaulle was in the first and final analysis a professional military man. None of his counterparts was in the same category: not Roosevelt, nor Churchill, nor Stalin, nor Hitler. Also, and in part from his military background, there was a bellicose, dominating strain in de Gaulle's personality that had a hardly neutral effect on other individuals (and on other nations). As Michel Debré, his prime minister in 1958–62, put it, "[General de Gaulle] had a taste for deciding, not for negotiating."[136]

But if de Gaulle was military by bearing and background, he was no mere military man: He was someone who considered himself capable of wielding state power. Indeed, de Gaulle drew a sharp distinction between those who are in charge of the "higher conduct of war" and those who are commanders in the field. De Gaulle undoubtedly saw himself as among the former, possessed, as he put it, of one of those "synthesizing minds, apt for generalizations, constantly capable of distinguishing between the essential and the accessory, and of attributing to each factor exactly the importance that it merits."[137] Not only were such minds rare, but it was even more extraordinary to find synthesizing minds combined with "those qualities of character in proportion to the immense responsibilities that the higher conduct of war constantly imposes."[138] Obviously, de Gaulle was thinking of himself or projecting himself into such a role.

"Isn't it true," de Gaulle wrote, "that strategists of modern times are no longer, as in former times, the leaders of armies but the leaders of peoples, for example, Churchill, Stalin, Roosevelt, or Hitler and Mussolini?"[139] There was no question that de Gaulle placed himself in the same category, at least potentially.

The famous dictum of military theorist Karl von Clausewitz, that war is the continuation of politics by other means, was another way of saying that politics is supreme. As sociologist and political commentator Raymond Aron pointed out in his essay On Clausewitz, "Even in time of war, politics, that is, the personified intelligence of the state, must retain its sovereignty."[140] De Gaulle echoed this view: "Only the government can stamp war with the general character that it must have."[141]

FREE FRANCE VERSUS VICHY

If de Gaulle could see the vast implications of the shame of Vichy's capitulation, why were so few others in France able to see them? De Gaulle had had the singular experience of challenging received French military doctrine in the 1920s and 1930s. But on the other side of the scale, the centralized French state traditionally tended in times of crisis to overwhelm the otherwise fractious political culture in France, as it did in the case of the Vichy government. Few dissenting voices were raised. Moreover, in France's hierarchical society, de Gaulle was not at the top level of the officer corps, from which he had only a few days earlier emerged to become a member of the government, and thus lacked the authority that might have won his protestations a broader hearing. Still, his position in the Reynaud government as a junior minister added to his uniqueness and provided the tenuous support on which he based his claim for a superior legitimacy. Essentially, de Gaulle asserted that he was in charge of the government of France from June 18, 1940, until January 20, 1946.[142]

Charles de Gaulle was later to describe, in his *War Memoirs,* this seeming act of levitation by which he seized control of "France" in 1940 or, as he was to put it, by which he "assumed" France:[143]

> This chief of state without a constitution, without electors, without a capital, who spoke in the name of France; this officer wearing so few stars, whose country's ministers, generals, admirals, governors, and ambassadors considered his orders indisputable; this Frenchman condemned to death by the "legal" government, vilified by many prominent men, opposed in battle by a part of his own troops, and before whom the flags dipped—he could not fail to amaze the conventional spirit of the British and American military men.[144]

But there was a limit to this act of levitation, as de Gaulle himself acknowledged, when it came time for him to leave the government not long after the end of World War II: "No man," said de Gaulle, "can substitute himself for a people."[145] He might have added the word *indefinitely* to more accurately describe his own experience.

The Vichy government, formed by Pétain and with Pierre Laval as its prime minister, wasted no time in declaring de Gaulle outside the law. Even before the armistice was signed, he was ordered by General Weygand to return to Bordeaux. De Gaulle replied on June 20, 1940, that he had received the order and would report to Weygand in twenty-four hours, "provided the capitulation has not been signed." But if it were signed, continued de Gaulle, he would continue the fight from abroad and recommended that Weygand do likewise.[146]

On July 4, 1940, the General was sentenced in absentia to four years in prison and a fine of one hundred francs for refusal to obey.[147] De Gaulle retorted with the following statement: "I hold the actions of the people of Vichy to be null and void. They and I will have it out after the victory."[148] A month later, on August 2, 1940, a military court in Clermont-Ferrand sentenced him to death in absentia "for having acted in secret agreement with a foreign power, in this case England and its agents, with the object of assisting the undertakings of this power against France."[149] De Gaulle had committed the ultimate sin of lèse-majesté in France's hierarchical society by defying a marshal of France, Philippe Pétain.

In London, de Gaulle found himself in an ambiguous and difficult situation. De Gaulle probably thought others, especially those in the French colonies, would be disposed to seek a "solution with honor," rather than the half-tempting peace that Hitler had presented to Pétain. De Gaulle telegraphed various authorities, civilian and military, in the colonies. On June 19 and 24, he sent messages to the key figure among them, General Charles Noguès, the French army commander in North Africa, offering to place himself under Noguès's orders, in the event that Noguès continued the struggle. Noguès had initially balked at the armistice, inviting Weygand to reconsider his order to implement it. But seeing that nearly everyone else was obeying Pétain and Weygand, Noguès gave in.[150]

Noguès did not reply to de Gaulle's two messages. Virtually alone, de Gaulle had no choice but to press on with his "solution with honor." Of all the authorities in the French Empire, only General Georges Catroux, governor-general of Indochina, and General Paul Legentilhomme, French military commander in Somaliland, dissented with the armistice, and these two were quickly removed from their positions by the Vichy authorities.[151]

In sum, very few people answered de Gaulle's appeal for resistance—particularly very few people who counted for anything in France. The class of the politically important people in France, loosely designated by the term *notables,* was not there.

Over the course of the war the so-called sword and shield theory emerged. This presented de Gaulle and Pétain as having, in effect, a distribution of roles. Pétain, who was widely, but falsely, rumored to be the godfather of his namesake, Philippe de Gaulle, was the shield who remained in France and protected the French population as best he could from the depredations of the Germans; de Gaulle was the sword who attacked German forces from the outside. Another version of this concept was the "eggs in two baskets" theory developed by William L. Langer, the head of the intelligence analysis element of the Office of Strategic Services (OSS), who was commissioned by U.S. Secretary of State Cordell Hull at the end of the war to assess the soundness of the administration's indulgent policy toward Vichy:

> France came out of her defeat much more fortunate than anyone could have expected. Not only were Hitler's terms remarkably lenient, permitting the continued existence of a French nation and a French government, but through de Gaulle France was to have at least some of the advantages of an exile government loyal to Britain and her allies. When through further developments of the war, Pétain's government became played out, de Gaulle and the Fighting French could take its place. So France was able to play both ends against the middle—France had eggs in two baskets.[152]

De Gaulle bitterly criticized the shield and sword theory, which tended to undermine his own uncompromising stance against the Pétain government. He had a disagreement over this issue after the war with Colonel Rémy (whose real name was Gilbert Renault), a Resistance follower of de Gaulle's who wrote an article claiming that the General in private conversations had lent some credence to this theory. In reference to this affair, de Gaulle later wrote tartly to Colonel Rémy: "Memories do not go away."[153]

In London de Gaulle's first idea was to set up the French National Committee, which would be composed of prominent French persons. When they did not materialize, this ambition had to be scaled back. Even de Gaulle had to admit that his movement did not gain much following at first. In a meeting with Winston Churchill on September 12, 1941, more than a year after he had made his initial appeal to the French people to continue the struggle, the General said he had all along wanted to put together a national committee representing all major French opinions and interests. However, he had come up against "the difficulty of finding a sufficient number of prominent persons representative enough and not tied to the enemy or to Vichy."[154]

So no national committee was formed, and instead, on June 28, 1940, de Gaulle was recognized by the British government as chief of the Free French in all British territory.[155] Soon, however, de Gaulle created, as a sort of substitute for a French national committee, the Council for the

Defense of the Empire, on October 27, 1940. The council was being formed, said de Gaulle, because the Vichy government was "neither constitutional nor free." The council would exercise all the powers that belonged to the "last constitutional and free government in [those] French territories [that] refuse to submit to the armistice."[156]

On September 22, 1941, a little more than a year after the fall of France, Charles de Gaulle, then fifty years old, finally announced the formation of the French National Committee. On the following day, in de Gaulle's first press conference of which a record exists,[157] he gave his rationale. The people's will, he said, was not able to manifest itself "because of the regime instituted by the invader and the usurpation of all national sovereignty by Vichy." The nation, he said, had "no other means than Free France to make its will known." The Free French movement would hold "a sort of delegation of national interest." It would be "an authority that we will exercise provisionally and that we will give back to the national representative assembly as soon as it will be possible to constitute one freely."[158]

De Gaulle added in his press conference that any infringement of French rights and interests resulting from France's "momentary collapse" would not be admitted and that these infringements would be rectified "by all the means that are—and perhaps one day by all the means that will be—in our power."[159]

De Gaulle's policy, spelled out in a memorandum at the end of 1941, was to "detach 'piece by piece' all French territories outside the Métropole [Metropolitan France] that are presently neutralized because of the existence and the action of a French government at Vichy."[160] Strategically, as de Gaulle put it, French territory had been split into three pieces: "One, occupied by the enemy; the other controlled by him and taken over by his collaborators, who have abused the people's confidence; and the third free and fighting, in Africa, in Asia, and in Oceania." It was up to the French in the latter territories "to speak and act in the name of the entire nation."[161]

The ambiguity of de Gaulle's situation was sharpened by the British attack on the French fleet at Mers-el-Kebir, Algeria, on July 3, 1940, after the French commander there refused to put his ships under British orders. This incident grew out of the lack of resolution of the problem of the French fleet at the time of the armistice. Embarrassed by the fact that 1,300 French naval personnel were killed or missing and 350 were wounded in the incident,[162] de Gaulle nevertheless felt compelled to issue a message of qualified support for the British action. The Vichy government, out of a sense of guilt partly at having deserted its alliance with Britain (despite the March 1940 agreement not to do so), but more particularly at having failed to secure the French fleet at the time it signed the armistice, turned with a vengeance on its former ally. Commenting on the incident and on the British motivation, de Gaulle wrote in his *War Memoirs:*

> It was clear that, in the British government and Admiralty, the fear caused by the danger they were in, the stale reek of an old naval rivalry, the resentments accumulated since the beginning of the Battle of France and brought to the point of paroxysm with the armistice concluded by Vichy, had exploded in one of those dark bursts by which the repressed instinct of this people sometimes smashes all barriers.[163]

Thereafter, in his attempts to rally "piece by piece" the various parts of the French Empire, de Gaulle met with opposition wherever he found sizable Vichy government forces. This started with an abortive operation against the French West African port of Dakar (September 1940), in which sudden reinforcements sent by Vichy made the taking of the city impossible. In de Gaulle's view, the Dakar issue was straightforward: According to the terms of the armistice, Vichy could not move any troops or ships without the agreement of the Germans. Therefore Vichy military moves at Dakar and other places were being carried out with the agreement of, and essentially on behalf of, the Germans.[164]

De Gaulle's aloof, lofty, and harsh style did not bring him popularity, especially in the early days of the Free French movement. Churchill's forthright endorsement of de Gaulle had been followed by the rude shock at Dakar. A similar situation occurred the following spring in the Levant, when a British-led joint operation with the Free French met with sharp though not successful resistance from the local Vichy forces. The British came to realize that their candidate to lead the French Resistance was not particularly well liked, certainly not within the upper levels of the French military. Thereafter, Churchill was determined not to associate de Gaulle with other British operations in French territories because this could make such operations more difficult. That consideration, in addition to de Gaulle's insistence on ensuring Free French political primacy in these areas of French influence, led Churchill to go it alone, seizing Madagascar (May 1942) to de Gaulle's bitter surprise. When the British then dealt independently and sympathetically with the Vichy commanders in these areas as they laid down their arms, de Gaulle was furious.

De Gaulle's ambivalent feelings about Churchill are evident in the portrait he sketched of the great Englishman in his *War Memoirs:*

> Certainly within the alliance itself Churchill did not deal gently with me, and later, with regard to the Levant, his behavior had been that of an adversary. . . . this great politician had always been convinced that

France was necessary to the free world; and this exceptional artist was certainly conscious of the dramatic character of my mission. But when he saw France in my person as an ambitious state apparently eager to recover her power in Europe and the world, Churchill had quite naturally felt something of Pitt's spirit in his own soul. Yet in spite of everything, the essential and ineffaceable fact remained that without him my efforts would have been futile from the start, and that by lending me a strong and willing hand when he did, Churchill had vitally aided the cause of France.[165]

A more unvarnished, less charitable view of Churchill was given to Alain Peyrefitte by de Gaulle in 1963: "Churchill was magnificent until [19]42. Afterwards, because he had exhausted himself by too heavy an effort, he passed the torch to the Americans and effaced himself behind them."[166]

The problem of the oath that the French military officers had sworn to their government authorities was to bedevil de Gaulle continually. He repressed discussing this problem but occasionally admitted it. The strong opposition he met "stems particularly from a certain aspect of professional honor on the part of the officers who have received a military mission and from an ingrained discipline." However, this in no way "reflect[ed] their sentiments, which, deep down, are favorable to our victory."[167]

Time and again the Vichy government's military establishment, in carrying out its duty, was to demonstrate its hostility to de Gaulle.

Both de Gaulle and Pétain, then, had laid claim to being the legitimate government of France. In the sense that Pétain, as the providential savior in the moment of the greatest national agony France had ever known, had the overwhelming support of the people, there is much to sustain Vichy's claim of legitimacy. Even de Gaulle admitted that Pétain's aim of a "national revolution," announced by the marshal on October 11, 1940,[168] had some merit:

> The social doctrines of "national revolution"—corporate organization, a labor charter, family allowances—embodied ideas that were not without their attractions. But the fact that this enterprise was identified with the capitulation could only influence the masses toward an entirely different mystique. That of Communism offered itself to their rage, and to their hopes.[169]

Indeed there is another dimension to legitimacy, beyond that of the people's support. Roger Filon, the American legal scholar, has pointed out:

"Legitimacy" in its narrower, legal sense, is simply a synonym for "legal." . . . This . . . however . . . is not the sense we ordinarily intend when we say that a government is legitimate or that some government action is illegitimate. What we mean, rather, is to make a *moral* claim.[170]

Here, of course, is where the Vichy claim for legitimacy broke down completely; most egregiously, Vichy even went beyond what the Germans asked for in rounding up Jews for deportation.

The Vichy regime at its apex—in the figure of Marshal Pétain—can be said to have represented in the main the last gasp of the conservative and Catholic Right in France, which had never accepted the results of the French Revolution. De Gaulle, although himself basically a man of the right (and a practicing Catholic), accepted the outcome of the French Revolution, that is, the Republic. As he later said to his information minister Alain Peyrefitte, "I don't like the Republic for the Republic['s sake], but because the French adhere to it, it is necessary to [do so]. They cannot imagine living except in a Republic."[171] Thus, with these contrasting strands of French thinking bound within him, de Gaulle can be truly said to represent a synthesis; therefore, in a curious way, he came to represent, over the course of World War II, the "general will" of the French people.

Despite his somewhat lugubrious temperament, de Gaulle maintained an outward long-term optimism, through sheer effort of will and the security of his conviction. In an article written on Bastille Day, July 14, 1940, shortly after the Mers-el-Kebir incident, de Gaulle stated, "In the depths of our abasement, this day should rally us together in faith, in will, and in hope."[172] In the very depths of his own personal abasement, right after the Dakar fiasco in September 1940, de Gaulle wrote to his wife: "At the moment, all the rubble is falling on my head. But the faithful are remaining faithful, and I remain optimistic about the future."[173] In July 1941, de Gaulle would write, "It is necessary, in fact, to have a soul of steel, so cruel are the events and so heavy the responsibilities."[174]

FREE FRANCE VERSUS WASHINGTON

De Gaulle's view of himself—as a counterpart of the other wartime leaders and therefore entitled to engage in the "higher conduct of war"— contrasted sharply with Franklin Roosevelt's view. The president had his first meeting with de Gaulle at the time of the Casablanca Conference in January 1943, which the General attended only under heavy British pressure. Roosevelt remarked to Ambassador Robert Murphy that the conversation left something to be desired and that de Gaulle had shown himself to be "rigid and unforthcoming regarding Roosevelt's wish to pursue the war energetically."[175] De Gaulle, on the other hand, saw the United States's constant invoking of the "exigencies of the military situation" as a way of denying him any political role.[176]

From the start, de Gaulle felt he had to establish his claim for legitimacy against that of Vichy. He threw down this challenge wherever an opportunity presented itself and, as we have seen, sometimes with disastrous results. De Gaulle's policy of regaining every bit of French territory piece by piece applied to obscure possessions such as the St. Pierre and Miquelon Islands in the North Atlantic and Clipperton Island in the Pacific, off the coast of South America!

Rallying St. Pierre and Miquelon to the Gaullist movement after a coup de main by Free French naval forces on Christmas Eve 1941 was a military success but a political disaster: In Washington, it seemed as though de Gaulle had violated the Monroe Doctrine just as the United States was entering the war and was increasing its convoys across the North Atlantic. Furthermore, the American administration was negotiating at the time with the Vichy authorities in Martinique about the use of French possessions in the Atlantic. Worst of all, Washington had been given to understand that de Gaulle would not move against the islands without prior notification.

On January 31, 1942, in the aftermath of the St. Pierre–Miquelon affair, de Gaulle, with an exaggerated bitterness, likened the issue to that of Munich. Washington was leaning toward taking the islands back from the Free French, as Neville Chamberlain and Edouard Daladier in 1938 had "[taken] the Sudetens away from the Czechs, for the same reasons and with the same consequences. . . . Our allies . . . seek to contest this rallying of France around us."[177]

De Gaulle seems to have had the notion that, as long as American public opinion was on his side, it would save his position vis-à-vis the U.S. government. Winston Churchill tried to disabuse him of this idea during a conversation on July 29, 1942; Churchill reproached him for the way he had conducted the St. Pierre–Miquelon operation. In de Gaulle's account of this meeting, Churchill said he saw no problem if de Gaulle occupied St. Pierre–Miquelon, Dakar, and even Paris. But de Gaulle had placed him in a very delicate position. Roosevelt and U.S. Secretary of State Cordell

Hull had thought de Gaulle had kept Churchill abreast of the operation. This situation was very irksome.[178]

"Yes," replied de Gaulle, "but nevertheless American opinion had reacted in favor of the Fighting French." Churchill observed that the relationship between public opinion and the government was not the same in America as in Britain. In the latter the government is obliged, sooner or later, to follow public opinion. In the United States, there is public opinion, and alongside it there is a "political machine," with no direct relationship between the two.[179]

As of September 1941, de Gaulle claimed that the Free French had fifty thousand men under arms,[180] but as far as London and especially Washington were concerned, de Gaulle's forces had little more than nuisance value militarily. It was not until the Battle of Bir Hakeim in May 1942 that the Allies came to realize that de Gaulle had managed to put together a credible fighting force of his own. In this battle, the First Free French Division (forty-four hundred men), led by General Joseph-Pierre Koenig, defended this North African desert post for fourteen days against first an Italian and then a German attacking force.

By the time of the Battle of Bir Hakeim, de Gaulle himself had become aware that the Free French movement was gaining in appeal. In the same month (May 1942), de Gaulle wrote that the Allies were becoming aware of growing support in France for the Free French movement. The Allies were not accepting it with good grace, however, as they preferred "a more malleable France than a France rallied around us." But the Allies had to accept the facts, and though they created obstacles for the Free French, they did not dare to go to an extreme. De Gaulle added: "A new and favorable element in this affair is the attitude of Russia. The Soviets are well informed on the state of mind in France, are chronically irritated by Anglo-Saxon hesitations, and are very disposed to support us diplomatically because the reconstituting of a great and strong France is essential to their future policy."[181]

But de Gaulle was an actor along a military and political front run by the Anglo-Americans, not by the Russians. And the dialectic between the General and his Anglo-American allies was such that restraint was imposed on the Gaullist side as well. Though applied to British policies in the Levant, the following passage from de Gaulle's war memoirs could be applied to the whole gamut of his relations with the British and Americans:

> Only the prospect of a rupture with us and the necessity of conciliating the feelings of France could impose on London a certain moderation. But

the same prospect and the same necessity similarly restricted our own freedom of action. The moral and material damage that separation from Great Britain would entail for us was bound, obviously, to make us hesitate.[182]

Nevertheless, despite the growing strength of the Gaullist movement and its military elements, the Allies, and especially Franklin Roosevelt, thought it would be unwise to associate de Gaulle with the North African invasion, which was planned for the fall of 1942. Accordingly, the Americans—the landing was to be primarily their affair—began looking for another French military figure whom the French army in North Africa could rally around or at least regard with neutrality. Roosevelt's emissary, Robert Murphy, first the chargé d'affaires, then the deputy chief at the American mission in Vichy, sounded out Maxime Weygand, who had been removed from his position as chief of staff at the insistence of the Germans. When Weygand proved reluctant, Murphy turned to Henri Giraud, a French general officer who had commanded an army corps in 1940 and had been captured by the Germans. Giraud, who had managed to escape German captivity, had returned to the Vichy-controlled zone.

Giraud did not prepare himself in time to have any effect on the North African invasion. He was in Gibraltar when the landings took place, and American troops generally met with stiff resistance from the Vichy forces. The Americans then turned to the second in command of the Vichy regime, the ardent collaborationist Admiral François Darlan, who happened to be in Algiers visiting his son. Darlan agreed to stop the conflict.

Part of the problem in this "Franco-French" infighting was that the Vichy officers, in order to join de Gaulle, would first have had to throw away their military careers. Some, however, saw the North African invasion as an honorable way out of the moribund Vichy regime, which now had direct control over no territory—since German troops had occupied the Vichy zone as a reaction to the invasion. De Gaulle had a dark view of these developments and saw behind them the desire of certain Vichy military officers "to ensure through an old comrade an honorable outcome for themselves in the present and in the future. It was for that [reason] that the departure of Giraud from France was so easy. It also explains the presence of Darlan at Algiers and his attitude."[183]

On November 16, 1942, less than two weeks after the North African invasion, de Gaulle told Churchill that Giraud, though still usable militarily, was of no value politically. First of all, Giraud had signed a sworn statement of loyalty to Pétain. When the American minister to Dublin, who was present at this conversation with Churchill, observed that Giraud had been taken to Germany and had reportedly been tortured by the Germans, de Gaulle retorted harshly that "if Giraud had preferred perjury to martyrdom, this was no reason to believe he had emerged enhanced from this adventure." But beyond this, said de Gaulle, "General Giraud has received his command from the American authorities, and that is unacceptable; certain procedures that are perhaps applicable for Peru are certainly not for France."[184]

In truth, Giraud's commitment to Pétain was compromising: In a letter of May 4, 1942, Giraud wrote to Pétain, "I give you my word as an officer that I will do nothing whatsoever to disturb our relations with the German government or to hamper the work you have charged Admiral Darlan and [Prime Minister] Pierre Laval to accomplish under your high authority."[185]

De Gaulle, who had had a history of contretemps with Giraud when he was under Giraud's command in the late 1930s,[186] found it essential not to accept Giraud ultimately as a political equal. To do so would have meant establishing Vichy on a par of legitimacy with the Free French movement. At the same time, de Gaulle realized that Giraud had acquitted himself honorably as a soldier in the 1940 campaign.

Whereas de Gaulle regarded Giraud with a mixture of suspicion and condescension (which was fully reciprocated), his attitude was quite different with Darlan. De Gaulle was furious at the American rehabilitation of Darlan, one of Vichy's most prominent pro-German advocates. On November 14, 1942, he wrote to Churchill in the following terms:

> The French nation sees the United States not only recognize, as it has done till now, a power founded on the betrayal of France and its allies, a tyrannical regime of Nazi inspiration, and men who have identified themselves with collaboration with the Germans, but now also associate itself on the ground with this power, with this regime, and with these men.[187]

On the following day, November 15, 1942, de Gaulle remarked to Admiral Harold Stark, the American representative in London to the Free French movement, "I can understand the United States's paying for the treason of traitors if this appears to be profitable, but this should not be at the expense of the honor of France."[188]

Four days later, in a note to Allied governments on November 19, 1942, de Gaulle wrote of the "stupor, anger, and disgust" aroused in French public opinion by "the political operation carried out in North Africa by an Allied power." This operation, stated de Gaulle, consisted of "using the so-called 'conversion' of Darlan to connect Darlan and his friends with the recovery of North Africa for the war of liberation. . . . The Vichyites, the Gaullists, and the Communists are all three exasperated."[189]

At a French National Day (Bastille Day) reception in London on July 14, 1942, Charles de Gaulle meets General Dwight D. Eisenhower. At Eisenhower's right is Admiral Harold Stark, the American representative to the Free French movement in London.

Indeed, de Gaulle was so agitated by Darlan's rehabilitation that he had even expressed indirectly some kind words for the Vichyites, one of the rare places that such words appear in his writings.

Darlan soon ceased to be a problem, however, as he was assassinated on Christmas Eve by a twenty-year-old French rightist youth, Fernand Bonnier de la Chapelle, himself executed less than two days later on Giraud's orders. The swiftness of the execution increased the rumors that the act had been politically sponsored. The French monarchists and Gaullists were most frequently mentioned, but these rumors were never proved.

In order to secure their North African rear, following the demise of Darlan, the Americans now saw it as imperative that Giraud be put in charge of the French population in the area and that de Gaulle be made to cooperate with him. Winston Churchill accordingly was prevailed upon to put heavy pressure on de Gaulle to come to the Casablanca Conference, where the famous picture of the stiff handshake between him and Giraud was taken.

On January 23, 1943, from inside the American barbed wire enclosure at the Casablanca Conference, de Gaulle sent out a letter to Captain Loys Tochon, one of his former students. In the letter, de Gaulle revealed the depths of his estrangement from American policy, starting with the demand that Free French forces be made subordinate to General Giraud. The real reasons for this, stated de Gaulle, were:

First, the desire of the Americans to ensure at whatever cost the triumph of the American team, whom you know. [The Americans] have been aiming since the armistice to maintain Vichy for the purpose of bringing her into the victory. This policy is referred to here in turn as Giraud, then Darlan, then Giraud again.

Second, the desire of the Americans to establish in North Africa and, if possible, throughout the [French] Empire, pending the establishment in France itself, of a French power that is completely beholden to them and consequently will not be able to refuse them anything. The Giraud combination is ideal for the Americans because it procures for them these realities under honorable appearances.[190]

The "American team" referred to by de Gaulle obviously meant Giraud, whose attitude, as described in the General's *War Memoirs*, was "a direct reflection of Murphy's suggestions."[191] As for Robert Murphy, he was portrayed in the *War Memoirs* as "skillful and determined, long familiar with the best society and apparently rather inclined to believe that France consisted of the people he dined with in town."[192]

In the letter to his former student, de Gaulle referred to the "ambiance created at Casablanca under the control of the Anglo-Saxons," which "recalled that of Berchtesgaden,"[193] the object being to force negotiations between de Gaulle and Giraud. Toward the end of the letter, de Gaulle stated, "In the extreme hypothesis of a rupture, there is no doubt that London and Washington will present things in their way—that is, in heaping blame on me." Since de Gaulle's means of getting his message out to the French people was limited, he asked Tochon to give the letter as much publicity as possible "if things turn completely bad."[194]

The "extreme hypothesis of a rupture" did not take place, but it nearly did in the aftermath of Casablanca. De Gaulle finally overcame the Allies' objections to letting him go to Algiers, where he arrived on May 30, 1943. On June 3, the French Committee of National Liberation (FCNL) was set up (to replace the London-based French National Committee).[195] Though de Gaulle had to compromise in that both he and Giraud were initially named copresidents of the FCNL, de Gaulle's presence on the ground in

North Africa immediately had its effect. Giraud was soon relegated to a purely military role.

Later, in 1950, de Gaulle recalled this difficult relationship with Washington in a letter to a friend:

> From the early signs of U.S. direct action in Europe (1941), I tried by my terribly reduced means to get American policymakers to acknowledge that it was in the interest of the world that it have a dialogue with Europe—which at the time meant essentially Free France. But the repressed passion of Roosevelt, the intrigues of the British, the equivocation that Vichy represented—all this prevented it from happening. The result was Tehran, Yalta, Potsdam.[196]

From one viewpoint, it would seem the ultimate in *outrecuidance* (extreme gall) for de Gaulle to claim to represent all of Europe (for after all, what did the Free French movement represent if not essentially the person of de Gaulle himself?). But to substantiate de Gaulle's claim there was the fact that of all the countries of Europe conquered by the Germans, the largest and most important was France. And to narrow the seeming breadth of his statement, in the de Gaulle perspective, Europe meant essentially continental Europe.

The wartime American view of de Gaulle grew most pejorative in the upper reaches of the Roosevelt administration, notably with the president himself. It was a curious situation: The rebarbative de Gaulle was largely scorned by the Allies (particularly by Franklin Roosevelt and his advisers), yet the shame and guilt lay with the Vichy leadership. For de Gaulle's reasoning was sound: France was the only country invaded by the Germans that had asked for an armistice. The Vichy regime had irrevocably compromised itself, at first by its surrender but later even more grievously by its identification with Nazi policies and its active persecution of Jews in France. As the American scholar Tony Judt has pointed out, Vichy France was the only country without a German military presence in which Jews were turned over to the Germans for deportation.[197]

In an apparent allusion to Nazi anti-Semitic policies, de Gaulle stated in May 1941, "We see the enemy installing [in France] his hatreds and his doctrines, [in order] to reorganize the whole French nation. This is the slope down which are likely rolling those who, having still the means to live, preferred to capitulate."[198]

Since the Vichy policy toward Jews in France could only have been exercised from the top down, anyone associated with that regime should have expected to be regarded as politically compromised. That Pétain could have said, in his only trip to Paris during the occupation (on April 26,

1944, to protest Allied bombings around the city), that on his next visit he expected to come unencumbered by German guards was fantasy. Said Pétain: "This is a first visit I am making to you today. I hope to come back later; and at that time I won't need to notify my guards. I will be without them, and we will be completely at ease. I will see you soon, I hope."[199]

Though large crowds acclaimed the eighty-eight-year-old marshal, even at that late date, this reception could not obscure the fact that he had irrevocably compromised himself and his regime with his obedience to Hitler.

But despite this flaw in Vichy's legitimacy—and the policy of persecution of the Jews had been set in motion as early as the summer of 1942[200]—the American government continued with its anti–de Gaulle policy. Secretary of State Cordell Hull, in a radio address on April 9, 1944, announced that the French Committee of National Liberation (FCNL) was not equivalent to the government of France, and at the end of military operations the French people would exercise their sovereignty in choosing for themselves the government that they wanted.[201] Later, on June 3, 1944, just before the Normandy invasion, the FCNL transformed itself into the Provisional Government of the French Republic, which was, however, not fully recognized by the United States until October 23, 1944. The Soviet and British governments followed suit at the same time.

THE "ASSUMPTION" OF PARIS, AUGUST 1944

On the afternoon of June 4, 1944, Charles de Gaulle, who had arrived in London that morning from Algiers, was officially informed of the Normandy invasion in a meeting at Portsmouth with Churchill and Eisenhower. De Gaulle had last seen Eisenhower on December 30, 1943, at which time he thought he had extracted a commitment from Eisenhower that it would be French troops who would take possession of the city of Paris when the time came.[202]

However, at the moment of the Normandy invasion, Free French army units were not included at the express wish of President Roosevelt—partly, presumably, out of animus toward de Gaulle and partly because of fears related to the Free French forces' reputation in Washington for a lack of secrecy.

Also at issue on the eve of the invasion were the currency the Allies would issue in Metropolitan France and a proclamation by Eisenhower, which stated that he would be the supreme authority in the country.

De Gaulle objected, in vain, to both of these procedures, describing the former to Churchill as "a so-called French currency, issued by foreign powers, which the Government of the Republic refuses to recognize."[203]

De Gaulle entered Metropolitan French territory for the first time since the fall of France in a brief visit to Bayeux on June 14, 1944, then returned to Algiers via London. He met Eisenhower again at the latter's Normandy headquarters on August 20, 1944. By this time the Free French Second Armored Division, commanded by General Philippe Leclerc, had arrived in Normandy on August 1 and had become engaged in the campaign.

At this point de Gaulle had to face—or thought he had to face—another unhelpful gambit of the Roosevelt administration: an attempt to resurrect the moribund National Assembly, which would be a way of deflecting a direct seizure of authority by the General in Paris. "No one doubted," wrote the General, "that if de Gaulle reached the capital without being met by some *fait accompli* there, he would be sanctioned by popular acclaim."[204]

The originator of the National Assembly idea, which de Gaulle claimed was favored by Roosevelt,[205] was Pierre Laval, who apparently thought the victors would give him some credit for his proposal. Laval's chosen instrument for carrying out this plan was the former Chamber of Deputies president Edouard Herriot, whom he brought to Paris on August 13. According to de Gaulle's *War Memoirs,* Herriot received encouragement in this venture from the Americans, specifically from the office of Allen Dulles in Berne through a French intermediary who was a friend of Herriot, a Mr. Enfière.[206]

In order for this desperate plan to be launched, Paris had to be kept quiet and free of military moves to regain it, and Laval, the master-mind of the plan, had to carry it off while retaining the acquiescence of the Germans and Marshal Pétain. In their meeting on August 20, de Gaulle sensed Eisenhower's discomfort at his query as to why the Allies were crossing the Seine but not moving on Paris, and he attributed this reluctance to Washington's continued efforts to make things difficult for him. However, according to de Gaulle, Eisenhower gave the order two days later for Leclerc's Free French troops to enter Paris.[207]

The danger, as de Gaulle saw it, came not only from his fear of American connivance in the Laval plan, which was never proven. (In any event, the plan did not receive enough support even to be launched.) A more present danger came from the National Council of the Resistance (CNR), which was strongly influenced by the Communists. Wrote de Gaulle:

They intended to appear at the [Paris] insurrection's head as a kind of Commune which would proclaim the Republic, answer for public order, mete out justice, and furthermore be sure to sing only the *Marseillaise*, run up no flag but the tricolor. On my arrival, I would find this "popular" government installed; it would bind my brow with laurel, invite me to assume the place it would show me to, and henceforth pull all the strings itself.[208]

De Gaulle, acutely aware, as always, of the importance of symbols, was later to write in 1953, "If de Gaulle hadn't entered Paris it would not have been a victory of the [French] Resistance."[209] What he meant, beyond his self-identification with France, was that the French Communists might have taken control of the capital, at least for a time.

Leclerc's division did get to Paris first, and in a ceremony on August 25 in the billiard room of the Paris prefecture of police, Leclerc accepted the surrender of the German commander in the Paris area, von Choltitz. Also present at the ceremony was Colonel Rol-Tanguy, commander of the Free French forces for the Paris area and a Communist. At a follow-up ceremony the same afternoon at the Montparnasse train station, at which time another document implementing the surrender was signed, Leclerc consented to have Rol-Tanguy cosign the agreement.[210] At this point, de Gaulle arrived and, furious that the Communist-dominated interior Resistance had worked its way into the ceremony, proceeded to dress down Leclerc.[211]

After leaving the Montparnasse station, de Gaulle chose not to go to the Hôtel de Ville, where the National Council of the Resistance (CNR) was reestablishing the machinery of the city government of Paris, but instead went straight to the Ministry of National Defense and War in a symbolic gesture aimed at physically "resuming" the reins of the national government. There, at the rue St. Dominique, de Gaulle found the building virtually the same as he and Paul Reynaud had left it when they had departed from Paris together on the evening of June 10, 1940.[212]

Having established his presence there, de Gaulle went to the Hôtel de Ville, where he was received by Georges Bidault and the other members of the CNR as well as some of the fighters from the internal Resistance. There Bidault asked him to proclaim the restoration of the Republic. De Gaulle replied that it was unnecessary: "The Republic has never ceased. Free France, Fighting France, the French Committee of National Liberation have successively incorporated it. Vichy always was and still remains null and void. I myself am the President of the government of the Republic. Why should I proclaim it now?"[213]

In other words, de Gaulle was saying that he had been carrying the mantle of legitimacy since the broadcast of June 18, 1940, and no one was going to take it away from him.

On the following day, August 26, 1944, in another symbolic gesture of great meaning at the time and for the future, de Gaulle was able to create an "irresistible national movement" in his favor, symbolized by a procession down the avenue des Champs-Elysées with himself at the head (he admonished Bidault to stay behind him).[214] The ceremony included elements of the Free French Second Armored Division, despite a stipulation by General Leonard Gerow, the American commander of the Fifth Army Corps and Leclerc's superior, that no French military units should be included.[215]

According to de Gaulle, some two million people[216] witnessed and participated in this great moment of national wonderment and elation embodied in this exclusively French spectacle. By that time scattered Allied units, which had passed through the Porte d'Italie at the time of the capture of the city, had moved on. As he passed by the statue of Georges Clemenceau, near the lower end of the Champs-Elysées, de Gaulle "hailed [him] in passing," and Clemenceau "looked as if he were springing up to march beside us."[217]

The Gaullist forces had brushed aside the Pétainists, the Communists, and even the Allies in this rush to seize the levers of national command in Paris. In the short period from June 4 until August 26, which began when de Gaulle was briefed at Portsmouth as a nonparticipant in the Normandy invasion and which culminated in a mass procession led by the General on the Champs-Elysées, de Gaulle's progress seemed irresistible. In between these two dates, de Gaulle had paid his first visit to Washington (July 6–10), where he had been unable to obtain full, de jure recognition[218] for his provisional government and had not measurably improved his relationship with Roosevelt. Throughout this period de Gaulle seemed buoyed by his confidence that mass support for him existed and needed only to be tapped at the right moment. As he wrote in his *War Memoirs,* "I found . . . [the] apparent stubbornness of Washington's policy quite depressing. But consolation was not far away. A great tide of popular enthusiasm seized me on my entry into Cherbourg [on August 20] and bore me onward."[219]

Even after he had "assumed," or taken responsibility for, Paris, for de Gaulle long wrangles lay ahead with the French Communists and with the Allied Command. There was also one bit of unfinished business with the Vichy government. An emissary from Pétain brought a written suggestion from the marshal that the two arrange a national reconciliation, "provided that the principle of legitimacy which I incarnate be pre-served."[220] De Gaulle wrote in his *War Memoirs*, "The only reply I could give him was my silence."[221]

As for the Communists, de Gaulle recorded in his *War Memoirs* that he had determined at the outset to assure the Communists of representation in the National Council of the Resistance (CNR) and at the decision-making level. "But I was quite as decided," said de Gaulle, "not to let them ever gain the upper hand, bypass me, or take the lead . . . ; all doctrines, all schools, all rebellions, have only one time. Communism will pass. But France will not pass."[222]

Allowing the Communists fully into the Resistance organization inside France was not without its risks, particularly because the Communists were so numerous among the fighters. For Georges Bidault, a Christian Democrat and the head of the "guiding body"—the CNR[223]—there was the risk, as de Gaulle saw it, of "find[ing] himself overpowered at the very heart of this Areopagus by a disciplined group experienced in revolutionary action and excelling in the use of conflict as well as camaraderie."[224]

Soon after its creation in 1943, the fifteen-member CNR had delegated its powers to a board of four, of whom two were Communists. The CNR had also instituted the "Action Committee," dominated by the Communists, to deal with military matters.[225] In April 1944, de Gaulle sought to achieve tighter control over the internal Resistance by naming one of his trusted military lieutenants, General Joseph-Pierre Koenig, to be in charge of relations with and supplies to the interior, operating out of London. Koenig, who was also the liaison with Eisenhower's headquarters, was given the title of commander of the French Forces of the Interior (FFI).

In a press conference after the war, de Gaulle was asked why his services in London had played politics with the internal Resistance, distributing arms to some and not to others. In his reply, de Gaulle flatly denied the charge and criticized those who were "now trying to divide those who were united in the common work of the Resistance—that is to say, of the National Defense."[226]

This statement, in fact, was the key to de Gaulle's handling of the internal Resistance. The Resistance was not to be considered an independent collection of partisans but a part of the government—the national defense. And de Gaulle, insisting that he had led the legitimate government since June 18, 1940, had only to prove it by arriving first in Paris with the Second Armored Division.

Despite the signing, after much delay, of an agreement between Eisenhower and Koenig on August 25, 1944, regulating the relations between the French administration and the Allied Command,[227] de Gaulle's difficulties continued beyond the ultimate Allied triumph in Europe in May 1945. The first major incident after the capture of Paris was de Gaulle's refusal to obey the orders of the Allied Command to evacuate Free French forces from Strasbourg in the midst of the Battle of the Bulge in December 1944–January 1945. De Gaulle, who regarded the symbol of Strasbourg, the capital of Alsace, to be of overriding importance, threatened to remove his troops from the Allied Command and finally succeeded in persuading Eisenhower to rescind the order.[228]

Another incident occurred in April 1945 regarding de Gaulle's reluctance to remove French troops from Stuttgart to make way for its occupation by American forces. De Gaulle ordered French troops to remain in the city "until the French occupation zone has been established by agreement among the governments concerned."[229] When the matter reached Eisenhower, "it lost a good deal of its sharpness," and though Eisenhower noted that the French were intervening in a strategic matter for political reasons, the French remained in Stuttgart for the time being and eventually got their own occupation zone.[230]

In a third incident, de Gaulle's forces drove into northwest Italy at the end of the war, causing the new U.S. president, Harry Truman, to demand on June 6, 1945, that the French forces withdraw forthwith.[231] De Gaulle pulled his forces out of the Valle d'Aosta, which he claimed he had never intended to occupy anyway, but in the end held on to two French-speaking towns, Tende and La Brigue, which had not been inside the French frontier in 1939.[232] In his account of this incident, as in general, de Gaulle did not indicate that he had had to back down.

De Gaulle wanted French forces to take part as much as possible in the campaign against Germany, reasoning that "Europe would have been lost if France had not been present at the victory."[233] At the same time, he was convinced that the Allies had deliberately limited the supply of arms to the new French units so that the French, in accordance with Roosevelt's wishes, would not be present at the final surrender.[234]

Although admitting that the reconstituted French army was of reduced proportions,[235] de Gaulle claimed that ultimately, French troops amounted to nearly one-fourth of those under Eisenhower's orders.[236] On February 11, 1945, on the occasion of a French-American military ceremony at Colmar after troops from the two countries had driven the Germans from Alsace, de Gaulle reflected, as though emphasizing the immutability of French-American friendship beneath all the quarrels, that patriotic zeal was mixed with another element of enthusiasm—the French and American soldiers' comradeship in arms. It was evident that this brotherhood had been raised to its highest pitch by the mutual success won. . . . Beneath the regiments' motionless silence, I sensed the pulse of friendship that links our two peoples.[237]

In a famous speech at Bayeux in June 1946, after he had led France out of the abyss and had left the helm of the French state, de Gaulle evoked the extralegal nature of his adventure:

If this great work was realized outside the previous framework of our institutions, it was because the institutions had not responded to national necessities and had themselves abdicated in the turmoil. Salvation had to come from outside.

Everywhere that the Cross of Lorraine appeared, it crumbled the structure of an authority that was only fictitious, although it was in appearance constitutionally founded.[238]

How the French state was reconstituted on a legal basis at the end of World War II and how de Gaulle proceeded a dozen years later to reorder French institutions will be the subject of the next chapter.

NOTES

[1] Charles de Gaulle, *The Complete War Memoirs of Charles de Gaulle*, vol. 3, *Salvation, 1944–1946*, trans. Richard Howard (New York: Simon and Schuster, 1964), 871 (all volumes hereafter cited as *WM*).

[2] Charles de Gaulle, *Lettres, notes, et carnets*, vol. 1 (Paris: Plon, 1980), 69 (all volumes hereafter cited as *LNC*).

[3] "The French people had for centuries grown accustomed to think of their country as the mastodon of Europe. It was this sense of their greatness and the responsibilities it entailed that preserved their unity." (From de Gaulle's account of what he said to Konrad Adenauer in their first meeting in France, in mid-September 1958 at de Gaulle's home at Colombey-les-Deux-Eglises, shortly after the General had returned to power.) Charles de Gaulle, "Renewal, 1958–1962," pt. 1 of *Memoirs of Hope: Renewal and Endeavor*, trans. Terence Kilmartin (New York: Simon and Schuster, 1971), 178.

[4] Leclerc was the *nom de guerre* of Philippe de Hautecloque, one of the few French army officers who rejected the Pétain armistice. A captain at the time of the fall of France, he managed, despite having been wounded, to escape German captivity. He obtained a false passport and arrived in London on July 25, 1940, via Spain and Portugal. Jean Planchais, "La mort de Leclerc, héros et victime du désert," *Le Monde*, Nov. 29–30, 1987, 2.

[5] Pierre Galante, *The General* (London: Leslie Frewin, 1969), 42 (hereafter cited as *PGTG*).

[6] Ibid., 39.

[7] *LNC*, vol. 1, 7–23.

[8] Ibid., 7.

[9] *PGTG*, 36.

[10] *LNC*, vol. 12 (1988), 162.

[11] *LNC*, vol. 1, 513.

[12] *LNC*, vol. 2 (1980), 11.

[13] From the speech at Bayeux, June 16, 1946. Charles de Gaulle, *Discours et messages*, vol. 2, *Dans l'attente, Février 1946–Avril 1958* (Paris: Omnibus/Plon, 1993), 310. The text of this speech, with only minor excisions, is in Part Two, The Documents. (In this study, the abbreviation *DM-OP* will indicate when the Omnibus/Plon edition is used. *DM* signifies the earlier Plon edition.)

[14] *PGTG*, 45.

[15] *LNC*, vol. 2 (1980), 284. This line is actually from a popular French song of the 1930s. De Gaulle's most famous line — "All my life I have had a certain idea of France" — with which he begins his *War Memoirs*, is actually borrowed in part from Maurice Barrès, an early-twentieth-century rightist writer who exerted a great influence on de Gaulle. See Alain Peyrefitte, *C'était de Gaulle* (Paris: Fayard, 1994), 279 (hereafter cited as *APCG*).

[16] *LNC*, vol. 2, 215.

[17] Ibid., 224.

[18] Ibid., 109.

[19] Ibid., 105. Elsewhere in de Gaulle's writings, these words are attributed to an unspecified biography of Hoche. Charles de Gaulle, *Le fil de l'épée* (Paris: Editions Berger-Levrault, 1944), 83–84 (hereafter cited as *CGFE*).

[20] Charles de Gaulle, *The Edge of the Sword*, trans. Gerard Hopkins (Westport, Conn.: Greenwood, 1960), 57 (hereafter cited as *CGES*).

[21] *LNC*, vol. 2, 41.

[22] Ibid.

[23] *LNC*, vol. 3 (1981), 405. "Boches" was a pejorative name the French used for the Germans during World War I.

[24] *LNC*, vol. 2, 295–310.

[25] *LNC*, vol. 1, 74.

[26] Ibid., 459.

[27] *LNC*, vol. 2, 342.

[28] *LNC*, vol. 1, 520.

[29] *LNC*, vol. 2, 30.

[30] Ibid., 72.

[31] De Gaulle delivered a series of three such lectures under Pétain's patronage. *LNC*, vol. 2, 310–11.

[32] *LNC*, vol. 12, 243.

[33] *LNC*, vol. 2, 472–73.

[34] Ibid., 477–80.

[35] *LNC*, vol. 4 (1982), 87.

[36] *LNC*, vol. 2, 397.

[37] Ibid., 397–98.

[38] *LNC*, vol. 3, 436.

[39] *LNC*, vol. 2, 402.

[40] Jean Lacouture, *De Gaulle*, vol. 1, *Le rebelle* (Paris: Seuil, 1984), 264–65 (all volumes hereafter cited as *JLDG*).

[41] *LNC*, vol. 3, 443–44.

[42] Ibid., 380.

[43] *LNC*, vol. 3, 422.

[44] *APCG*, 264.

[45] In 1536, a formal alliance was concluded between the Ottoman sultan Suleiman the Magnificent and Francis I, against the Hapsburg emperor Charles V, who had been crowned Holy Roman Emperor and king of Italy six years earlier, in what was the last imperial coronation by a pope. *LNC*, vol. 2, 442.

[46] Maurin, who resigned in 1936, was hostile to de Gaulle's proposal for a large and

autonomous armored force for the French army. *Dictionnaire commenté de l'oeuvre du général de Gaulle* (Paris: Plon, 1975), 532.

[47] Ibid., 447.

[48] Ibid., 484.

[49] *LNC*, vol. 3, 448. The *Reichswehr* was the term for the German army under the Versailles Treaty, which Hitler denounced in 1935.

[50] *LNC*, vol. 2, 486.

[51] "Chronologie: Charles de Gaulle et son temps," in *CGFE*.

[52] *LNC*, vol. 3, 472–73.

[53] "Chronologie: Charles de Gaulle et son temps," in *CGFE*.

[54] *LNC*, vol. 3, 442.

[55] *LNC*, vol. 1, 460.

[56] *LNC*, vol. 2, 499.

[57] Ibid., 497.

[58] Ibid., 496.

[59] *LNC*, vol. 3, 476–77.

[60] Camille Chautemps, *Cahiers secrets de l'armistice* (Paris: Plon, 1963), 129 (hereafter cited as *CS*).

[61] "Chronologie: Charles de Gaulle et son temps," entry for 11 June 1940, in *CGFE*.

[62] *LNC*, vol. 4, 214.

[63] *WM*, vol. 1, *The Call to Honour, 1940–1942*, trans. Jonathan Griffin, 73.

[64] *Foreign Relations of the United States*, 1940, vol. 1 (U.S. Government Printing Office, 1959) 247 (hereafter cited as *FRUS*).

[65] L'Institut Charles de Gaulle, *Chronologie de la vie du général de Gaulle* (Paris: Plon, 1973), 22.

[66] *FRUS*, 1940, vol. 7, 248–50. President Roosevelt's reply, although expressing support for France, stressed that no military commitment could be made, as this could be done only by Congress. Ibid., 255–56.

[67] *LNC*, vol. 3, 477–78.

[68] Ibid., 477.

[69] *WM*, vol. 1, 73–74.

[70] Ibid., 75–77.

[71] Ibid., 78.

[72] *JLDG*, vol. 1, 343.

[73] Cordell Hull, *Memoirs*, vol. 1 (New York: Macmillan, 1948), 793.

[74] *JLDG*, 342.

[75] *WM*, vol. 1, 80.

[76] Ibid., 78.

[77] Ibid., 81.

[78] *WM*, vol. 3, 750.

[79] *WM*, vol. 2, *Unity, 1942–1944*, trans. Richard Howard, 580.

[80] The text of de Gaulle's declaration can be found in Part Two, The Documents.

[81] *LNC*, vol. 3, 14.

[82] *LNC*, vol. 2, 173.

[83] It was Adm. Horatio Nelson who defeated the French in the naval Battle of Trafalgar in 1805. *CGES*, 45.

[84] The French National Assembly under the Third Republic consisted of two houses, the Chamber of Deputies and the Senate.

[85] Jules Jeanneney, *Journal politique: Septembre 1939–Juillet 1942*, ed. Jean-Noël Jeanneney (Paris: Armand Colin, 1972), 315 (hereafter cited as *JP*). To the list of those opposed must be added the twenty-seven parliamentarians who had boarded the ship *Massilia* at Bordeaux, bound for North Africa, in the expectation that the war would be continued from there. Jean-Pierre Azéma, *1940, l'année terrible* (Paris: Seuil, 1990), 181.

[86] The text of the Constitutional Law of July 10, 1940, is contained in Part Two, The Documents.

[87] *JP*, 314.

[88] From a text proposed by de Gaulle, dated June 23, 1940. The text was to have been part of a British statement recognizing the new French National Committee under de Gaulle, but the committee was not formed at the time because few prominent French persons rallied to de Gaulle. *LNC*, vol. 3, 14.

[89] *FRUS*, 1940, vol. 1, 259–60.

[90] "Chronologie: Charles de Gaulle et son temps," in *CGFE*.

[91] *LNC*, vol. 4, 207–8.

[92] *DM-OP*, vol. 5, *Vers le terme, Janvier 1966–Avril 1969*, 1006–7.

[93] "L'histoire en direct," *France Culture*, July 3, 1989 (voice of Philippe Pétain).

[94] *LNC*, vol. 7 (1985), 15.

[95] Radio broadcast from London on June 26, 1940, addressed to Marshal Pétain. Charles de Gaulle, *Discours et messages*, vol. 1, *Pendant la guerre, Juin 1940–Janvier 1946* (Paris: Plon, 1970), 9.

[96] *LNC*, vol. 3, 59.

[97] *WM*, vol. 2, 665.

[98] *WM*, vol. 3, 951.

[99] Ibid.

[100] *CS*, 135, 240.

[101] From Churchill's speech to the Canadian House of Commons in Ottawa in Dec. 1941. James C. Humes, *The Wit and Wisdom of Winston Churchill* (New York: HarperCollins, 1994), 128.

[102] *WM*, vol. 1, 131.

[103] Ibid., 240.

[104] Ibid., 242.

[105] *WM*, vol. 2, 318.

[106] Ibid., 331.

[107] Ibid., 597.

[108] *LNC*, vol. 4, 213.

[109] *WM*, vol. 1, 201.

[110] *LNC*, vol. 2, 172.

[111] *LNC*, vol. 3, 159.

[112] *LNC*, vol. 4, 161.

[113] Ibid., 93.

[114] Ibid. The Jacobin political grouping, advocating egalitarian democracy imposed through centralized control from Paris, gained the ascendancy over its rivals and ran France during the period of the Terror (1792–94).

[115] *LNC*, vol. 12, 351–52.

[116] On April 22, 1961, elements of the French army staged a coup d'état in Algiers in protest against de Gaulle's self-determination policy for Algeria, which had been approved in a referendum by the French people. The attempt fizzled out in four days after de Gaulle exerted his authority from Paris. *DM-OP*, vol. 3, *Avec le renouveau, Mai 1958–Juillet 1962*, 736.

[117] The expression is that of Georges Pompidou, de Gaulle's prime minister, 1962–67. See *APCG*, 267.

[118] Michel Debré, *Entretiens avec le général de Gaulle, 1961–1969* (Paris: Albin Michel, 1993), 162 (hereafter cited as *MDE*).

[119] *LNC*, vol. 4, 212.

[120] *WM*, vol. 3, 721.

[121] *CGES*, 27.

[122] *MDE*, 11.

[123] Stanley Hoffmann, "The Man Who Would Be France," *The New Republic*, Dec. 17, 1990, 34.

[124] "At this moment, the worst in her history, it was up to me to assume the burden of France." *WM*, vol. 1, 88.

[125] *WM*, vol. 3, 672.

[126] *WM*, vol. 2, 443.

[127] *DM*, vol. 5, 179.

[128] "Les schèmes qu'on abat," *Commentaire*, no. 63 (Fall 1993) and no. 64 (Winter 1993–94). See also notes 28 and 55 in chap. 1. The article's title is a play on words on André Malraux's conversation with de Gaulle near the end of the General's life, described in an article entitled "Les chênes qu'on abat" ("The oaks that are struck down").

[129] Ibid., no. 63, 469–70.

[130] Sheila Mathieu and W. G. Corp, trans., *The Speeches of General de Gaulle*, vol. 1, *June 18, 1940–December 31, 1941* (London: Oxford University Press, 1941), 63–64 (all volumes hereafter cited as *SCDG*).

[131] *LNC*, vol. 3, 167.

[132] This term originated with the Italians. It refers to the charge of the French gendarmes who forced a passage in the Apennines for the French forces of Charles VIII who were returning from Italy in 1495. Albert Malet and Jules Isaac, *L'histoire* (Paris: Editions Marabout, 1993), 298 (hereafter cited as *LH*).

[133] *SCDG*, vol. 2 (1942), 45.

[134] *LNC*, vol. 3, 228.

[135] *LNC*, vol. 4, 325.

[136] *MDE*, 26.

[137] *LNC*, vol. 1, 461.

[138] Ibid.

[139] *LNC*, vol. 4, 460.

[140] Raymond Aron, *Sur Clausewitz* (Paris: Historiques, Editions Complexe, 1987), 63.

[141] *LNC*, vol. 1, 469.

[142] Jan. 20, 1946, is the date de Gaulle resigned from the postwar government. He left office the following day. *LNC*, vol. 6 (1984), 264.

[143] *WM*, vol. 1, 88.

[144] *WM*, vol. 2, 600.

[145] *WM*, vol. 3, 931.

[146] De Gaulle had this reply delivered through the French military attaché in London and received it back in Sept. 1940 with the typewritten notation, "If retired Colonel de Gaulle wishes to communicate with General Weygand, he must do it through normal channels." *WM*, vol. 1, 331.

[147] *LNC*, vol. 3, 26.

[148] Ibid., 27.

[149] "Chronologie: Charles de Gaulle et son temps," in *CGFE*.

[150] *WM*, vol. 1, 86.

[151] Ibid.

[152] William L. Langer, *Our Vichy Gamble* (New York: Knopf, 1947), 65. This is the book version, based on the report Langer submitted to the State Department.

[153] *LNC*, vol. 7 (1985), 224.

[154] *LNC*, vol. 4, 63.

[155] *LNC*, vol. 3, 34.

[156] Ibid., 151.

[157] *LNC*, vol. 4, 72.

[158] Ibid., 73–74.

[159] Ibid., 76.

[160] Ibid., 161.

[161] *LNC*, vol. 3, 320.

[162] *DM*, vol. 1, 13.

[163] *WM*, vol. 1, 91–92. Years later, de Gaulle confided to Alain Peyrefitte that he would have done the same thing had he been in the British position. *APCG*, 145.

[164] *LNC*, vol. 3, 133.

[165] *WM,* vol. 3, 900. "The four years in which William Pitt [the Elder] remained in power [1757–61] were marked by the triumph of England [over France] on the sea, in Canada, and in India." *LH,* 492.

[166] *APCG,* 370.

[167] *LNC,* vol. 3, 357.

[168] *DM,* vol. 1, 175.

[169] Corporate organization, or corporatism, refers to organizing society into industrial and professional organizations that serve as organs of political representation and exercise a degree of control over their members. *WM,* vol. 3, 775.

[170] Roger Pilon, "Individual Rights, Democracy and Constitutional Order: On the Foundations of Legitimacy," *Cato Journal* 11, no. 3 (Winter 1992): 377.

[171] *APCG,* 280.

[172] *LNC,* vol. 3, 36.

[173] Ibid., 127.

[174] Ibid., 375.

[175] *FRUS,* Conferences of Washington and Casablanca, 696.

[176] *WM,* vol. 2, 386.

[177] *LNC,* vol. 4, 192–93.

[178] Ibid., 333.

[179] Ibid., 333–34.

[180] Ibid., 77.

[181] Ibid., 270–71.

[182] *WM,* vol. 1, 206.

[183] *LNC,* vol. 4, 425.

[184] Ibid., 435.

[185] Ibid.

[186] *JLDG,* 265–66.

[187] *LNC,* vol. 4, 429.

[188] Ibid., 434.

[189] Ibid., 438–39.

[190] *LNC,* vol. 4, 505–7.

[191] *WM,* vol. 2, 385.

[192] Ibid., 314.

[193] This is a reference to the Czech crisis of 1938, when Hitler had Neville Chamberlain come to his mountain retreat in Bavaria for negotiations.

[194] *LNC,* vol. 4, 507.

[195] The French National Committee had been formed on September 24, 1941, at which time the role of the Council of the Defense of the Empire had become consultative only.

[196] *LNC,* vol. 6 (1984), 461.

[197] *The New York Review of Books,* Nov. 3, 1994, 10.

[198] *LNC,* vol. 3, 294.

[199] André Kaspi, "Pétain à Paris," *Le Monde,* Apr. 17–18, 1994, 2.

[200] The original law, requiring that Jews be separately identified, was passed by Vichy as early as October 1940.

[201] *LNC,* vol. 5 (1983), 192.

[202] *WM,* vol. 2, 545. Eisenhower, virtually alone among the American leadership, enjoyed a cordial relationship with de Gaulle. Wrote de Gaulle: "I discovered on the American commander-in-chief's part a comprehension which the political pressures of his country refused me." (*WM,* vol. 2, 375). At this same meeting on Dec. 30, 1943, as Eisenhower told him that the unfavorable reports he had originally heard about de Gaulle were wrong, the General replied, "You are a man! For you know how to say, 'I was wrong' " (*WM,* vol. 2, 545).

[203] Ibid., 557–59.

[204] Ibid., 628.

[205] Ibid., 637.

[206] Ibid., 630. Dulles, at Berne, headed the principal post in continental Europe of the Office of Strategic Services (OSS), the U.S. wartime intelligence service.

[207] Ibid., 641.

[208] Ibid., 631. The reference is to the Paris Commune, in which a disparate group of left-wing radicals tried to take control of Paris in the aftermath of the armistice concluded with the Prussians in 1871.

[209] *LNC*, vol. 7 (1985), 154.

[210] *Le Monde*, Nov. 29–30, 1987, 2.

[211] *WM*, vol. 2, 647.

[212] Ibid., 648.

[213] Ibid., 650.

[214] *JLDG*, 837.

[215] *WM*, vol. 2, 652.

[216] Ibid., 653.

[217] Ibid., 655.

[218] De facto recognition was accorded shortly after his visit.

[219] *WM*, vol. 2, 637–38.

[220] Ibid., 663.

[221] Ibid., 665.

[222] *WM*, vol. 1, 269.

[223] In June 1943, Bidault was elected by the CNR as its president, without de Gaulle's having been consulted (*WM*, vol. 2, 490). He replaced de Gaulle's hand-picked man, ex-prefect Jean Moulin, who had been betrayed to the Germans, tortured, and executed.

[224] Areopagus means "high court." *WM*, vol. 2, 490.

[225] Ibid., 491.

[226] *DM-OP*, vol. 2, 347–48.

[227] *WM*, vol. 2, 648.

[228] *WM*, vol. 3, 833–39.

[229] Ibid., 862.

[230] Ibid., 862–63.

[231] Ibid., 875–76.

[232] Ibid., 877.

[233] Ibid., 920.

[234] Ibid., 704.

[235] Ibid., 707.

[236] Ibid., 818.

[237] Ibid., 841.

[238] *DM-OP*, vol. 2, 310.

3

De Gaulle and the Reordering of the French State, 1946–1962

Having attested that victory had been won for the nation thanks only to an authority which rose above all its divisions . . . I saw that henceforth my great battle would be to endow it with a Republic capable of matching up to its destiny.[1]

—*Charles de Gaulle*

REPLACEMENT OF VICHY BY THE PROVISIONAL GOVERNMENT

During World War II, Charles de Gaulle started thinking about postwar arrangements for France and how to avoid repeating the mistakes of the past. By mid-1942, the Gaullist movement seemed at last firmly anchored, after the Free French troops had fought their first major engagement, at Bir Hakeim, Libya, in late May–early June. At the end of June, General de Gaulle sent a letter to the president of the French Senate, Jules Jeanneney. Noting that provisional arrangements should be made for a government to represent the country, de Gaulle asked Jeanneney for his confidential opinion of how the French state should be reconstituted as France re-entered the war.

In his letter dated June 30, 1942, de Gaulle paid tribute to the spirit of Georges Clemenceau, for whom Jeanneney had worked as cabinet director in 1919, by saying that Fighting France would never give up, and he assured Jeanneney that he would safeguard democracy in France.[2]

Jeanneney replied in October 1942. He began by expressing his opinion regarding the National Assembly's decision on July 10, 1940, to give Marshal Pétain power to amend the constitution. (The National Assembly was the designation under the Third Republic that encompassed the two houses [Chamber of Deputies and Senate].) Although Jeanneney had been present at that session, his opinion was that the National Assembly did something that it was not permitted to do. According to the Constitution of 1875, it is to . . . [the National Assembly] alone that this power belongs . . . a competence that it is obligated to exercise itself. The National Assembly's delegation is therefore not valid. The wrongly delegated power was, in explicit terms as well as in the minds of the principals, in the context of a republican constitution. However, the power was used against the institutions of the Republic, even to the extent of changing its designation. Since this power has been abused, it should be revoked.[3]

The juridical basis for Jeanneney's argument was the organic (or constitutional) law of February 25, 1875, which had established the Third Republic. This law stated that the two houses of the National Assembly were to meet together to revise the constitutional laws, which then had to be passed by an absolute majority of their combined membership.[4] Jeanneney's contention was that the National Assembly had repudiated the law by its illegal delegation of constituent powers to Pétain, which in turn had resulted in the demise of the Third Republic. On July 11, 1940, the day after Pétain took charge, he issued Constitutional Act No. 3, which prohibited Parliament from meeting unless convoked by him.[5]

Jeanneney's conclusion therefore was that national sovereignty could not legally be exercised by the still-existing (but nonfunctioning) National Assembly. This body had defaulted on its responsibilities, and consequently, it was up to the "nation" to assume sovereignty, by the medium of a free vote to determine the institutions and the leadership of France. But since a free vote could not be arranged until order had been restored, prisoners of war returned, and voting lists established, a provisional government would have to be set up to govern in the interim and eventually arrange for such a vote.[6]

There was no alternative, said Jeanneney, but to "cross the Rubicon" and create a provisional government until a new assembly could be elected.[7] Pending the holding of general elections for a new assembly, the provisional government would take the form of a committee of national safety of the French Republic and would rule the country, exercising both legislative and executive powers. This committee would be composed of seven members who would themselves elect a president and an alternate president. The committee would legislate through a vote of a majority of four. The earlier constitutional laws for setting up a government (February 24–25 and July 16, 1875) would be suspended.[8]

However, a rival thesis surfaced at around the same time (late 1942–early 1943), espoused by General Henri Giraud and supported by Jean Monnet, who acted as an adviser to Giraud in that period. This thesis had its roots in the so-called Tréveneuc Law of February 15, 1872, which stated that if the National Assembly were illegally dissolved or prevented from meeting, the general councils in each of the French departments[9] should immediately meet. They would each designate two representatives, and provided this procedure were followed in at least half of the departments, these representatives would form an assembly. This assembly would ensure order and provisionally carry out administrative measures primarily aimed at the restitution of the National Assembly's full powers. After the restoration of the National Assembly, this ad hoc assembly would be dissolved.[10]

The Tréveneuc thesis became a public issue in the spring of 1943 after de Gaulle had proposed to Giraud that they organize together a new central governing power for France, along with a consultative assembly of the Resistance. De Gaulle at the time was physically blocked by the Allies from leaving London[11] in the aftermath of the Casablanca Conference, while Giraud was the leading French authority in North Africa, under Allied sponsorship.

The underlying premise of de Gaulle's proposal for unity was that the 1940 armistice would have to be considered null and void. One of the consequences of this determination would be that certain leading Vichy officials in North Africa and West Africa could not be retained in their posts.[12] In de Gaulle's view, keeping these individuals in place served to "disqualify" the Free French movement.[13]

Giraud's reply to de Gaulle, on April 10, 1943, was that he, as French military chief operating under the Allied Command, would be dependent on no French political authority. De Gaulle commented on Giraud's answer as follows:

> This strange apparatus [headed by Giraud] was to operate as long as the war lasted. After that, far from proceeding at once to a national plebiscite, there were plans to invoke a law dating back to 1872, the so-called Tréveneuc Law, which provided that in the absence of a National Assembly it devolved upon the general councils to provide an administration and appoint a government. All in all, according to the memorandum signed by General Giraud, everything would transpire as if France no longer existed as a state, at least until the victory. Such was indeed Roosevelt's intention.[14]

The main lines of the Tréveneuc thesis became the policy of the Roosevelt administration (under the coaching of Jean Monnet) because it seemed the fairest way to constitute a new authority in France at the end of the war. As Roosevelt wrote to General George C. Marshall on June 2, 1944, four days before D-day:

I have a moral duty that transcends "an easy way." It is to see to it that the people of France have nothing foisted on them by outside powers. It must be a French choice—and that means, as far as possible, [of] forty million people. It carries with it a very deep principle in human affairs.[15]

However, from the Gaullist point of view the Tréveneuc thesis accepted the continuity and legitimacy of the Vichy experience; it would be holdover officials of the Vichy government—the members of the general councils in the departments—who would elect the new representatives. Vichy, by de Gaulle's standards, had forfeited its claim to legitimacy. "The legitimacy of a governing power," wrote de Gaulle, "derives from its conviction and the conviction it inspires, that it embodies national unity and continuity when the country is in danger."[16]

Furthermore, subordinating the Free French movement under Giraud's command, as the Allies wanted, would have similarly legitimized Vichy on the military plane, as de Gaulle pointed out: " 'I should have done so with all my heart,' I told them [the Allies], 'had Giraud been in command of North Africa on June 18, 1940, and had he continued the war by repudiating Pétain's and Weygand's injunctions. But today the facts are there. The French nation has taken cognizance of them.' "[17]

Giraud's problem was that he had not answered the "call to honor" on June 18, 1940. Indeed, he was in no position to do so since he was in German captivity at the time. But even if he had had a free choice, he almost certainly would not have acted against Pétain. If he had been in command of North Africa, in the position of General Charles Noguès, his reaction might not have been very different from that of Noguès, who bent to the will of Pétain and Weygand. In addition, Giraud would not have associated himself with a venture of de Gaulle's, quite apart from Giraud's much higher rank: Dating back to the 1930s, no love was lost between the two men, and a colleague of Giraud had once described de Gaulle to a visiting parliamentary commission at Metz as "the stupidest officer in the French army."[18]

But now it was 1943, and for de Gaulle to have resubordinated himself to Giraud would have taken some of the luster off his "call to honor" in 1940. In a way, it would have conceded that de Gaulle's action had been misguided, albeit well-intentioned, and had, moreover, been an incitement to rebellion against the French state.

Thus, under the Tréveneuc thesis, those who had stayed behind in the Vichy administration would have constituted the foundation of the new French state. Though they recognized the practical difficulties involved in creating a provisional administration from the ground up—given the intense rivalry among Vichyites, Communists, and Gaullists at the time—

those who espoused the Tréveneuc thesis did not reckon on the tidal wave of desire for expiation that rose up from the French people and swept out of power many of these Vichy officials at the war's end.

In the final analysis, de Gaulle was able, in imposing the "Jeanneney thesis" over the "Tréveneuc thesis," to uphold the legitimacy of the Gaullist movement over those who had stayed behind and had become part of the Vichy administration.

A third approach to reconstituting the government after the occupation, espoused for a time by Vichy, was to reestablish it through the National Assembly of 1940: In the event of the demise or disappearance of Pétain, powers that the National Assembly had conferred on him in 1940 would revert to this same assembly.[19] To materialize, this project would need to be connected with a prominent person. We have seen in the previous chapter how Pierre Laval sought to coopt Edouard Herriot, the speaker of the Chamber of Deputies, to reconvene the assembly in August 1944. De Gaulle thought this abortive effort had American support, though this has never been proven.[20]

According to de Gaulle, there was an earlier attempt by the Allies to use President Albert Lebrun, who had never resigned the presidency, as a symbol of the restored legitimacy of France (and thereby bar the route to de Gaulle). This plan was initiated in connection with the Italian armistice negotiations in August–September 1943, when Lebrun was living in the Italian occupation zone, but Lebrun refused to be a party to the enterprise.[21]

THE RESTORATION OF "REPUBLICAN LEGALITY"

As we have seen in the previous chapter, de Gaulle proclaimed the Provisional Government of the French Republic (GPRF) on June 3, 1944, just before the Normandy invasion, and then proceeded to establish it in Paris two and a half months later behind the vanguard of the Second Armored Division. Forming such a government was done against great odds, not the least of which was the Communist attempt to set up, in effect, a new commune in Paris.

But de Gaulle's new governmental authority in Paris was strictly provisional and was created only for the purpose of restoring the French Republic.[22] De Gaulle was to say later, "I fought the war in order to obtain victory for France, but I did it in such a way that it was also the Republic's victory."[23] This remark was a way of saying (as he maintained more explicitly on other occasions) that he *could* have set up a dictatorship at the war's end but did not.

But though he did not attempt to set up a dictatorship, de Gaulle wanted to be sure that he was at the helm of affairs in France when the transition from war to peace took place. He felt fully justified in seeking this position in view of what he had accomplished for France and what others had not. Contrasting his behavior, on the one hand, with that of Pétain and Weygand, on the other, he wrote:

> If a disaster sweeps away government while a country is without valid institutions, then there is no longer anything [interposed] between the warrior and the nation. May God then prevent the soldier from assuming the mantle of national renunciation. On the contrary, may God help him to transcend his basic nature [as a soldier] and serve as guide to the people and as a recourse to the state, for the struggle, for salvation, and for grandeur.[24]

De Gaulle wrote these words in 1954, long after he had been through the World War II experience that he described in such grandiose terms. De Gaulle's desperate move in June 1940 in casting his lot with the British was not just an honorable action of keeping faith with an ally. True, an Allied victory was indispensable; but de Gaulle's main aim was the "salvation" of the French nation and the restoration of the former French "grandeur."

Yet France would never return to grandeur without a profound reform of the French state structure, as de Gaulle asserted in a letter to Paul Reynaud, the last prime minister of the Third Republic before Philippe Pétain took over the government on the evening of June 16, 1940. The occasion for the letter was the publication in January 1952 of Reynaud's memoirs, entitled *Au coeur de la mêlée (In the heart of the struggle)*, which de Gaulle found "worthy of the great events it evokes." In the letter, de Gaulle wrote that

> in my view, the misfortune of France at the time was that, first before the threat and then in extreme peril [in 1940], its political regime was powerless to fulfill its elementary duty, that is, to defend the country. It was this regime (a nonexistent chief of state, discontinuity of the government, confusion in the Parliament, political games and rivalries) that in large part paralyzed you, while the regime collapsed in capitulation and abdication. It was in its absence that we were able to, in spite of everything, bring about a cruel victory.

How, after such experiences, would proven patriots not judge today that the first condition of redressment and salvation is the profound reform of a regime that has been reestablished in [its] absurdity [in the Fourth Republic] and is more impotent than ever?[25]

Because from the outset of the fall of France, de Gaulle wanted to effect the "profound reform of a regime," he was intent on being in charge of a French provisional government that would set the transition from war to peace. In his way, however, lay the problem of the Allies, particularly Washington, where, as de Gaulle had recognized early on, "our situation is extremely delicate."[26] A conviction was growing in the Roosevelt administration that de Gaulle was a potential threat to the practice of democratic government in France.

In December 1941, de Gaulle sent out a policy directive on the issue of the Free French movement's position toward democracy. This directive was contained in a letter to Adrien Tixier, the chief of the Free French delegation in Washington:

We are firm supporters of democratic principles such as those that triumphed in the French Revolution and in the world. We accept neither a plot for a monarchical restoration nor a dictatorship of any person, group, or social class. The government of the people should proceed from the people and the people only. But we think, along with the great majority of Frenchmen, that the democratic regime that existed before the war was bad and must be profoundly reformed. However, it is not up to us to pronounce these necessary reforms. This will be the role of a freely elected national assembly, which should be convoked as soon as possible.[27]

A few months earlier, de Gaulle had been even more blunt, in a letter to one of his followers in London, Professor René Cassin:

We must continue to be very prudent in stating our political position, despite the inconvenience that this semi-obscurity can present for us now in the United States. If we simply proclaim that we are fighting for democracy, perhaps the Americans will praise us, but we will lose in the French context, which is the principal one. The French masses confound the word *democracy* with the parliamentary regime that existed before the war. Our own supporters . . . and especially our soldiers are in the vast majority convinced of this. This regime is condemned by the facts and by public opinion. Besides, we are the sworn enemies of the Hitlero-fascist system. The proof is that we are fighting [the system] everywhere and first of all in France, and that to destroy it and drive it away we do not shrink even from civil war.[28]

In his public statements as well, de Gaulle did not shrink from the idea of revolutionary change in France. These remarks tended to confirm Washington's impression of de Gaulle as an antidemocratic figure.[29]

As de Gaulle surveyed the postwar perspective and his own chances for changing the country, he saw a France that could rise to the occasion but more often than not was a collection of quarrelsome Gauls. It was both a conservative country and a country of protest against government, having as de Gaulle said, "[a] contentious and at the same time conservative character."[30] Therefore, he maintained, "everyone feels that to lead the French in the terrible circumstances in which they find themselves, it is necessary to have a strong government."[31]

The key to the difference between French and Anglo-American perceptions of democracy was the fact that in the latter countries the public powers were separated and functioned in a sort of prudential symbiosis. In France, this was not the case. The French, as de Gaulle viewed them, "are in the habit of splitting into irreconcilable factions"[32] because of the many invasions and revolutions the country had gone through. In Great Britain and the United States, it was altogether different. De Gaulle noted in a speech to the British Parliament in April 1960: "How much of your success has depended on the value of your institutions! At the worst moments, who in your country contested the legitimacy and the authority of the state?"[33]

In de Gaulle's view, apart from a civil war, the United States did not share the experiences that had brought forth France's divisive tendencies. The United States had only two main political parties, not much different from each other.[34] But in France, if the two powers, legislative and executive, "were erected face to face behind theoretically impregnable ramparts . . . the inevitable result would be either the submission of the President to the demands of the deputies or else a pronunciamento. How then could one speak of balance?"[35]

To de Gaulle, the system of government in prewar France, which the Tréveneuc Law would in effect restore, was based on the control of public power by private interests:

> The crime of the present system is that it passes the public powers intact to representatives of individual interests, which means that public affairs are utilized for these individual interests. Therefore, these parties should not have public powers.[36]

This was another way of saying that public powers, in the sense of executive powers, should not be exercised by the Parliament. Instead,

Parliament should be *separated* from executive power, which should proceed from the chief of state.

In fact, de Gaulle had learned to muffle his disdain for Parliament; in his younger days, it came through quite strongly, as in a letter to his mother in 1915: "The Parliament is becoming more and more odious and stupid. . . . We will be victorious as soon as we have swept away this scum, and there is not a Frenchman who would not shout for joy, especially those who are fighting. . . . I would be very surprised if this regime survives the war."[37] In the same year, on December 31, 1915, de Gaulle wrote in a similar vein: "Doubtless the enemy will be able to prolong [the struggle] some more, thanks to his energy and discipline and the irremediable inferiority of our republican—parliamentary—regime."[38]

In his later public career de Gaulle was to use code words to express his disapprobation of parliamentary supremacy in France. He called it "the exclusive regime of the parties." On rare occasions he made the connection explicit: "I considered it necessary for the government to derive not from Parliament, in other words, the parties, but, over and above them, from a leader directly mandated by the nation as a whole and empowered to choose, to decide and to act."[39]

THE POSTWAR STRUGGLE OVER PARLIAMENTARY SUPREMACY

Even though de Gaulle did not succeed in his first attempt (1944–46) to reform the French political system, he made two important innovations at the start of the process. In a referendum on October 21, 1945, French voters were asked two questions at the polls during the election for a new assembly. The first asked whether they wanted the assembly to be constituent—that is, to draw up a new constitution—which would mean the end of the Third Republic and the start of a new one. The vote was 96.1 percent affirmative. The second question concerned the powers of the assembly and, among other things, asked the voters whether they wanted to ratify the constitution themselves: 66.3 percent voted yes, despite a vigorous campaign, especially by the Communists, to secure a negative answer. As the authors of *Histoire de France* noted, "Thus de Gaulle broke with the tradition of a solely sovereign Constituent Assembly [empowered] to give the country its institutions."[40]

De Gaulle was entirely conscious of the important stake that the 1945 referendum represented for the future. He recalled this event in his *Memoirs of Hope,* written after his final departure from power in 1969:

[In 1945], with an eye to the future, and before the [Constituent] Assembly had been elected, I introduced the referendum system, made the people decide that henceforward, its direct approval would be necessary for a Constitution to be valid, and thus created the democratic means of one day founding a good one myself, to replace the bad one which was about to be concocted by and for the parties.[41]

Moreover, the October 1945 referendum, with its 96.1 percent vote in favor of the new assembly's being constituent, repudiated the previous regime in order to create a new Republic. Also, it covered and in effect endorsed the parenthesis of illegality that marked the Gaullist cause from June 18, 1940, onward, or what the General referred to more euphemistically as "this great work . . . achieved outside the former framework of our institutions."[42]

That de Gaulle was very conscious of the ramifications of these actions is evident in an interview he gave toward the end of his public career, in which he characterized the October 1945 referendum in these terms: "I had the country on the one hand legitimate the action carried out during the war, and on the other hand adopt what was immediately needed in order to reestablish democracy and prevent the threatening advent of a totalitarian regime."[43]

The reference to the French Communist party was not an idle one. The Communists, it turned out, became the largest party in the Constituent Assembly in the October 1945 elections, winning 160 seats. Therefore it was of major importance to de Gaulle, both from the political and the constitutional point of view, that the National Assembly not be the final arbiter of a new constitution.

The question of the National Assembly's sovereignty—and what power could be more sovereign than one that creates a constitution?—was at the heart of the French Revolution. Essentially, two actions defying royal prerogatives had created the Revolution: the declaration of the delegates of the third estate that they alone—to the exclusion of the king, the nobles, and the clergy—sufficed to form the National Assembly (June 17, 1789); and the Tennis Court Oath (June 20, 1789), whereby the delegates agreed to continue meeting until a new constitution was established. Through this oath, enshrining the principle of parliamentary supremacy, the eventual downfall of the monarchy was set in motion.

De Gaulle struck at the foundations of this revolutionary tradition in staging the referendum of October 1945 before the Constituent Assembly was even in place. He set up the referendum through an ordinance of the provisional government on August 19, 1945.[44] For the first time the French people had been asked whether they preferred to have the opportunity to ratify a constitution drawn up by a constituent assembly. By setting up this referendum, de Gaulle had whittled away some of the National Assembly's sovereign power, established by the traditions of the Revolution. In this and other actions, he can be said, historically speaking, to have restored some of the monarchical—that is, executive—powers, though he did not seek to restore the royal house of France itself.

Though the precedent of referring constitutions to the people now had been set, the voters rejected the Constituent Assembly's draft constitution, and a new Constituent Assembly was elected in June 1946. This assembly reduced the possibility of making such referenda perennial by stipulating in its draft constitution that no referendum would be required for a revision of the constitution if two-thirds of the National Assembly agreed to such a revision.[45] This second draft constitution was approved by the voters in October 1946,[46] thus inaugurating the Fourth Republic. In this new constitution, the legislature was known overall as the Parliament, and the two houses were called the National Assembly and the Council of the Republic (the former Senate).

Later, in a press conference on November 17, 1948, de Gaulle mused on the tension between parliamentary supremacy on the one hand, and the referendum procedure on the other:

> Apparently one is seditious today when one asks that the country be consulted. . . . [This becomes] a danger for the Republic. In sum, the Republic has to be protected against universal suffrage. I claim, on the contrary, that the Republic should be founded on universal suffrage.[47]

For insisting that the constitution be approved in a referendum by universal suffrage, de Gaulle was attacked by his enemies as having "Bonapartist" tendencies. A century earlier, in the wake of the Revolution of 1848, the first election in France by universal suffrage produced a constituent assembly; it in turn created a constitution calling for the election of a president by universal suffrage for a term of four years. Napoléon's nephew, Louis-Napoléon Bonaparte, was elected president, but since his term would run out in four years, he staged a coup d'état in December 1851 and proceeded to sanction his authoritarian regime by three plebiscites, in 1851, 1852, and 1870. (Four months after the third plebiscite [May 1870], this "Second Empire" [Napoléon's was the first] perished in the shock of the Franco-Prussian War.)

De Gaulle was acutely aware, as he put it, of "the passionate prejudices which, since Louis-Napoléon, the idea of a plebiscite aroused in so many sectors of opinion."[48] He was also aware of charges that he was a "man on horseback" waiting for a chance to seize power. In a speech at Nice in

September 1948, de Gaulle declared, "No, I am not Bonaparte! I am not Boulanger! I am General de Gaulle!"[49] Still, in the same speech de Gaulle maintained that it was "a usurpation to pretend to defend [the Republic] today against universal suffrage."[50]

THE FIRST PRESIDENCY
OF CHARLES DE GAULLE

De Gaulle may have thought in 1944–45 that he could reform the French constitution, become president, and then as such enjoy full executive powers. However, France's presidency under the previous (Third) Republic had been largely ceremonial, and the existing political parties wanted to keep it that way. At the war's end, de Gaulle, despite his immense prestige, was in a relatively weak position politically: He had no party of his own to use in the parliamentary debates over the framing of a new constitution.

Also, de Gaulle had to contend with another force of immense prestige after the war: the French Communist party, which referred to itself as the "party of the seventy-five thousand executed," claiming that this was the number of its members killed in the Resistance. Though de Gaulle had succeeded after the liberation in disarming the Communist militias and incorporating some of them into the reconstituted French army, "the Party," as it was called in the postwar period, held preponderant influence in French public life, as it indeed had in the internal Resistance during the war. Additionally, the Party was reinforced by the immense prestige of the Soviet Union because of the latter's role in the defeat of Nazi Germany.

In forming his provisional government after the capture of Paris, de Gaulle chose to govern with the Communist party. He allowed Maurice Thorez, the self-exiled Communist leader and a powerful public speaker and organizer, to return from the USSR. De Gaulle also brought into his government Georges Bidault and the latter's newly formed Mouvement républicain populaire (MRP), which represented for the first time the appearance of a Christian Democratic party in preponderantly anticlerical France. The third major element in the postwar coalition was the Socialist party (Section française de l'internationale ouvrière—SFIO), which, though partly discredited as the result of its presence in prewar French governments, was not lowered to the same degree as its governing partner at the time, the Radical (middle-class) party.

De Gaulle's provisional government, though including Christian Democrats, was weighted toward the left. And probably in part to protect himself against Soviet attempts to disrupt his regime by manipulating the French Communist party, de Gaulle signed a treaty of friendship with the USSR on December 10, 1944.

But de Gaulle did not remain long at the head of the provisional government after the war. Exasperated at the prospect of the return of Parliament's supremacy over the executive branch, which to him symbolized all the past ills of France, he resigned as a new constitution was still being developed, on January 20, 1946. Said de Gaulle to his ministers: "The exclusive regime of the parties has reappeared. I disapprove of it, but aside from establishing by force a dictatorship which I do not desire and which would certainly end in disaster, I do not have the means of preventing this experiment. I must therefore withdraw."[51]

Twelve years later, on May 19, 1958, when he was about to return to power, de Gaulle recounted the experience of his first resignation:

When I saw that the parties had reacted like the *émigrés* of old, that is to say that they had forgotten nothing and learned nothing, and that consequently . . . any Government was impossible, I withdrew. I did not try to force their hand. Subsequently they drew up a poor constitution. . . . I did not attempt to violate it in any way.[52]

With this figure of speech, de Gaulle stood the revolutionary argument on its head, by comparing Parliament to the royalist émigrés who returned to France after the Bourbon restoration in 1815—whereas he presented himself as the man who had saved the French *Republic*. In this de Gaulle sought to embody the "general will" of the nation against the "factions" represented by the political parties in the Parliament.

In a further irony, it was this notion of the "general will," emerging from the thought of Jean-Jacques Rousseau (1712–1778), that the triumphant Jacobins of the French Revolution had used so effectively to stifle dissent, acting from their positions that derived from the Convention (1791–94)— that symbol of parliamentary supremacy run amok.

THE BAYEUX SPEECH

Five months after his resignation and immediately following the election of the second Constituent Assembly, de Gaulle made a seminal speech at Bayeux in June 1946, aimed at influencing the deliberations of the new assembly toward the kind of constitution he had been advocating. In it, de Gaulle described the definitive form of government that he wanted to establish. First of all, de Gaulle wanted to see to it that "legislative, executive, and judicial [powers would] be clearly separated and be in strong mutual equilibrium."[53]

As for the legislative branch, said de Gaulle, it was clear that laws should be voted on and budgets approved by an assembly elected by direct and universal suffrage. But since reactions in this kind of politically charged assembly would not be, at least initially, "clairvoyant" and "serene," there should be a second chamber. The first chamber, or Chamber of Deputies, would represent the main political currents in the country. The second chamber would represent more local interests, both in Metropolitan France and in the empire, and members would be elected in a different manner.

The second chamber would consist of three parts. Mainly it would include representatives of the general councils of the French departments and the municipal councils, as the former Senate had. It would also include representatives of economic organizations and family associations, and intellectuals. A third group would be composed of members of the local assemblies from the French overseas territories. Meeting together, these three elements would constitute the High Council of the French Union (the new name for the French Empire).[54]

Executive power would be distinct from the legislative power vested in the two chambers, which together would make up the Parliament. Unity, cohesion, and discipline could not be maintained over the long run "if executive power emanated from the other power that it is supposed to balance against, and if each of the members of the government . . . were only . . . the representative of a party."[55] (Though de Gaulle did not say so outright, separation of powers meant in effect a diminution of parliamentary power. He indicated as much in a later speech in January 1959 [after he had put into effect a new constitution], in which he said that henceforth "Parliament would devote itself to its legislative task.")[56]

Moreover, de Gaulle told his audience at Bayeux, a chief of state must be placed above the parties ("above political contingencies [there should] be established a national arbitration that would bring continuity in the midst of [political] combinations").[57] The chief of state, or president, would be voted on by an electoral college, which would include the Parliament but also other representatives, so that the chief of state would be president of the French Union as well as of Metropolitan France. Executive power would be vested in this chief of state, who would promulgate laws, name ministers, and preside over councils of ministers. Furthermore, "in moments of grave confusion, [he would] invite the country to express its sovereign decision through elections. It would be his duty, if the nation was in peril, to guarantee the national independence and the treaties France had concluded."[58]

The latter phrase was a direct reference to 1940. It was a prefiguration of what became Article 16 in de Gaulle's eventual Constitution of 1958, which enabled the chief of state to assume emergency powers. (Doing so had not been possible during the fall of France, and de Gaulle later turned this provision into reality when he invoked these powers during the revolt of the generals in Algiers in April 1961.)

Though he did not spell out his view on the judiciary in the Bayeux speech, he did so three months later on September 29, 1946, at Epinal, in the course of a broad attack on the new draft constitution, which had just been passed by the second Constituent Assembly. The judiciary, de Gaulle maintained, should be administered by the Council of the Magistrature, which would be independent of political influence.[59]

Here again, in calling for an independent judiciary, de Gaulle was running up against the tradition of a totally sovereign National Assembly. In this case, the second Constituent Assembly had recommended in the new draft constitution that the Council of the Magistrature be composed of fourteen persons, including the president and the minister of justice; six of these members would be elected by the National Assembly.[60] De Gaulle was also confronting a strong tradition in France against a powerful judiciary, dating back to the ancien régime, when judges were viewed as willing instruments of the monarchy.

The Constitution of the Fourth Republic, passed in October 1946, was not what de Gaulle had proposed. Instead of a second chamber with three parts, as he had envisaged it, the constituents split the three apart: The old Senate, with less power, was resurrected under the name of the Council of the Republic; the corporate element became the Economic and Social Council; and a separate assembly was created for the French Union. More important, the president of this new Fourth Republic had powers not very different from the presidents under the Third Republic.

In the political program he had set forth at Bayeux, de Gaulle had reached very far, and his ideas were not to be realized for a long time. Throughout he stuck to the idea of a strong executive and a weakened Parliament, and in the end, in 1962, he achieved this goal.

THE RETURN OF DE GAULLE, 1958

During World War II, Gaullist Resistance leader Pierre Brossolette recommended that de Gaulle form a mass party at the war's end, before the prewar parties had a chance to get organized, and govern on the basis of it. But this proposal would have encouraged a one-party dictatorship, and de Gaulle rejected it.[61] However, after the Constitution of 1946 had reestablished parliamentary supremacy in France, de Gaulle, by then out of office, inaugurated a movement whose aim was to propagate the reform of the French state. It was a movement, he emphasized, and not a political party. He called it the Rally of the French People (Rassemblement du peuple français—RPF). "If we created the [RPF]," de Gaulle stated in a speech in June 1952, ". . . it was with the principal, the capital, idea of bringing about a complete change in this bad constitution."[62]

De Gaulle not only did not call his RPF a political party, he did not condone the idea that deputies elected under this banner might join the government. De Gaulle acknowledged the criticism that this attitude aroused: "They said, 'You will not change the constitution while remaining outside the system of the majority' "[63] (that is, in refusing to join the ruling parties in the government). This de Gaulle refused: "At no price will we enter into a bad system . . . [which] is deplorable and ruinous to the country's interest."[64]

But the RPF experiment failed. After a high point in October 1947, when the RPF received some 40 percent of the vote in the municipal elections, the movement was never able to match that promise. By the early 1950s it had begun a downward slide, in part bedeviled by the question of whether to enter into ruling coalitions, which caused defections among its ranks as some Gaullists began entering the government as ministers. The RPF gradually dissolved while its remnant successor, the Républicains sociaux, saw its share of the vote dwindle to 5 percent and go completely out of existence in September 1956.

In 1953, in the middle of his political wilderness, the so-called crossing of the desert, de Gaulle mused on his failure to reform the French state:

The left abandoned me in the wake of the liberation because it is against the state. The right abandoned me subsequently because it is against the people. However, neither the right nor the left has really succeeded in governing since my departure. They will not be able to do so today. Sooner or later, the fall [of the regime] lies at the end of these national recantations.[65]

De Gaulle had correctly foreseen that nothing less than a political upheaval could propel him back to power. The option of returning by parliamentary majority was out. He evoked images of a volcanic eruption or an earthquake, as in this letter in December 1951 to his only son, Philippe: "If [the political situation] deteriorates before I die or am beyond the capacity to act, the force of events will be such that great responsibilities will befall me." If, however, he were dead or incapacitated at the time of the "eruption of the volcano," it would be up to his son "to become the de Gaulle of the new drama." It was important, therefore, that Philippe remain in a respected milieu, that is, the military.[66]

By the mid-1950s de Gaulle had retired to his modest country home in eastern France, at Colombey-les-Deux-Eglises, where he devoted himself largely to the completion of his *War Memoirs*. The three volumes, published in 1955, 1956, and 1957, fell upon a public astonished to discover in a military figure a master of French prose and a savant of history. The memoirs formed an essential, if undefinable, step in his return to power later in the decade, in the midst of a crisis in Algeria that threatened to plunge France into civil war.

Curiously, Charles de Gaulle subsequently came to power in June 1958 under conditions somewhat similar constitutionally to those when the vote at Vichy was held on July 10, 1940: In the midst of a national trauma over how to deal with a nationalist revolt in Algeria, he was elected to office by the National Assembly by a vote of 329–224 on June 1, 1958. (It was the first time he had been the subject of a vote of this kind. Previously, he had been in effect the self-proclaimed president of the provisional Republic.) The following day, by roughly the same majority, de Gaulle was given full powers for six months in addition to constituent power, which authorized him to arrange the drafting of a new constitution to be ratified in a national referendum.

This parliamentary action was taken in spite of the fact that, according to Article 90 of the Constitution of the Fourth Republic, it was up to the National Assembly "to elaborate a draft law involving revision of the constitution."[67] This article had to be (and was) amended by the National Assembly in order that de Gaulle himself could proceed with the drafting of a new constitution, which was presented to and approved by the voters in a referendum on September 28, 1958, without having been discussed and voted by the National Assembly.[68]

Despite the juridical similarities between the parliamentary actions of July 10, 1940, and of June 1, 1958, the political circumstances were entirely dissimilar. In 1958, de Gaulle came to represent the only constitutional alternative to civil war in France, and this fact was recognized and ratified by the Parliament. In 1940, the Parliament handed over power to the "party of surrender," as de Gaulle referred to the Vichy government, and did so, in a manner of speaking, under the gun of the Germans (although technically, two-fifths of France had been left under the direct control of Vichy and was free of German troops).

It is also worth pointing out that 1958 was only the second time in French history that a constitution was drafted by a small group instead of by a constituent assembly. The other time was under Louis-Napoléon Bonaparte, in 1852, after his coup d'état. However, the historian René Rémond, in noting this parallel, pointed out that in 1958, unlike 1852, democratic means were associated with the framing of a new constitution: It was submitted to a consultative committee made up of a majority of parliamentarians, and after it was drawn up the text was put to a referendum. If the 1958 constitution had failed in the referendum, it would not have gone into effect.[69] Napoléon III, on the other hand, sanctioned his rule with two plebiscites, nearly a year apart: one to approve his coup d'état and the next to approve his designation as emperor. In between he had a new constitution framed. (Much later, in 1870, he staged a third plebiscite for approval of his rule.)

The 1958 constitution, passed by 79 percent of the voters, ushered in the Fifth Republic and essentially ended the tradition of parliamentary supremacy in France. The groundwork for this process had been laid by de Gaulle in the referendum he conducted in the immediate aftermath of the war, on October 21, 1945, when the people voted in favor of being consulted electorally on a new constitution. Though this was in part modified by the constitution of the Fourth Republic that was eventually adopted,[70] de Gaulle in 1958 definitively took away from Parliament sole sovereignty over French constitutions: The Constitution of the Fifth Republic made a referendum mandatory for any revision of the constitution.

Thus de Gaulle modified the most fundamental innovation of the French Revolution: that to prevent the resurgence of the monarchy, sovereignty must henceforth reside in the people, and specifically in the representatives of the people. It was this assembly of people's representatives (the Parliament), through its passage of laws, including constitutional laws, that was the final arbiter of the destiny, indeed of the human rights, of the French.[71]

In his declaration to the National Assembly on June 1, 1958, de Gaulle announced a proposal to amend Article 90 on constitutional revision, so that he could draw up a new constitution. He also enunciated three principles that would underlie the new constitution: Universal suffrage is the source of all power; there must be a separation of powers between the executive and the legislature; and the government must be responsible to the Parliament.[72]

Though de Gaulle paid obeisance to the third principle, his private view was that "in fact, the government depends essentially on the President."[73] Indeed, a sea change took place with the formal inauguration of the new constitution on October 5, 1958. Fifteen days later, with the Parliament still in recess, as it had been since June 3, 1958, de Gaulle held a press conference in which he stated that Parliament was "no longer omnipotent." He added: "The people who drafted the Constitution of 1958 . . . place[d] strict limits and powerful brakes on future Assemblies. The nation has ratified their work. . . . the needs of national renovation absolutely prohibit a return to the confusion of times past."[74]

It was the president who now became the heart of the governmental system, with notable powers. But de Gaulle, who was elected president on December 21, 1958, interpreted these powers as requiring constant affirmations of his own legitimacy: Since the presidency, as it now existed, was the result of his own initiative and "the sentiment which existed toward me in the national consciousness," it was necessary to maintain an accord between himself and the people, through the medium of the referendum.[75]

As de Gaulle would describe it, "The very principle of the referendum [is] that the response of the people, in deciding on the question, tells whether the people give confidence or not to the one who poses it."[76] De Gaulle tested the barometer with the French people in six referenda, starting with the one on October 21, 1945, and ending with the one on April 27, 1969. These were exercises in political Russian roulette, and in the final one, when the majority went against him (53.71 percent to 46.78 percent), de Gaulle took it as a vote of no confidence and immediately resigned. In the first, fifth, and sixth of these referenda (1945, 1962, 1969), de Gaulle bypassed the Parliament completely. In the others, the Parliament voted in favor before the text was put to a referendum.[77]

The various referenda were staged in order to get the people's approval of policies that de Gaulle was instituting—policies that generally happened to be those the parliamentarians were reluctant to endorse or to which they were openly hostile. The device was important to de Gaulle because, although as of November 1958 the majority of representatives in the new National Assembly came under the name of his new political formation, the Union for a New Republic (UNR), he was not assured of support on all issues.

Whatever the circumstances, the practice of staging referenda over crucial issues had the effect of downgrading the role of Parliament, since Parliament was being bypassed at these critical moments. De Gaulle was aware of this and, according to him, the banalized debates in the National Assembly produced in him a certain melancholy: He had always revered, he said, the oratorical talents that had enlivened the French parliamentary scene. But, he added, perhaps with a touch of irony, that he consoled himself by "reflecting on the disorder created by the parliamentary 'games, poisons, and delights' which were the keynotes of the Third and Fourth Republics and which destroyed them both."[78]

As in 1944, de Gaulle in 1958 had to draw from the traditional political parties in forming a governing coalition. The cabinet team that de Gaulle put together in June 1958 was more centrist than the one he had formed in the wake of the liberation in 1944; it was composed largely of ministers and notables from the Fourth Republic. The 1958 coalition was formed with the assistance of the Christian Democrats (MRP) and the Socialists (SFIO), the latter chiefly in the person of Guy Mollet, who earlier in the 1950s had had the longest tenure of any prime minister of the Fourth Republic.

In 1944–46, de Gaulle governed with a coalition of parties predominantly of the left and stood in a politically weak position himself, having no party of his own. He had rejected a suggestion that he form his own mass party at the war's end.[79] This time, immediately after the Constitution of the Fifth Republic was passed, de Gaulle resurrected his "movement" in preparation for the legislative elections of November 1958. The new political formation of the Gaullists was called the Union for the New Republic (UNR) and gained 194 seats in the 537-member National Assembly. Unlike his situation in 1944–46, de Gaulle now had a base in Parliament.

The following month, de Gaulle was elected president under the new constitution, and the Socialists left the governing coalition. De Gaulle, who had tried to govern with a heavy hand in 1944–46 and became the most likely target for grievances, now seemed to realize that he had to delegate most of the day-to-day running of the government to a strong prime minister. In January 1959, he named Michel Debré, who remained prime minister until the settlement ending the Algerian War in 1962.

THE FINAL ACT, 1962:
THE MONARCHY OF THE REPUBLIC

The 1958 constitution made the president the head of the French state with powers that de Gaulle was later to describe in a radio-television address on September 20, 1962. They included the right to choose the prime minister and the other ministers and to preside over the Council of

Ministers; to issue decrees and ordinances; to appoint civil servants, military officers, and judges; to command the armed forces; to invoke emergency powers in a crisis; and to call for a referendum, or new parliamentary elections, or both.[80]

But the constitution was lacking one major element, from the Gaullist point of view: It did not invest the president with the authority of a chief executive elected by universal suffrage. Though the president was not elected by the Parliament and therefore was not beholden to it, he was not chosen by the people as a whole either. Under the 1958 constitution, the president was chosen by a college of about eighty thousand electors.[81] On December 21, 1958, de Gaulle was elected president by 78.5 percent of the votes of this electoral college.

De Gaulle acknowledged that at Bayeux in 1946 and in putting together the Constitution of 1958, he had not specified that the chief of state be elected by universal suffrage. For this last, and definitive, assault on parliamentary supremacy, he had to bide his time. As he wrote in his *Memoirs of Hope*, it was best that he not do everything at once. Having placed the presidency rather than the Parliament at the center of the state, "it would be as well to postpone the final completion of this vast mutation." In particular, he needed to demonstrate to the people that the presidency could be conducted "without any suggestion of dictatorship," adding "But in any event, for the sake of the future I was determined to finish off the edifice in this respect before the end of my seven-year term."[82]

Though not above ruse, de Gaulle tended to give forewarning of what he would try to effect next, for the very reason that his policies, both foreign and domestic, were generally consistent and formed part of an ensemble. One such moment occurred during his press conference of April 11, 1961, when he spoke of "possible provisions for the day when I shall have disappeared." De Gaulle explained:

> I know that many consider that the method of electing the President of the Republic by an electoral college limited only to elected representatives . . . would hardly be consistent for the person who would have to succeed me. . . . In order to correct this, in strengthening, if I may put it this way, "the personal equation" of the future President, it may be thought that he should be chosen by the nation through universal suffrage. . . . If I myself have the time and the opportunity for it, I could, at the opportune moment, put this point on the agenda, a very important point for the future of France.[83]

The "opportunity" came in the wake of the shocking attack on de Gaulle's motorcade outside Paris on August 22, 1962, by a group of fanatics in the

Secret Army Organization (OAS) who were bitterly hostile to de Gaulle's Algeria policy. De Gaulle's vehicle was struck by fourteen bullets, but miraculously none of the four occupants—the General, his wife, his son-in-law, and his chauffeur—was hit. After this shattering experience, Yvonne de Gaulle, with formidable aplomb, emerged from the car to inquire whether the chickens in the trunk had been hurt. As for de Gaulle, who had refused to crouch down during the attack (which paradoxically may have saved his life), he insisted on reviewing the guard at Villacoublay Airport before the party proceeded by plane to the General's family residence.[84]

The prospect of an untimely disappearance of de Gaulle raised suddenly the question of succession. Given de Gaulle's unique personality and authority, which could not be matched by any successor, an election by universal suffrage would certainly give a boost to a successor's authority. De Gaulle was concerned that a successor might cede powers to the Parliament, as Marshal Mac-Mahon had done during the Third Republic.[85] At the same time, de Gaulle rejected the idea of an American-style vice president who, having no mandate from the people because the office was not separately elected, would not be able to rule effectively after the death of a president. This was all the more true in de Gaulle's eyes because France was an unruly country and difficult to govern.[86]

On this new occasion for constitutional reform, de Gaulle had a more difficult time than he had had in pushing through the new constitution in 1958. De Gaulle described the issue of the 1962 referendum as a clash between two republics, "the republic of yesterday, whose hopes of a rebirth were discernible behind the bitter diatribes of the partisans, and the republic of today, which was personified by me and whose survival I was endeavoring to ensure."[87] And yet such a clash was not surprising to de Gaulle: "How could one doubt that this profound transformation, which had given the Republic a Head that it had never had organically before, would eventually be undermined by all the vested interests?"[88]

De Gaulle knew that the Parliament would never agree to the diminution of its authority that the election of a president by universal suffrage would require: "It was only from the mass of the nation, and certainly not from parliament, that it was possible to hope for the adoption of such a measure."[89] And therefore de Gaulle embarked on a different procedural route. Against very strong objections, he staged a referendum without its being first voted on by the Parliament. This had happened before, in 1958, but at that time with Parliament's approval.

De Gaulle's argument was based on Article 11 of the Constitution of 1958, which stated that "the President of the Republic may, at the proposal of the government, submit to referendum any bill dealing with the organization of the public authorities."[90] De Gaulle's position was that the constitution, and particularly the method of electing a president, fit under this rubric. He also pointed out that "the constitution of 1875 which inaugurated the Third Republic was precisely called: 'Law concerning the organization of the public authorities.' "[91]

De Gaulle emphasized that he was the inspiration behind the Constitution of 1958. He argued that calling for a constitutional amendment by the use of Article 11 was completely consistent with it. Finally, he maintained, if the people had been consulted on the 1958 constitution without its having been voted on by the National Assembly, why shouldn't they be consulted on an amendment to it? "Above all, since the 1958 constitution derived from the direct suffrage of the people, by what authority were they to be denied the power to alter what they had themselves created?"[92]

Perhaps de Gaulle intended all along to accomplish the change in this manner and intentionally included Article 11 in the 1958 constitution as a contingency for this purpose. The evidence suggests otherwise; Article 89 of the 1958 constitution stated definitely that, in order for the constitution to be amended, both houses of Parliament would have to agree to the amendment, which would then be submitted to the country in a referendum.

De Gaulle, following the pattern of 1958, announced in September 1962 a referendum (on the election of the president by universal suffrage), which would then be followed by elections for a new National Assembly: "Just as in 1958, although in circumstances that were clearly very different, I was calling upon the country first of all to pronounce judgment on our institutions, and then to provide itself with a new Chamber."[93]

On October 1, 1962, the Council of State, which rules on the validity of procedure, issued an opinion that was unfavorable to de Gaulle's recourse to Article 11 for the holding of a referendum on the election of the president by universal suffrage.[94] The argument against de Gaulle held that Article 89 provided for constitutional revision through parliamentary channels. Since no other article was specifically devoted to revision of the constitution, to initiate such revision through channels other than this article was contrary to law and therefore unconstitutional.[95]

Not only the Council of State but the Parliament opposed de Gaulle. A motion of censure against the government passed by a vote of 280–200 in the National Assembly on October 5, 1962. De Gaulle went ahead anyway, dissolving the assembly, staging the referendum, and then holding new elections to the assembly. The referendum on election of the president by universal suffrage passed by 62 percent of the vote. De Gaulle saw it as proof that the traditional political parties did not represent the nation: "They gave clear and terrible proof of it in 1940, when the regime abdicated in the midst of disaster. They illustrated it once more in 1958, when they ceded power to me on the brink of anarchy, bankruptcy, and civil war. They have now confirmed it in 1962."[96]

As a measure of its powerlessness at the time, the Constitutional Council, which rules on the constitutionality of laws, had also, by majority vote, registered an unfavorable opinion when it addressed the issue before the referendum. However, it desisted from making a judgment requested after the referendum. (It was only in the 1970s that the council, formed in 1947, began to play an effective role in judging the constitutionality of laws passed by the Parliament.)[97]

The "hidden monarchy," or the "Monarchy of the Republic," as François Furet has characterized it, was now in place. The apogee of the de Gaulle presidency was reached in the declarations he made during his biennial press conference on January 31, 1964, well before his humiliating descent: a second-round runoff with François Mitterrand in the presidential elections the next year, the massive student protests of May 1968, and his repudiation by the voters a year later, when his favorite device—the referendum as plebiscite—was turned against him. In that press conference at the beginning of 1964, de Gaulle incanted point by point the recommendations he had made in the Bayeux speech nearly twenty years earlier, which he had now turned into reality.[98] But in that high moment, de Gaulle went even further in the direction of absolutism. He declared to his listeners that "the indivisible authority of the State is entrusted completely to the President by the people who elected him. . . . there is no other authority—either ministerial, civilian, military, or judicial—which is not entrusted and maintained by him."[99]

As to the paradox of a government formed by the supreme authority (the president) who was still responsible to the Parliament, de Gaulle offered the following formula to his listeners. The president already has the confidence of the people, confirmed through his election. If the Parliament censures the government, the president ensures continuity by having the people decide on the dispute—either by general elections, a referendum, or both. "Thus there is always a democratic way out."[100]

It was clear that, because of the 1958 and 1962 constitutional mutations, the president held the instruments of political change in his hands: dissolution of Parliament (though not more than once in a year), calling for new elections, or calling for a referendum. But despite de Gaulle's assertion, there was no "democratic way out" for removing a president, except for waiting for the end of the seven-year term. Unless, of course, the president chose to call for a referendum as a test of confidence, which was precisely what happened in 1969. Not all of de Gaulle's successors have followed that example.

Even with the sea change produced by the October 1962 referendum, de Gaulle believed that two pieces of unfinished business regarding the constitution remained: the problem of the relationship between the president and the prime minister and the problem of the Senate. The former problem resided in the ambiguity created by Article 20 of the constitution, which states that "the government decides and directs the policy of the nation. It has at its disposal the administration and the armed forces."[101] Though this article would seem to give full powers to the prime minister as head of the government, it is contradicted by two other articles. Article 5 states that the president ensures respect for the constitution and provides for the functioning of public authorities and the continuity of the state.[102] Article 15 states that the president is head of the armed forces and presides over the higher councils and committees of national defense. In addition, Article 16 confers special power on the president in the event of a national emergency.[103]

This ambiguity, in turn, reflected the disparate outlook of the framers of the 1958 constitution and in particular the influence of Michel Debré, who was distinctly more Parliament-oriented than de Gaulle. Though de Gaulle wanted to clear up this ambiguity, he never did bring himself to do it, and his personal authority over his prime ministers was sufficient to preclude the need for another constitutional revision.

De Gaulle specifically wanted the constitution to clearly allow the president to dismiss the prime minister.[104] In fact, this power has never been questioned in practice in the Fifth Republic, particularly so in that a change of prime minister has only taken place when the prime minister and the president have come from the same ruling coalition.

The problem of the obstructive potential of the Senate continued to gnaw at the General until the end of his political career. The problem was partially resolved by the October 1962 referendum: By the successful use of Article 11, which in the final analysis was not contested by the Constitutional Council, neither house of Parliament could now block the president's recourse to a referendum for constitutional change.

This change was particularly important as regards the Senate, which was not a representative body in the national sense. Its members were drawn from representatives of local councils.

Georges Pompidou, de Gaulle's prime minister from 1962 to 1968 whose overall approach was less harsh than that of de Gaulle, thought that since the people had approved the resort to Article 11, the Senate had been effectively short-circuited, so there was no need to seek further change in its role or makeup.[105] But de Gaulle felt that the Senate, as it was then constituted, represented an anachronism. It was no longer needed to balance against the National Assembly; a new and strong presidency was doing just that.

De Gaulle's sense of the primacy of unity was such that he probably never seriously considered—or did not want to consider—the possibility of cohabitation, in which the representative of one party held the presidency, while the representative of another party enjoying a majority in the National Assembly held the prime ministership. The General's vision of the future, as he stated it in a press conference on February 21, 1966, was quite otherwise. The president, said de Gaulle, must have a government "proceeding from him," in order to carry out his policy; he must have a Parliament "made up of a majority faithful to [the majority] which exists in the nation . . . around [the president]. This is at present the French situation and the whole of the future depends on its lasting."[106]

De Gaulle had his own method for obviating cohabitation: the referendum as a test of popularity. If he won, the resulting legislative elections would confirm his victory. If he lost, he would resign, and the newly elected president would almost certainly see a majority for his party in the ensuing legislative elections. But events subsequent to de Gaulle's departure did not work that way. In 1972, Georges Pompidou staged a referendum on the entry of Britain into the Common Market but did not make it a test of popularity of his regime. (The referendum passed.) In 1984, François Mitterrand stayed on after his party lost the parliamentary majority, and a member of the new majority, Jacques Chirac, took over the prime ministership. Though the periods of cohabitation (1984–86 and 1993–95) did not fundamentally undermine the primacy of the president, they did reveal the limits of his power when a rival party holds the premiership. Further, these periods exposed the contradiction in the 1958 constitution concerning the roles of the president and prime minister.

THE FALL OF DE GAULLE

Through years of effort, de Gaulle had succeeded in creating a "Monarchy of the Republic." But additionally, he had put his personal stamp of authoritarianism on it, and in this respect the Gaullist reign was to be an ephemeral institution. For de Gaulle, the dilemma was acute: He could institutionalize a system, but he could not institutionalize de Gaulle. His legitimacy was only mystical and therefore fragile:

> Under the monarchy . . . the King was by heredity the sole source of authority. The plebiscites that installed each of our two Emperors [Napoléon I and III] conferred on them total authority for life. . . . But in my case it was without hereditary right, without a plebiscite, without an election, but simply in response to the silent but imperative call of France, that I had formerly been led to take the responsibility for her defense, her unity, and her destiny.[107]

One way to alleviate the problem of succession would be to enhance the successor's legitimacy, either by a connection to de Gaulle or a connection to an earlier legitimacy; de Gaulle seems to have given some passing thought to these ideas. We have seen that de Gaulle thought his son Philippe might take over his mantle someday.[108] But the son was not the father and had been confined to a career of military service. So this possibility, or what could be called the Bonapartist option, appears never to have been more than a wish projection of the General.

De Gaulle seems to have thought longer and harder about the Orléanist[109] count of Paris, with whom he corresponded throughout his public career in tones of respect and cordiality. In fact, the correspondence between the two, published as a separate book in 1994,[110] can be read as a striking display of monarchist nostalgia on de Gaulle's part. Shortly after his repudiation by the French people in what has been referred to as the "suicide referendum" of April 1969, de Gaulle responded as follows to an expression of support by the count of Paris:

> Your judgment about the events that concern me would be for me in any case the most precious possible. But let me [also] say to You in this instance that, in my eyes, it is the only one that really counts. Your judgment expresses, in effect, the voice of eternal France, whatever may be the discordant appraisals of the French of today.[111]

In a later letter, at the end of 1969, de Gaulle wrote, "You, monseigneur, remain intact, clairvoyant, and permanent, as [does] France. . . . You personify that which is supreme in her destiny."[112]

The "Monarchy of the Republic" had hardly been put in place, with the referendum of October 1962, when the first signs of the public's restiveness with de Gaulle's authoritarian rule began to appear. In the late winter of 1963, a strike in the public sector among the coal miners broke out and dragged on for weeks before finally being settled. In the meantime, the parties of the left began to unify their efforts to challenge de Gaulle in the presidential elections of 1965, the first to be held under the universal suffrage amendment. A consensus developed around François Mitterrand (who was later to unite the various strands of socialism into a single party) as the best candidate to challenge de Gaulle. Mitterrand, de Gaulle's most persistent critic, had observed to the National Assembly in April 1964 that "the present system makes one think more of the relationship between a master, who holds absolute power, and his favorite, than of a Constitution, which is valid for all its citizens."[113]

Mitterrand's challenge to "the monarch" in December 1965 was more serious than generally anticipated. He forced de Gaulle into a second-round runoff, which humiliated the seventy-five-year-old General even though he won handily with 54.5 percent of the vote. The next electoral test came in the legislative elections of early 1967. The first round gave promise that the Gaullist coalition would easily stay in power, but the second round saw the parties of the left judiciously combine their efforts, imposing party discipline so that the weaker of the candidates desisted from the runoff. The governing coalition lost forty seats and wound up with only a three-seat majority in the National Assembly.

By early 1968, despite the overall strong performance of the French economy, early signs of social malaise emerged. Unemployment had begun to rise slightly, and strike activity was on the increase. By this time, de Gaulle had been in power for nearly ten years, and his unchallenged rule had begun to seem stifling. "France is bored," wrote Pierre Viansson-Ponté in a memorable editorial in *Le Monde* on March 15. On April 28, de Gaulle told his aide-de-camp, François Flohic, "I no longer find this very entertaining; there is no longer anything difficult, or heroic, to be done."[114]

The precipitate cause of the events of May 1968, which appeared seemingly out of nowhere and left Paris paralyzed for the better part of the month, was France's exploding student population. The General seemed out of touch with the following grievances of the students: the slow pace of modernization of French education; the overcrowded classrooms; the limited opportunities for upward mobility because of the extreme competitiveness for the prestigious *grandes écoles* at the top of the educational hierarchy; the rigidities of the system introduced by the Fouchet Law of 1967, which placed young students into categories of schools from which they could not easily switch; and the prospect that the egalitarian aspects of the university system, whereby all degrees were theoretically considered to be equivalent, would be undermined through a differentiation process known as "selection."

In the ideological context, the late 1960s saw the beginning of the fossilization of Soviet Communism and the rise of Third World, or Maoist, Communism. Thus, the 1968 student uprising in Paris was put together by a vanguard of unorthodox socialists, Trotskyites, and Maoists, and even when the trade unions later joined in the fray, the French Communist party held back and in this sense can be viewed, as Jean Lacouture has put it, as having been in an objective alliance with the government.[115]

The government was torn between the hard-liners, mostly represented by wartime comrades (*compagnons*) of de Gaulle who believed they were carrying out his wishes, and a more pragmatic approach that came to be embodied by Prime Minister Georges Pompidou. The crisis was not aided by the absence of the president and the prime minister from the country at various times. On May 25, the government, under the direction of the prime minister, opened negotiations with the workers and made substantial concessions, only to have them rejected. A radio and television broadcast on May 24 by de Gaulle—appealing for order when he himself had been a cause of the disorder—fell flat, by de Gaulle's own admission. All he had to offer was a new referendum aimed at giving him a new mandate for change.

The demonstrations continued in their intensity, and on May 28, François Mitterrand announced he was ready to assume the presidency in the event of a "vacancy of power." On the following day de Gaulle made an unannounced flight to Baden-Baden, West Germany, for a visit of a few hours to his old military comrade, General Jacques Massu—demonstrating to the French people, whether intentionally or not, that they could suddenly lose their helmsman. Only then did the fever begin to subside.

Though the long reign of de Gaulle was at the core of the amorphous "happening" that constituted the crisis of May 1968 ("Ten years is enough" became the principal slogan of the demonstrators), the French people came to their senses. A massive progovernment demonstration along Paris's avenue des Champs-Elysées on May 30 turned the tide. The National Assembly was dismissed, and in the ensuing legislative elections, the governing coalition won its greatest electoral victory, gaining 356 of 485 seats.

Immediately after the tumultuous events of May, de Gaulle, in a televised interview with the journalist Michel Droit, spoke of various times in his career when he had been seized with a "wave of sadness" and was tempted to give up what he was doing. He recounted a series of events, starting with the Dakar fiasco in 1940 and ending with his flight from Paris to Baden-Baden in the midst of the disturbances of the previous month.[116]

De Gaulle was mortally wounded politically by the May 1968 experience, and he made things worse for himself by immediately replacing Pompidou, who had emerged as the hero of the settlement, with the technocrat foreign minister Maurice Couve de Murville. De Gaulle, who had been persuaded by Pompidou in the midst of the crisis not to conduct a referendum, as he had publicly promised, but to hold legislative elections instead, came back to the referendum idea ten months later.

In this last referendum of April 1969, which de Gaulle used, characteristically, as a test of his own popularity, the issue was not one of central concern to the French people. The referendum document, a long and complicated one, dealt with a plan for reviving the former regions of France as an echelon between the departments and the central administration, and with a reform of the Senate along the lines of what he had advocated in his Bayeux speech in 1946: to include in it representatives of economic and social organizations and to make it a purely consultative body.

On April 10, 1969, shortly before the referendum was to take place, in another interview with Michel Droit, de Gaulle confirmed to the journalist that he was making the referendum an issue of confidence: "The response that the country will make to what I ask will determine, obviously, either the continuation of my mandate or my immediate departure."[117] De Gaulle said that for thirty years he had been taking risks and initiatives concerning the destiny of France and had always submitted these to the country, which had given him its approval. "One day someone will gauge what collapses, what abysses, the nation was spared by how profoundly the people accepted me when I asked for their approval."[118]

De Gaulle's last effort failed, as the referendum went against his proposals by a margin of 53.71 percent to 46.78 percent. He immediately resigned (April 28, 1969) with the briefest of announcements, never to make a statement in public again. A year and a half after this fatal and final referendum, de Gaulle died, on November 9, 1970. In the interim, he wrote his *Memoirs of Hope*, which covered the period following his return to power in 1958. He finished the first volume (1958–62) and was two chapters into the second (1962–65) when death intervened. Before his death, de Gaulle had also planned to write a series of imaginary dialogues with French figures of the past (Joan of Arc, Napoléon, Louis XIV, and others), comparing their actions with his—an ultimate expression of mysticism and historical perspective that was left unaccomplished.

THE GAULLIST IDEOLOGY

What de Gaulle saw as basically wrong with the French polity (and French society) was its lack of unity. Only once in de Gaulle's lifetime—the period of the "sacred union" of World War I—had the pattern been reversed: The French people in effect rose as one in response to the outbreak of war, and the baton was passed to a series of remarkable leaders: Raymond Poincaré, Ferdinand Foch, Georges Clemenceau . . . with some breaks in between, during which French morale sagged, sometimes dangerously.

This lack of unity went at least as far back as the revolutionary origins of the modern French state. The Revolution, led by elements of the French bourgeoisie, who were supported by mobs who occasionally went out of control, declared that what had gone on before the Revolution in 1789— the ancien régime—was null and void. The country was starting anew, from a clean slate (tabula rasa), and French society was to be recreated from top to bottom.

The tabula rasa theory ultimately meant that a monarch had no place in French society. Nor was there any special place for the nobility, whose privileges were removed at one stroke on the night of August 4, 1789, by the National Assembly (which by this time included nobles and clergy as well as the third estate). Neither was there a special position for a Catholic Church that maintained its obedience to Rome.

According to the French revolutionaries, the vacuum left by the liquidation of these "corrupt" institutions was to be filled by a single concept, based in virtue: There is no power superior to the will of the people. The expression of such will was to be manifested through the people's representatives, that is to say, the National Assembly. The idea that supreme power in France could be vested in a national Parliament of hundreds of people was a prescription for chaos that led to bloody dictatorship and terror in the early years of the revolutionary experience.

The revolutionaries' rewriting of history was contested throughout the nineteenth century and attacked ideologically by groups who had been excluded from their special status in French society by the phenomenon of the tabula rasa. These groups included the legitimists, who wanted to restore the Bourbon monarchy to France (and did so for a brief period after the Napoleonic Wars) and the Orléanists, who emerged with a rival claim to the throne, billing themselves as being more disposed to the Revolution (so much disposed to it that a member of the line, Philippe Egalité, voted for the beheading of the Bourbon king Louis XVI; he made his own trip to the guillotine later during the Terror). The Orléanists did in fact displace the Bourbons and ruled from 1830 to 1848.

The Revolution was also contested on structural grounds—in the sense that the problem to be attacked was the supremacy of the French Parliament and the chaos therein. A strong state could be fashioned under a single leader who would represent the people as a whole, not any particular party or faction, and at the same time would not be a descendant of the ancien régime. This led to the Bonapartist experiment, described by the historian François Furet as part meritocratic and part deriving from the former landed aristocracy—an experiment brought down by Napoléon's unchecked ambition. But it had such a nostalgic resonance that it was tried again—except, as François Furet points out, the leader of this Second Empire, Louis-Napoléon Bonaparte, did not have the qualities of the first.

The parties that emerged from the French Revolution and represented the French bourgeoisie reflected an element of the French experience noted by Professor Stanley Hoffmann and by Raymond Aron, a leading French intellectual of the postwar period: the split between liberals (in the European sense) and democrats. In general, the liberals were more interested in personal liberty than equality, and the democrats were more interested in equality than liberty.

The democrats, embodied in the nineteenth century in the Radical party, were essentially an egalitarian group, holding the principle of equality of opportunity and education, yet lacking an ideological agenda except for anticlericalism. As the nineteenth century wore on, other parties emerged outside the bourgeois context—utopian parties (Saint-Simonians, Fourierists, and others) and then Marxist ones (Blanquistes, Socialists of the Second International, and Communists of the Third International)—all claiming lineage in the French Revolution.

The France into which Charles de Gaulle had been born had seesawed throughout the nineteenth century; power was passed from Bonapartists to legitimists, to Orléanists, to democratic revolutionaries (1848), and then to the Bonapartists again. The brief period of the extremist Commune uprising in Paris in the wake of the disaster of the Franco-Prussian War dissolved into the seemingly final triumph of the Republic under the Radical party, only to be disturbed temporarily by an apparent avatar of Bonapartism—the "man on horseback," General Georges Boulanger, in the years just before Charles de Gaulle was born.

France was an unfinished society constitutionally and a contested society from within. The principle of revolution, carried to its extreme, meant that revolution could never end; therefore a constitutionally stable state would never emerge. And since the society was contested from within, any party that triumphed momentarily could introduce a new constitution.

Still, it seemed that the Third Republic had firmly anchored the republican principle in French society. But the disaster of the Battle of France overturned this longest-lived French constitution (1875–1940), and again the organization of the French political society became an open question. Charles de Gaulle was not a man of the tabula rasa. To him, denying the first thirteen hundred years of French history was to deny a large part of French grandeur. De Gaulle incorporated, and exalted, both the ancien régime and the Revolution, whenever and in the measure that these experiences brought glory and power to France. His symbolic figures were Louis XIV and Lazare Carnot: Louis XIV for ensuring French supremacy in Europe before his successor set about squandering the legacy; Carnot for directing the French war effort against a coalition of European monarchies in the revolutionary wars of the early 1790s.

De Gaulle was a synthesizer, and as such he attempted to be all things to all people. The Gaullist movement, therefore, did not have a strong ideological cast. The General described his movement as revolutionary, though not in the ideological sense. Instead he meant a rotation of elites — a new elite rising to oust an established and corrupt one. We have seen earlier that de Gaulle described his Free French movement as an "elite begun from nothing."[119] It was not surprising that the Gaullist outlook was upsetting to the elites in France's entrenched society, the so-called notables. This designation means roughly "the important people" and is a term that harks back to the postrevolutionary system of French elections, in which communes elected one-tenth of the residents as "communal notabilities," and the next higher administrative area, the *arrondissement,* elected in turn its "notabilities."[120]

The notables remained wary of de Gaulle to varying degrees, up to and including the act of his political demise. The failed referendum of 1969 was lost partly because he wanted, through the referendum, to change the nature and diminish the power of the Senate, a stronghold of the notables.

As a synthesizer, de Gaulle incorporated other elements of the French tradition, notably that of *dirigisme,* the leadership of the state over the economy, which, though it predated the Revolution, dovetailed with the centralizing thrust of the dominant Jacobin strain in the revolutionary movement. As we have seen, the Jacobin tradition, both determinedly revolutionary and wedded to the idea of a strong central government, had its roots in the thought of Jean-Jacques Rousseau — particularly the idea that there is such a thing as the *general will* of a people, which must be identified and acted upon. Though de Gaulle was ambivalent about Jacobinism because of its tie to the Revolution's notion of parliamentary supremacy (he once referred in this context to "these peculiar Jacobins"),[121] its centralizing legacy appealed to him. This was reflected in the series of nationalizations that de Gaulle carried out when he headed the provisional government at the end of World War II.[122]

De Gaulle sought to be nearly all things to all French people: He was resolutely republican; he was nostalgic about "the grandeur of our Monarchy"; and he had a sneaking admiration for Napoléon Bonaparte, especially his military victories. De Gaulle made it hard for historians and political scientists to put him in one place along France's complicated political spectrum. But there was one thing he was not: He was not a partisan of parliamentary supremacy, which had been so much the watchword of the left in France since the Revolution.

Although virtually from the outset a category of "left Gaullists" were noted for their nonconservative social policy and for their neutralism in foreign affairs, de Gaulle remained a man of the right, if for no other reason than his distaste for the tradition of parliamentary supremacy and his implacable opposition to the French Communist party, after a brief but fruitless experience with Communist members in his postwar provisional government. With his eye forever on French unity, de Gaulle relentlessly dismissed the Communists as "separatists" under the influence of a "Slavic power." In a speech at Rennes on July 21, 1947, de Gaulle remarked: "This is where we are. On our soil, in the midst of us [there are] men who have made a vow of obedience to the orders of a foreign enterprise of domination, directed by the masters of a great Slavic power."[123]

De Gaulle even went so far as to say, in reply to a question at a press conference on October 1, 1948, "I consider that if it should happen that the separatists entered into what is still acceptable to call the government of France, from that moment on it would completely depart from legitimacy."[124] (The Communists did not occupy a place in the cabinet for a generation—not until the first Socialist government of the Fifth Republic, in 1981, under President François Mitterrand.)

Also with his eye on achieving unity, de Gaulle was in favor of a strong government with a strong leader at the head of it. In his view, the various corps of the French civil service agreed: "For the most part [they] appreciated the sort of revolution which had given the Republic a head."[125] No one could better fulfill that role than himself. No successor would have the same "personal equation."[126]

At the same time, de Gaulle was wise enough, and understood the French people well enough, not to become associated in the public mind with Caesarism, or absolutist government. He did not try to disband Parliament or turn it into a nonrepresentative body, as his predecessor of a century earlier, Louis-Napoléon, had done in staging a coup d'état and then "legitimizing" it with a plebiscite. Instead, de Gaulle sought to force Parliament to his will.

We return to the theme of the introduction: unity and aggrandizement. There is so little ideology in de Gaulle's thinking (indeed he constantly placed ideology in unfavorable juxtaposition to nationalism)[127] that his role models become easily identified as those who unified (and centralized) France and contributed to its aggrandizement: Louis XIV, Carnot, Napoléon, Clemenceau, Foch. This lends credence to Stanley Hoffmann's formula: that de Gaulle was part monarchist, part Jacobin, and part Bonapartist.[128]

The first line of de Gaulle's second book, *The Edge of the Sword,* contains a quotation he attributed to *Hamlet:* "To be great is to sustain a great quarrel."[129] In the final analysis, de Gaulle's "great quarrel" was his unflagging effort to sustain the independence of France and, at the same time, to return France to its former position of grandeur. But the word *quarrel* had a larger meaning for him. It was the "quarrel of humanity" — that is, the improvement of humanity:

> In our time, the only worthwhile quarrel is that of mankind. It is mankind that must be saved, made to live and enable[d] to advance. . . . Let us . . . improve the chances of life and peace. How much more worthwhile that would be than the territorial demands, ideological claims, [and] imperialist ambitions that are leading the world to its death?[130]

De Gaulle's primary concentration, which was on the advancement of the French nation and the French people, seemed to push ideology into the background. As Stanley Hoffmann has noted, de Gaulle's ideology was France itself, and this helps explain the ideological poverty in his thinking.[131] To de Gaulle, the national impulse was at the base of all political action: At a press conference on July 29, 1963, when asked about the Sino-Soviet split, de Gaulle observed that it seemed to be ideological but was in effect political, adding, "In reality, the standard of ideology only covers ambitions."[132]

"ASSOCIATION": THE MESSAGE THAT DID NOT TAKE

In a speech in 1950, when he still had hopes that the political movement he had created, the Rally of the French People, would propel him back to power, de Gaulle described what he called the three "flames" of France: the Christian religion, the "traditions" of France, and the "social flame" — the faintly ideological notion of "association."[133]

De Gaulle openly proclaimed his (and France's) attachment to Christianity, meaning Catholicism, "the historic religion of the French nation, which remains that of the great majority of Frenchmen," as the historian René Rémond has put it.[134] Said de Gaulle: "We are a Christian country. It's a fact. We have been for a very long time. It is the case that we have been more or less, but more rather than less, shaped by that source."[135]

De Gaulle was Catholic most particularly in his awareness of the symbiotic relationship between Catholicism and French "grandeur," a leading symbol of which was the coronation of the first Capetian "king," Hugh Capet, at Reims in 987. De Gaulle was not anticlerical. He was not "Catholic against the church," a phrase sometimes applied to Charles Péguy, who along with another French nationalist thinker, Maurice Barrès, had great influence on de Gaulle. Nor was de Gaulle a nationalist to the point of being exclusionary, as Barrès, an anti-Dreyfusard and anti-Semite, most certainly was. De Gaulle was aware of the hybrid makeup of France, and indeed there is only one place—in de Gaulle's early writings—where a trace of anti-Semitism appears (though tactfully excised by his editors). In a letter to his mother, describing the scene in Warsaw in 1919, he wrote:

> And in the middle of all this innumerable [. . .], hated to the death by all classes of society, all enriched by a war from which they have profited at the expense of the Russians, the Boches, and the Poles, and rather well disposed toward a social revolution in which they would pick up a lot of money in exchange for a few bad blows.[136]

De Gaulle was a regularly practicing Catholic, he wrote in respectful terms to the French clergy, and he paid homage to Pope John XXIII in a visit to the Holy See in June 1959. But at the same time, de Gaulle bristled at any intrusion of the church into politics. When asked in a press conference in Brazzaville whether he was a practicing Catholic, de Gaulle shot back, "*Oui, et après?*" ("Yes, and so what?"), as though this were not an appropriate question for the public arena.[137]

When de Gaulle attended a Te Deum for the liberation at the Cathedral of Notre Dame after his triumphal march down the Champs-Elysées on August 26, 1944, he directed that the cardinal-archbishop of Paris, Emmanuel Suhard, not be present. Suhard had received Pétain during the marshal's visit to Paris in March 1944,[138] and a month later had officiated at a funeral ceremony at the cathedral for Philippe Henriot, a notorious Vichy official who had been assassinated.

When in 1951 the Vatican newspaper *Osservatore Romano* came out in

favor of the Christian Democratic party in France, the Mouvement républicain populaire (MRP), rather than de Gaulle's movement, the Rally of the
French People, the General issued a scathing denunciation of the
article.[139]

The concept of "association," the third of the "eternal flames" of France,
echoed the idea of the French Revolution's "fraternity" in de Gaulle's
mind. In the nineteenth and twentieth centuries the concept became
expressed in the term "solidarity," which had been adopted as a byword of
the French left. De Gaulle sought to incorporate the morality implicit in
fraternity in finding a middle route between an overly selfish capitalism and
an overly regimented socialism. Association, virtually the sole ideological
motif in Gaullist thought, was one of the General's unrealized goals
throughout his public career. It flowered and developed emphasis in the
post–World War II period and was a continuing preoccupation for him; he
eventually came to call the concept "participation." It was a major factor in
the staging of his final referendum in April 1969 (although, curiously, it was
removed from the text of the referendum, which was concerned with
regionalization—recreating the old provinces of France as regions—and
the reform of the Senate).

In the postwar period, de Gaulle described association as an idea that,
"though invented in the nineteenth century, could not develop before the
Rallying."[140] This was a reference to the Rally of the French People
(RPF), whose coming to power, de Gaulle averred, was essential for the
full expression of association. The rationale behind association was its
twofold opposition to, on the one hand, "capitalism, long intoxicated with
its own accomplishments, and on the other, the champions of the class
struggle, full of illusions about what would result from a dictatorship of the
proletariat."[141]

De Gaulle seems to have visualized association as a remedy for traditional human, and particularly French, fractiousness. Workers and their
employers would not base their relationship on exploitation but would act
together on the basis of a mutual contract. In a speech in the worker town
of St.-Etienne in January 1948, de Gaulle spelled out this idea:

> In the same group of enterprises, all those who were a part of it—
> employers, white collar staff, and workers—would together establish as
> equals, under an organized arbitration, the conditions of their work,
> notably their salaries. And they would fix them in such a way that
> everyone, from the employer to the manual worker, would receive by
> law and according to a hierarchical scale a remuneration in proportion to
> the overall profits of the enterprise. Then the elements of moral order

that give honor to a vocation—authority for those who direct it, a taste for a job well done among the workers, a professional capacity for everyone—would take on their full importance, because they would control the profits, that is, the common benefit. Then one would see emerge, inside the professions, a psychology other than that of the exploitation of some by others, or that of the class struggle.[142]

Moreover, it was de Gaulle's idea to incorporate association (or, under its later term, participation) into the institutions of the state. Representatives from commercial and industrial enterprises would sit alongside elected officials in the local councils. At the top level of the state, they would sit in the upper chamber (the Council of the Republic under the Fourth Republic, the Senate under the Fifth), along with representatives from the local councils. This change in the composition of the Senate was to form part of the referendum of 1969. However, the idea was neither grasped nor accepted by the French people as a whole, and the Senate correctly interpreted the provisions of the referendum as an attempt to weaken its authority and therefore opposed it.

De Gaulle's association seems to have been partly an adoption of the corporatist idea in French thinking—represented by Latour du Pin in the nineteenth century and Charles Maurras, the principal French rightist thinker in the interwar period, in the twentieth—as well as the social Christian doctrine embodied in the encyclical of Pope Leo XII in 1893; and partly a transcendence of traditional trade unionism. "Association," said de Gaulle, "calls for a renovated trade unionism—that is to say, professional, free, constructive, [and] cleansed of all politics."[143] It was a question of arranging things "so that men who have to work together are close enough to understand each other, explain things to each other, and associate with each other. That is what participation is!"[144]

In the moral sphere, both communism and capitalism were lacking, according to de Gaulle. Communism imposed a distribution system based on "constant moral and material constraint—in other words, an implacable and perpetual dictatorship."[145] Concerning capitalism, de Gaulle was only slightly less condemnatory:

> Capitalism says: Thanks to profits that initiative stimulates, let us create more and more wealth, which, through distribution in the free market system, raises the level of the social body as a whole. But, however, the ownership, the management, the profits of enterprises in the capitalist system belong only to capital. And so those who do not possess it find themselves in a sort of state of alienation inside the very activity to which they contribute. No, capitalism from the point of view of humanity does not offer a satisfactory solution.[146]

Both when he was in power immediately after the war, and after he returned to power in 1958, de Gaulle sought to establish, by ordinance, worker participation in company committees and later, in profit sharing. But his ideas in this area never came to fruition and fell into oblivion with the referendum of 1969 and his departure from power.

In the same speech in 1950 in which he spoke of the "three flames" of France, de Gaulle stated that, besides association, there were two other things France needed in the postwar period: the reform of the French state and the reestablishment of France's external position.[147] We have seen in this chapter how de Gaulle accomplished the most profound reform of the French state since the Revolution. We will examine in the next chapter how de Gaulle accomplished the reestablishment of France's external position and in the process set a lasting stamp on what is referred to variously (and often with puzzlement outside France) as the French "specificity," or the French "difference."

NOTES

[1] Charles de Gaulle, "Renewal, 1958–1962," pt. 1 of *Memoirs of Hope: Renewal and Endeavor*, trans. Terence Kilmartin (New York: Simon and Schuster, 1970), 6 (hereafter cited as *MH*).

[2] Letter dated Oct. 30, 1969, to Jean-Marcel Jeanneney. Charles de Gaulle, *Lettres, notes, et carnets*, vol. 12 (Paris: Plon, 1987), 343–44 (all volumes cited hereafter as *LNC*).

[3] Jules Jeanneney, *Journal politique: Septembre 1939–Juillet 1942*, ed. Jean-Noël Jeanneney (Paris: Armand Colin, 1972), 315 (hereafter cited as *JP*).

[4] L. Duguit, H. Monnier, and R. Bonnard, *Les constitutions et les principales lois politiques de la France depuis 1789* (Paris: Librairie générale de droit et de jurisprudence, 1952), 292 (hereafter cited as *DLC*).

[5] See Part Two, The Documents, for the text of this law.

[6] *JP*, 315.

[7] Ibid., 314–15. "Crossing the Rubicon," as Caesar did in 49 B.C. when he crossed from Gaul into Italy, meant there was no turning back from this irrevocable action.

[8] Ibid., 317.

[9] Departments are administrative divisions of France that were established after the French Revolution, replacing the old French provinces.

[10] *DLC*, 288.

[11] Charles de Gaulle, *Discours et messages*, vol. 1, *Pendant la guerre, Juin 1940–Janvier 1946* (Paris: Plon, 1970), 258 (all volumes hereafter cited as *DM*).

[12] Charles de Gaulle, *The Complete War Memoirs of Charles de Gaulle*, vol. 2, *Unity, 1942–1944*, trans. Richard Howard (New York: Simon and Schuster, 1964), 407 (all volumes hereafter cited as *WM*). Among the cases that interested de Gaulle was that of Pierre Boisson, who had been retained by Adm. Darlan as governor-general of French West Africa at Dakar. Boisson had successfully led the resistance to the attempted Anglo-French landing there in Sept. 1940. However, Boisson had helped rally French West Africa to the

Allies after the Nov. 1942 invasion. When Churchill referred to this in a conversation with de Gaulle on Apr. 2, 1943, the latter's rejoinder was that "it was only a question of knowing whether Governor Boisson has served France" (*LNC*, vol. 12, 373). At the end of 1943, de Gaulle succeeded in having Boisson arrested. See note 4. Chapter 1.

[13] *LNC*, vol. 4 (1982), 586.

[14] *WM*, vol. 2, 412–413.

[15] "The View from Hyde Park," *The Franklin and Eleanor Roosevelt Newsletter*, Winter 1989. Review of the book by Raoul Aglion, *De Gaulle et Roosevelt: La France libre aux Etats-Unis* (Paris: Plon, 1984).

[16] *MH*, pt. 1, 3.

[17] *WM*, vol. 2, 411.

[18] Jean Lacouture, *De Gaulle*, vol. 1, *Le rebelle* (Paris: Seuil, 1984), 266 (all volumes hereafter cited as *JLDG*).

[19] *WM*, vol. 2, 485.

[20] See p. 56. In November 1943, Pétain had the idea of convening the National Assembly to decide on the question of his successor, but the Germans indignantly squelched the plan.

[21] *WM*, vol. 2, 485–86.

[22] See Part Two, The Documents, for excerpts from the key document (Ordinance of August 9, 1944) that annulled the Vichy period and restored "Republican legality."

[23] Press conference of May 19, 1958. *Major Addresses, Statements, and Press Conferences of General Charles de Gaulle, May 19, 1958–January 31, 1964* (New York: French Embassy Press and Information Bureau, 1974), 2 (hereafter cited as *MASPC*).

[24] *LNC*, vol. 7 (1985), 208.

[25] Ibid., 60. By this time de Gaulle had resigned, having failed to effect his reforms.

[26] *LNC*, vol. 4, 141.

[27] Ibid., 147–48.

[28] *LNC*, vol. 3 (1981), 385.

[29] See Part Two, The Documents, for the passage in de Gaulle's speech in London on Apr. 1, 1942, in which he talks about a transformation in France through his movement's "revolution."

[30] *MH*, pt. 1, 293–94. See also p. 8.

[31] *LNC*, vol. 5 (1983), 60.

[32] "Endeavor, 1962–," pt. 2 of *MH*, 324.

[33] Charles de Gaulle, *Discours et messages*, vol. 4, *Avec le renouveau, 1958–1962* (Paris: Omnibus/Plon, 1993), 669. (In this study, the abbreviation *DM-OP* will indicate when the Omnibus/Plon edition is used. *DM* signifies the earlier Plon edition.)

[34] *MH*, pt. 2, 323.

[35] Ibid., 324.

[36] *LNC*, vol. 7, 151.

[37] *LNC*, vol. 1 (1980), 273–74.

[38] Ibid., 286.

[39] *MH*, pt. 1, 6.

[40] Jean Carpentier and François Lebrun, ed., *Histoire de France* (Paris: Seuil, 1987), 346.

[41] *MH*, pt. 1, 7–8.

[42] *DM-OP*, vol. 2, *Dans l'attente, Fevrier 1946–Avril 1959*, 310.

[43] Interview with Michel Droit, Apr. 10, 1969. *DM-OP*, vol. 5, *Vers le terme, Janvier 1966–Avril 1969*, 1141.

[44] *DM-OP*, vol. 3, 818.

[45] *DM-OP*, vol. 2, 323.

[46] Since the second draft constitution modified the people's total right to be consulted on constitutional change, de Gaulle characterized it as a "questionable" referendum. Alain Peyrefitte, *C'était de Gaulle* (Paris: Fayard, 1994), 485 (hereafter cited as *APCG*).

[47] *DM-OP*, vol. 2, 439. The French Communist Party in particular sought to hang the label of would-be dictator on de Gaulle and referred to him in its statements as "General Seditious." Ibid., 319.

[48] *MH*, pt. 2, 307.

[49] De Gaulle was referring to Napoléon I, not his nephew, Louis-Napoléon Bonaparte (Napoléon III). Gen. Georges Boulanger was an intriguer who sought unsuccessfully to overthrow the parliamentary regime of the Third Republic in the late 1880s. *DM*, vol. 2, 203–4.

[50] Ibid., 204.

[51] "The exclusive regime of the parties" was de Gaulle's way of describing parliamentary supremacy. See page 76. *WM*, vol. 3, *Salvation, 1944–1946*, trans. Richard Howard (New York: Simon and Schuster, 1964), 993.

[52] *MASPC*, 3.

[53] Charles de Gaulle, *Discours et messages*, vol. 2, *Dans l'attente, Février 1946–Avril 1958* (Paris: Omnibus/Plon, 1993), 309–14. Large extracts from the Bayeux speech are contained in Part Two, The Documents.

[54] Ibid., 313. Although de Gaulle wanted a senate, and not a single assembly, he did not want to see repeated what he regarded as a major error of the Third Republic: The Senate could oppose indefinitely the decisions of the National Assembly. Said de Gaulle: "In the final analysis, this blocked urgent reforms, particularly in the social area." (*DM*, vol. 1, 611). In de Gaulle's view, it was the chief of state who should balance against the National Assembly, and not the Senate (*DM-OP*, vol. 5, 1104).

[55] Ibid., 10. "The other power" refers to the Parliament.

[56] *DM*, vol. 3, 77.

[57] *DM-OP*, vol. 2, 312.

[58] *DM*, vol. 2, 10.

[59] *DM-OP*, vol. 2, 321.

[60] Ibid.

[61] *APCG*, 33.

[62] *LNC*, vol. 7, 86.

[63] Ibid.

[64] Ibid., 87.

[65] *LNC*, vol. 7, 143.

[66] Ibid., 44.

[67] *DLC*, 569.

[68] *DM-OP*, vol. 4, *Pour l'effort, Août 1962–Décembre 1965*, 816. Roughly the same procedure had been recommended to de Gaulle for the postwar period by Jules Jeanneney, president of the Senate: that the provisional government draft a new constitution, have it debated by a committee of wise men, and then submit it to the people in a referendum. De Gaulle did not do this because he had promised the people there would be a constituent assembly elected after the war was over. *APCG*, 33–34.

[69] René Rémond, *La politique n'est plus ce qu'elle était* (Paris: Calmann-Lévy, 1993), 132 (hereafter cited as *RR*).

[70] See p. 78 and notes 45 and 46.

[71] Article 4 of the Declaration of the Rights of Man and of the Citizen of Aug. 26, 1789, reads as follows: "Liberty consists of being able to do everything that does not harm others. Thus the exercise of the natural rights of each man is only limited by that which assures other members of the society the enjoyment of the same rights. These limits can only be determined by the law." *Les constitutions de la France depuis 1789*, ed. Jacques Godechot (Paris: Garnier-Flammarion, 1970), 34.

[72] *MASPC*, 8.

[73] *APCG*, 448.

[74] *MASPC*, 23.

[75] *MH*, pt. 1, 270–71.

[76] *DM-OP*, vol. 5, 1139.

[77] The normal procedure, per Article 89 of the Constitution of the Fifth Republic, is that a

constitutional amendment, before it goes to a referendum, has to be passed by both houses of Parliament in identical terms.

[78] *MH*, pt. 1, 277.

[79] See pp. 82–83.

[80] *MASPC*, 191.

[81] *DM-OP*, vol. 4, 814.

[82] *MH*, pt. 2, 307.

[83] *MASPC*, 125–26.

[84] *APCG*, 209–12.

[85] Marshal Mac-Mahon, elected president of France for seven years by the National Assembly in 1873, gave up the office in the wake of a new constitution voted by the assembly in 1875. Ibid., 213.

[86] Ibid., 213–14.

[87] *MH*, pt. 2, 320.

[88] Ibid., 306.

[89] Ibid., 309.

[90] Ibid., 314.

[91] Ibid.

[92] Ibid.

[93] Ibid., 321.

[94] Ibid., 316.

[95] Ibid., 313.

[96] Ibid., 333.

[97] The Constitutional Council was created as a body to pronounce on the constitutionality of laws, but, as François Furet has pointed out, it did not begin asserting its influence until the 1970s. It is still up against a general French reluctance to strike down a law passed by Parliament. This reluctance has its roots in the historical prejudice against magistrates, who had a privileged position under the ancien régime after they were ennobled during the reign of Louis XIV.

[98] For an excerpt from the press conference dealing with this subject, see Part Two, The Documents.

[99] *MASPC*, 248.

[100] Ibid., 249.

[101] William Pickles, *The French Constitution of October 4th, 1958* (London: Stevens & Sons, 1960), 14.

[102] Ibid., 4.

[103] Ibid., 8.

[104] *APCG*, 449.

[105] Ibid., 481.

[106] *DM-OP*, vol. 5, 991.

[107] *MH*, pt. 1, 270.

[108] See pp. 83–84.

[109] The count of Paris is the descendant of the Orléanist king Louis-Philippe, who replaced the legitimist (Bourbon) king Charles X in 1830 and ruled until he himself was overthrown in the Revolution of 1848.

[110] Henri, Comte de Paris, *Dialogue sur la France* (Paris: Fayard, 1994).

[111] Letter to the Count of Paris, May 5, 1969. *LNC*, vol. 12 (1988), 17.

[112] Ibid., 83.

[113] As it happened, the contradiction between the "parliamentary" and "presidential" aspects of this constitution, made sharper by the "universal suffrage" referendum of 1962, did not come into full light until the mid-1980s, when France first experienced "cohabitation" (president from one party, prime minister from another). *JLDG*, vol. 3, *Le souverain* (1986), 616.

[114] François Flohic, *Souvenirs d'Outre-Gaulle* (Paris: Plon, 1979), 212.

[115] *JLDG*, vol. 3, 672.

[116] Interview of June 7, 1968. *DM-OP*, vol. 5, 1083. For an extract from this interview, see Part Two, The Documents.

[117] *DM-OP*, vol. 5, 1140.

[118] Ibid.

[119] Speech at Bayeux, June 16, 1946. *DM-OP*, vol. 2, 310. Also see p. 18.

[120] "Notabilities" is an earlier term for notables. *LNC*, vol. 12, 211.

[121] "These peculiar Jacobins . . . had no favorable word for the civilizing function France had fulfilled." This was a reference to the near-unanimous sentiment in the Consultative Assembly against his attempts to secure the French presence in the Levant, June 1945. WM, vol. 3, 892.

[122] This postwar wave of nationalizations in France involved electric companies, insurance companies, several banks, Air France, and Renault.

[123] *DM*, vol. 2, 99.

[124] *DM-OP*, vol. 2, 418.

[125] *MH*, pt. 1, 288.

[126] See p. 88.

[127] "He always warned his Western interlocutors against the temptation to see ideology as the principal cause of the major conflicts of the day." *JLDG*, vol. 3, *Le souverain* (1986), 409.

[128] Remarks made by Prof. Hoffmann during a seminar he conducted at Harvard University in the fall of 1992.

[129] Charles de Gaulle, *Le fil de l'épée* (Paris: Plon, 1972), 3.

[130] Press conference of Mar. 25, 1959. *MASPC*, 44–45.

[131] Stanley and Inge Hoffmann, "De Gaulle as Political Artist," in Stanley Hoffmann, *Decline or Renewal* (New York: Viking, 1974), 217.

[132] *DM*, vol. 4, 125.

[133] *LNC*, vol. 6 (1984), 402–6.

[134] *RR*, 53.

[135] *LNC*, vol. 6, 405.

[136] *LNC*, vol. 2, 28.

[137] *JLDG*, vol. 1, 444.

[138] See pp. 54–55.

[139] *DM*, vol. 2, 447–48. For an excerpt from this statement, see Part Two, The Documents.

[140] *LNC*, vol. 6, 339.

[141] Ibid.

[142] *DM-OP*, vol. 2, 400.

[143] Ibid.

[144] *DM-OP*, vol. 5, 1131.

[145] Ibid., 1088.

[146] Ibid.

[147] *LNC*, vol. 6, 402.

4

De Gaulle, Man of the Traditional European Concert, 1962–1969

After the terrible lacerations she had undergone in the last thirty years . . .
Europe [after World War II] could find equilibrium and peace only by an
association among Slavs, Germans, Gauls, and Latins.[1]

—*Charles de Gaulle*

The earthquake that Charles de Gaulle predicted would propel him back into power had taken place in 1958, perhaps later than he had expected. Just as de Gaulle was almost too young and inexperienced to "assume" France in 1940, so he was almost too old—age sixty-seven—by the time he returned to power a dozen years after the end of World War II. Not only did he not have much time to accomplish the rest of his mission; after a few years of his rule, a perception set in that he was getting too old to lead the French state. In the end de Gaulle sensed this and, whether consciously or not, arranged his own—forced—abdication. Thus de Gaulle's "reign," although lengthy (1958–1969) cannot match the tenure of François Mitterrand (1981–1995), though it far exceeded Mitterrand's in importance. Nor was it as long as the public tenure of his Allied counterparts in World War II, Franklin Roosevelt and Winston Churchill. But all these former giants had moved off the scene, leaving de Gaulle almost on center stage. Therefore, in a sense de Gaulle's last decade—the 1960s—was "his" decade. In the 1960s de Gaulle's foreign policy expressed the French "difference" with stridency and worldwide impact.

THE GAULLIST WORLDVIEW

Charles de Gaulle applied realism and the balance-of-power principle in his approach to the outside world ("States have only interests, not friends," was his harsh motto), striving to arrest France's trend from an earlier grandeur to a panicky decline. However, though it cannot be denied that

111

de Gaulle was a French nationalist, a larger theme imbued his actions—the resurgence of Europe. His desire to promote this resurgence led de Gaulle to accept the European Common Market when he came to power a year after its creation in 1957, to change from a repressive policy toward Germany after World War II to a rapprochement with Konrad Adenauer in the late 1950s, and to attempt détente with the Soviet Union in the 1960s.

Moreover, Charles de Gaulle himself was not against the idea of a European union per se. He advocated that "the largest possible number of [European] nations ensure in common the organization of their security, their economic development, and the progress of their culture."[2] However, he visualized this union not as a tight *federation* but as a loose *confederation,* in which each European state, while keeping its own national character, would delegate part of its sovereignty in matters of defense, the economy, and culture.[3] Most important, this process would take place as a matter of negotiation between sovereign European states and not as a result of a delegation of these powers to a supranational authority.

In external relations, de Gaulle was the man of the traditional European concert, a term that dates back to the Congress of Vienna in 1815, when the great powers of Europe, acting in concert, created an equilibrium that was to last throughout the century, although the German Empire, united under Bismarck, began to disrupt it after 1860. "My policy," said de Gaulle, "[is] aimed at the setting up of a concert of European States which in developing all sorts of ties between them would increase their interdependence and solidarity."[4] In this concert, the "cooperation of states,"[5] not ideology, would constitute the key fact of public life. These states would balance against each other and strive to maintain (or regain) their rank. As Raymond Aron has pointed out, "There exists in Europe a tendency toward equilibrium, of which the survival, for a thousand years, of the principal states constitutes the best proof."[6]

But France, in the Gaullist worldview, was the key to this equilibrium. The existence of France "in its independence and grandeur" was "necessary for the equilibrium of the world," de Gaulle wrote.[7] In a lecture at the Senior War College in 1927, de Gaulle had stated, "France feels that it is, for better or for worse, the guardian of the new continental order."[8]

The European system had gradually come apart over the course of the nineteenth century. In his early writings, de Gaulle had described the second half of that century as a time when "hatreds and ambitions were accumulating . . . the European equilibrium painfully constituted by the old diplomacy to avoid or put off the horror of armed conflicts had only produced discontentment . . . rancors, and unsatisfied greed."[9]

France was in a vulnerable position among the countries of Europe and therefore had every interest in restoring stability: "Consider the French hexagon. The sea borders three [of the] sides. Mountains—the highest in Europe, bar two others. But the sixth is wide open [and] just at the side where the most warlike of our neighbors lives."[10] De Gaulle had no illusions about the difficulties that post–World War II France would face in trying to restore stability to Europe and, in so doing, return France to a position of security.

Following his return to power in 1958, de Gaulle repeatedly spoke of the need to preserve equilibrium in Europe. During John F. Kennedy's visit to France in May–June 1961, de Gaulle said:

Anything that upsets [the balance of power], and in particular the German situation, would plunge the world into serious danger. Therefore, when Khrushchev summons you to change the status of Berlin, in other words to hand over the city to him, stand fast! This is the most useful service you can render to the whole world, Russia included.[11]

A year earlier, de Gaulle had said much the same thing to Nikita Khrushchev during the latter's March 1960 visit to France: If West Germany were to change sides, the European balance would be upset, and this could be the signal for war.[12]

In the Gaullist vision of a "European concert," gradations of rank arose, and de Gaulle held that France should be in the lead. All his actions, usually a mixture of careful coercion and intransigence in a manner reminiscent of Bismarck, were aimed at maximizing the relative power of the French state.

At the apex of the Western system were what de Gaulle termed "the world powers of the West"—that is, the United States, Great Britain, and France. They were the only three Western powers with worldwide interests, as the phrase "world powers of the West" implies, and as such they should together coordinate the West's strategic approach to the world.

Second, in the Gaullist lexicon, "Western Europe" meant "continental Europe," a concept that placed France in the leading European position. The distinction, of course, was that Great Britain was not to be included, for historically, "Albion could not accept that there be established on the Continent any kind of hegemony because the state that achieved this would have become a pretender to the empire of the sea."[13]

Whether by design or not, de Gaulle's rhetoric consistently banishes Britain, twenty-three miles away, from the Continent. We have seen this exclusionism in the quotation at the beginning of this chapter,[14] and we see it also in the following: "There exist in Europe more than 300 million people who are neither English, nor Russian, nor Chinese, nor citizens of the United States."[15] Even more glaring is this observation from de Gaulle's press conference of July 23, 1964:

It is clear that things have changed. The western states of our Ancient Continent have remade their economies. They are reestablishing their military forces. *One of them, France, has acceded to nuclear power.* Particularly, they have become conscious of their natural links. In brief, Western Europe appears capable of constituting a capital entity, full of values and means[16] (italics added).

Within the councils of the "world powers of the West" was occasional room for discussions with a fourth power—Federal Germany—but only on specific Germany-related and European-related subjects. Germany was not to be a regular member of these councils.

After Germany, in a further gradation, came the lesser European powers, the first of which was Italy: In December 1959, four-power consultations were held in Paris (Americans, British, Germans, and French) in preparation for an East-West summit to be held in 1960. On November 10, 1959, de Gaulle stated in a press conference:

I am quite pleased by the fact that four-power meetings have been set for December. . . . I believe that the beginning of Spring will be a suitable time for a further meeting, when our Governments will have worked on the bases which, I hope, we are going to set, and when they will have had the leisure to consult the Atlantic allies, particularly Italy.[17]

Italy, therefore, was in no way assumed to be the equal of France, and furthermore, Italy was permanently compromised because of its tendency to follow the lead of Britain and the United States.

This, then, was the Gaullist worldview, aimed to secure the predominance of France on the continent of Western Europe by the approach of the 1970s, by which time de Gaulle would have made France's nuclear arsenal operational.

One of the clearest and most succinct statements of Gaullist foreign policy aims is contained in the following passage of his *Memoirs of Hope,* which, however, was a backward glance (the General wrote them following his final departure from power in April 1969):

My aim, then, was to disengage France, not from the Atlantic Alliance, which I intended to maintain by way of ultimate precaution, but from the integration realized by NATO, under American command; to establish relations with each of the States of the Eastern bloc, first and foremost Russia, with the object of bringing about a *détente* followed by understanding and cooperation; to do likewise, when the time was ripe, with China; and finally to provide France with a nuclear capability such that no one could attack us without running the risk of frightful injury. But I was anxious to proceed gradually, linking each stage with overall developments and continuing to cultivate France's traditional friendships.[18]

THE ALGERIAN INCUBUS

Charles de Gaulle had been brought into power in 1958 by a frustrated and helpless French political class in order to solve the Algerian problem and restore public tranquility to France. He had to do this before he could step out on the world stage and use the instruments of the French state to, among other things, settle old scores with the British and the Americans. His sense of biding his time was evident long before, as in this letter of October 11, 1942, about the difficulties he was having with his Anglo-American allies: "The goal of the moment is to exist, I repeat, to exist, with the means at our disposal. Later we will see if we have an interest in working together with the British or with the Americans."[19]

The tumult in Algeria was the reason the National Assembly had approved de Gaulle as chief of government with extraordinary powers, by a vote of 329–224 on June 1, 1958. At that moment, though not in a position to assert French power in the world, de Gaulle was aware of how "an expansion toward the exterior is essential to the world situation of France."[20]

Not only did de Gaulle proceed to make a stronger French government, as we saw in the preceding chapter; he also had to cast off the Algerian incubus, which was not only threatening French society from within but crippling France's image abroad. For the next four years, de Gaulle was to wrestle with this problem, torn between the illogicality of one million Europeans' ruling nine million Algerians (at a time when decolonization was gaining sway throughout the world) and the sad fate of those Europeans, mostly French, who were in danger of being harassed, or worse, and ultimately faced the prospect of being forced out of the country, thus ending the French presence in Algeria that had lasted since 1830.

The war, begun by the Algerian nationalists on November 1, 1954, had dragged on for nearly four years by the time de Gaulle returned to power. As de Gaulle later observed in his *Memoirs of Hope,* "It was not without uneasiness and some impatience that [the French people] endured the costly struggle that was being waged there, and if they had condemned the Fourth Republic, it was above all because that republic had failed to extricate them from the struggle."[21]

The impasse in Algeria carried the risk that "outcomes [would] be imposed on us from the outside,"[22] as de Gaulle noted in a speech on May 19, 1958. This was a veiled reference, at a moment when de Gaulle was positioning himself for a return to power, to the recently concluded Anglo-American Good Offices Mission. This mission had attempted to mediate between France and Tunisia earlier in the year, after a French plane, on February 8, 1958, had attacked a border village suspected of harboring Algerian insurgents. The mission's recommendations were unsatisfactory to the French, who were hoping for an outcome that would effectively close the Tunisian-Algerian border to insurgent activity. The fact that the Fourth Republic government of Félix Gaillard accepted these recommendations under duress led to its downfall and shortly thereafter to de Gaulle's return to power.

Evidence exists that, as early as 1957, a year before de Gaulle came back to power, he realized that the only course was to let Algeria become independent. He told his wartime colleague Christian Pineau, who had been a member of several cabinets in the Fourth Republic, that independence for Algeria, probably in the short term, was inevitable. Pineau exclaimed: "But General, say as much [publicly]; this will finally clarify the situation." De Gaulle replied, "It's too early. . . . It's out of the question for me to speak before I have the means to act!"[23]

However, in de Gaulle's first visit to Algeria after returning to power, he announced that "as of today, France considers that in all of Algeria there is only one single category of inhabitants: There are only full-fledged Frenchmen . . . with the same rights and the same duties."[24] Whether or not he actually believed it at the time, the myth of "ten million Frenchmen of Algeria"[25] was unsustainable. Neither the French of Metropolitan France nor the French of Algeria were willing to accept nine million Algerians of native origin on a basis equal to themselves. Perhaps de Gaulle introduced this theme—or myth—immediately after his return to power in order to prod his countrymen into reality and into a search for other solutions. He was also clearly trying to reach out to the Muslim Algerians.

Four months later, the public expression of the myth was beginning to come apart. De Gaulle held out an olive branch to the Algerian insurgents who were contesting France's right to remain in Algeria: "I say unequivocally that, most of the men of the insurrection have fought courageously. Let the peace of the brave come, and I am sure that all hatred will fade away and disappear."[26]

In a press conference on September 16, 1959, de Gaulle mentioned publicly for the first time the fateful term "self-determination." It was to be realized by means of a referendum to be held in Algeria after the fighting had stopped. The Algerians would be given three choices.[27] The first was "francisation," or what is now called "integration." Every Algerian would become a full-fledged French citizen with the same weight of vote and the same rights.

The second alternative was "association," in which France would manage Algeria's defense and foreign policy—an arrangement akin to what de Gaulle had already offered to the other French colonies in Black Africa and Madagascar in a referendum on September 28, 1958. All the states opted to stay within the French Community (the new name for the French Union)—except Guinea under its leader Sékou Touré. Algeria had voted in a referendum on the same date. But its vote, which was an extension of the one in Metropolitan France, was strictly on whether to accept the new French constitution.[28] Algeria was not given the choice, as were the other French-zone African states, of whether to stay inside the French Community or become independent.[29]

But it was not long before the African states decided to have their cake and eat it too. One by one, they chose to remain in the French Community but to become independent also, making the situation in Algeria, which had not even been offered the choice, politically untenable. De Gaulle's evocation of an ensemble consisting of Algeria closely associated with Metropolitan France, which would be "completed by the Sahara [and which] will link itself, for the common progress, with the free states of Morocco and Tunisia,"[30] illustrated the flaw in the policy of "association." Were the Algerians less entitled to independence than the Moroccans and Tunisians? Were the Algerians not entitled to the petroleum riches of the Sahara, interposed as the Algerians were between the Sahara and France?

The third alternative, as outlined in de Gaulle's press conference of September 16, 1959, was "secession," which would produce, warned the General, "the most appalling poverty, frightful political chaos, widespread slaughter, and soon after, the warlike dictatorship of the Communists. But this demon must be exorcized, and this [exorcism] must be done by the Algerians themselves."[31] Secession would also involve a regrouping and resettlement of the European population and of those Algerians who wished to remain French. This "regrouping," as the concept gradually jelled in de Gaulle's mind, would take place around Oran and Algiers.[32]

A year later, in his press conference of September 5, 1960, de Gaulle seemed to have dropped the first alternative, francisation (or integration), altogether. The only question remaining, said de Gaulle, was to determine whether "Algeria will be Algerian against France—through secession or a breaking away from her—or will be Algerian in association with, in a friendly union with, France."[33]

Thus the choice had become between, on the one hand, association with France, which meant a diminished sovereignty without the privileges of full French citizenship, and, on the other, independence. It was not hard to divine what the native population of Algeria would choose. This was recognized by de Gaulle's own prime minister at the time, Michel Debré, who was loyal to the General but heartsick at the latter's decision in favor of according self-determination to Algeria.

By 1961, de Gaulle was hinting publicly that Algeria was headed for independence: "It is difficult to claim that the Algerian masses, as a whole, wish to be part of the French people. . . . France has no objection and intends to raise no obstacle to the fact that the Algerian populations would decide to form a State that would be in charge of their country."[34]

The only stumbling block, albeit a major one, was the one-million-strong European population in Algeria. The European community in Algeria began to stir once more after de Gaulle's announcement on September 16, 1959, of a forthcoming referendum in which the Algerians would be permitted to decide their status.

In the end, de Gaulle ceded completely to the nationalist Algerian forces, while managing, in part because of his overpowering personality, not to appear to do so. No countrywide elections were held prior to the establishment of a native-origin government in Algeria. Originally, de Gaulle had insisted on such elections, as he had not done for the reconstitution of the French government in 1944, on the grounds that Algeria had never before existed as a country on its own. There was no regrouping of the European population and the pro-French Muslims into a separate enclave in Algeria. Despite the Evian Accords of March 1962, which protected the rights of the Europeans, the removal of the French army, together with anti-Muslim terrorism carried out by diehard settlers under the banner of the Secret Army Organization (OAS), produced a reaction against the European population, and a great stampede into southern France took place in the summer of 1962. A part of the native population that had fought the uprising on the side of the French (the *harkis,* mostly of Kabyle [Berber] origin) was transported to France, but the remainder suffered reprisals by the Algerian nationalists of the Front de la libération nationale (FLN). And finally, no special provisions were accorded to France for the Sahara, neither in the matter of mineral rights nor nuclear-testing facilities.

How did de Gaulle avoid looking like a failure after ceding so much ground? De Gaulle stuck to a vision, despite tactical deceptions along the way, as in his famous statement to the throng assembled in the Forum at Algiers, during his first visit in June 1958 immediately after returning to power: *"Je vous ai compris!"* ("I have understood you"). He said neither *what* he had understood nor to whom he was specifically addressing these remarks—the European population (presumably) or the Muslims. But he did make clear in the same speech that the relegation of Muslims to second-class status would have to change, which implied a great deal.[35]

De Gaulle held that France could not return to greatness except by projecting a world role for itself,[36] and the Algerian incubus had to be cast off in order for France to assume this role. International opinion could not tolerate France's holding nine million Muslims against their will. Detaching Algeria from France, de Gaulle told Alain Peyrefitte a month after his call for self-determination in September 1959, "may perhaps be the greatest service I will have rendered to France."[37]

Keeping the vision meant that de Gaulle had to be extremely firm with the European population of Algeria, and he was. De Gaulle had long given up hope that the Europeans would accept the Muslims as equals. He alluded to this regret in a press conference on November 4, 1960, in which he indicated that although France had aided Algeria economically, it had not done much for the Algerians themselves: "In sum, if we have done much in Algeria and for Algeria, we have not done in time other things that were necessary to do. The result was that the pot boiled over."[38]

De Gaulle's firmness with the European population gave his Algerian policy an impression of strength, even as he was gradually making one concession after another to the Algerian nationalists. His prestige intact after twelve years out of power, de Gaulle held firm through a string of crises.

From the beginning, when the disturbances in Algiers projected him onto the scene as the sole alternative to chaos in France, de Gaulle did not let these problems get completely out of hand. On May 28, 1958, even before he had been voted back into power, he summoned a representative from the military command in Algiers to his retreat at Colombey-les-Deux-Eglises to make the point that he would not be under the control of the insurrectionist officers poised to take power in Metropolitan France. He preferred to come back to power by the "regular process."[39]

On two subsequent occasions, as the French army (or at least the nondraftee side of it) reacted with sympathy toward the settlers *(colons)*, who were traumatized by the prospect of self-determination for Algeria, de Gaulle intervened to hold the army in check. The first occurrence was the revolt of January 1960, the "week of the barricades," in which a group of armed Europeans formed themselves into a redoubt, calling for de Gaulle's departure from power. In a television address on January 29, 1960, de Gaulle intoned: "As you know, I have the supreme responsibility. It is I who bear the country's destiny. I must therefore be obeyed by every French soldier."[40]

The second incident was the far more serious "revolt of the generals" in April 1961, after a referendum had passed in France and Algeria with 75 percent of the votes in favor of self-determination for Algeria. De Gaulle, donning military uniform and denouncing on television this putsch by "a quartet of retired generals,"[41] was able to bring the French army in Algeria to heel and break the revolt in four days. Article 16 of the constitution, giving the president emergency power, was instituted and remained in effect for five months.

Some French people, and not only reactionary ones, felt de Gaulle had betrayed the promise that had brought him to power. But most French people and most of the world felt that the resolution of the human tragedy of the Algerian War represented a personal and political triumph for de Gaulle. France ceased to be the target of Third World, and particularly Arab, wrath. France, the traditional haven in Europe for political exiles of all kinds, could now press with renewed vigor, and without shame, its universalist message of human rights and democracy, inherited from the Enlightenment and the Revolution (at least the part of the Revolution that preceded the Terror).

Shortly after the signing of the Evian Accords, de Gaulle told his cabinet on April 25, 1962: "Napoléon said that in love, the only victory is flight. In the matter of decolonization also, the only victory is to go away."[42] Half a year later, when some eight hundred thousand Europeans had fled Algeria for France, de Gaulle told Alain Peyrefitte, "This page was as painful for me as anyone. But we have turned it. It was necessary for the salvation of the country. Later, people will understand it."[43]

After the referendum of April 8, 1962, had given a 90 percent approval to the recently concluded Evian Accords granting independence to Algeria, de Gaulle could at last say that "France's policy is prompted as much as possible by common sense and—let us speak plainly—by modesty."[44] Gone were the images of French paratroopers (the *"paras"*) torturing Algerian civilians in the wake of terrorist café bombings. But more fundamentally, in a later press conference de Gaulle could assert that "the nation is at peace in the world where, at the present time, it is not engaged in any conflict of any kind. . . . This situation, so new for France, allows her to consider and deal serenely with the important matters that concern her."[45]

In the meantime, while the Algerian crisis was slowly, with its many twists and turns, leading to the rehabilitation of France's world image, de Gaulle was trying to lay the basis for a new relationship with the main Western powers. He brought with him a long history of frustration in such attempts and with it a spreading reputation for rancor.

THE PROPOSAL FOR A STRATEGIC TRIDOMINIUM

Soon after his return to power, in the so-called Memorandum of the Directory,[46] de Gaulle sought to call forth an alliance of the "world powers of the West": Britain, France, and the United States. De Gaulle had taken office determined to break the Anglo-American monopoly on Western decision making, a monopoly he had observed as a frustrated outsider during World War II but that in reality had diminished in the postwar period. Referring to the wartime period, de Gaulle observed in his memoirs, "It is understandable how eagerly I desired to penetrate the mystery in which . . . Americans and British alike wrapped their plans."[47]

In simultaneous letters to President Dwight D. Eisenhower and Prime Minister Harold Macmillan, dated September 17, 1958, de Gaulle proposed a codirectorate (which came to be known as the "tridominium") of the three powers to consult and decide on strategic matters, including nuclear strategy. De Gaulle had experienced a long history of not being consulted by the Anglo-Americans on matters of war and peace, starting shortly after the Battle of France in 1940; in the summer of 1958 he criticized U.S. actions to protect Quemoy and Matsu Islands in the Formosa Straits and more especially the U.S.-British military interventions in Lebanon and Jordan, which had raised cold war tensions to a degree unprecedented since the early months of the Korean conflict. De Gaulle thought that developments in these two areas, the Middle East and the Formosa Straits, were evidence that the Western alliance was not working well: "The solidarity in the risks incurred does not correspond with the cooperation [that is] indispensable, both in terms of decisions taken and responsibilities."[48] As the General later was to explain publicly, on September 5, 1960, "We feel that, at least among the world powers of the West, there must be an arrangement . . . as to their political conduct, and should the occasion arise, their strategic conduct outside Europe, especially in the Middle East, and in Africa, where the three powers are constantly involved."[49]

The fact that France was about to acquire nuclear weapons made it all the more imperative, as de Gaulle wrote in his *Memoirs of Hope*, "that the alliance should henceforth be placed under a triple rather than a dual direction."[50] Failing that, France would either demand a reform of NATO or leave it, as it had the right to do under Article 12 of the Washington Treaty, which had created the Atlantic Alliance.[51] And de Gaulle added, "As I expected, the two recipients of my memorandum replied evasively. So there was nothing to prevent us from taking action. But circumstances decreed that we should act with circumspection."[52]

Whether de Gaulle ever intended his tridominium proposal, to which he returned again and again, to be anything more than a negative testing of his Anglo-American allies is open to question. The foregoing citation from his *Memoirs of Hope* suggests he did not. Furthermore, de Gaulle told Alain Peyrefitte later, in 1963, that the memorandum was only a "procedure of diplomatic pressure."[53]

Parenthetically, it is worth noting that de Gaulle's great strength, as well as his weakness, was that he had a taste for deciding and not for negotiating, according to Michel Debré, a man who knew him better than most.[54] It is hard to visualize de Gaulle in the process of negotiating a satisfactory tridominium compact. In any event, de Gaulle never did receive a satisfactory answer. Eisenhower, in a brief message on October 20, 1958, told him that it would not be fair to have a three-way decision-making group at the top that left the other alliance members marginalized.[55]

De Gaulle saw no contradiction in forming a tridominium of the leading Western powers without Germany because the latter, whatever the value of its military contribution, would not be able to possess nuclear weapons. It would be at a level *down* from the Big Three. Put another way, there was no contradiction between de Gaulle's having invited Adenauer to his home at Colombey-les-Deux-Eglises on September 14, 1958, for what was to be the opening curtain for the French-German Alliance and de Gaulle's having sent a message three days later to the Anglo-American powers proposing a tridominium—precisely because Germany was to remain on another level and was intended to be the junior member of the Franco-German Alliance.

De Gaulle continued to be put off by the United States and Britain on the tridominium issue, and he began signaling his displeasure in a series of actions. This process would culminate some eight years later with

France's withdrawal from the military structure of NATO. The "dialogue of the deaf"—the process of the two sides talking past each other—continued as well. The French ambassador in Washington, Hervé Alphand, who had been approached by his American counterparts concerning exploratory discussions about a strategic dialogue, was instructed by de Gaulle on December 10, 1958, to inform them that two principles had to be established first: a common plan of political action among the three Western powers, to prevent being seen as merely reacting to the initiatives of the Soviets; and a three-way strategic plan for acting in concert in case war arose, including decisions on the use of nuclear weapons.[56]

De Gaulle was aiming very high, impossibly high, from the viewpoint of Washington. He was demanding that France be put on a par with Britain in the eyes of the United States. He was in effect asking that France be given access to American nuclear weapons data[57] and proposing that France be consulted on the employment of nuclear weapons, a privilege that even the British would never be accorded. And all the while France had not even exploded its first atomic device. Britain had, in 1952.

The tridominium was a theme to which de Gaulle would return again and again, both in his correspondence with President Eisenhower and his subsequent correspondence with President Kennedy. As a concept, the tridominium functioned passably well in moments of high tension with the Soviet Union (the U-2 incident, in which an American reconnaissance plane was shot down inside Russia; the Berlin crisis; the Cuban missile crisis) precisely because de Gaulle was called upon, as an equal, by the other two. De Gaulle described the U-2 incident as showing "the deep-seated solidarity which exists among the Western powers. . . . We three [de Gaulle, Macmillan, Eisenhower] . . . did not have much trouble in reaching agreement, in wisdom and in firmness. Our alliance appeared a living reality." But he added, "In order for it to become even more so, France must have her own role in it, and her own personality."[58]

Less than four months later, however, after the start of the American-inspired intervention in the Congo, de Gaulle again registered public disappointment at the failure to institute the tridominium: "[It] is what I proposed, as you know, to President Eisenhower and to Mr. Macmillan two years ago. This has not yet been done. . . . I am convinced that the Western States . . . must take council together continually—at least the *Western world powers* must do so"[59] (italics added).

De Gaulle went on to say that the Congo was conclusive proof of his thesis. The United States, Britain, and France should have agreed upon their positions from the beginning of the crisis and compelled an arrangement between the Congolese and the Belgians rather than play second fiddle to the United Nations.[60]

CASTING OFF THE BURDEN OF NATO

Throughout de Gaulle's writings, one gains the impression that the tridominium, with its implicit equality, was an ideal to be achieved, whereas NATO, born under the threat of a Soviet attack and not an organization among equals, was a burden to be cast off. In a related context, de Gaulle drew a contrast between the Atlantic Alliance, which remained sacrosanct or at least was paid obeisance in public statements, and NATO as a defense organization with an integrated command, which was to be attacked with increasing vigor.[61] Said de Gaulle in 1963, "[An] American protectorate was organized in Europe under the cover of NATO."[62]

During his long period in the political wilderness (January 20, 1946–June 1, 1958), de Gaulle saw created without him two Western European institutions that were to have immense significance for the future: the Atlantic Alliance and the European Economic Community (EEC). The former was created on April 4, 1949, by the Washington Treaty and was followed up by the North Atlantic Treaty Organization (NATO) a year later. The EEC came into being with the Treaty of Rome on March 25, 1957. Neither of these institutions was to de Gaulle's liking because he saw both NATO and the EEC as under the ultimate direction of Washington. They both violated de Gaulle's eventual vision of a "Europe from the Atlantic to the Urals," which would essentially exclude the United States: "If the Western half of the Old World remained subordinated to the New, Europe would never be European, nor would she ever be able to bring her two halves together."[63]

De Gaulle had reservations about the Washington Treaty from the outset. He welcomed it as a "meritorious and salutary expression of intentions by the United States," but he added that "the French nation should reserve its overall judgment." It remained to be seen what arms France would receive, how it would be aided in case of aggression, and what commitments it would have to make as to the security of others.[64]

Before long de Gaulle's concerns became manifest. In the following year, in May 1950, NATO was created, and by the end of the year, on December 19, a supreme allied commander for Europe (SACEUR) had been designated—General Eisenhower. More significant, in order to obtain German rearmament, which was deemed vital for the defense of Europe, a scheme had been developed by the European-minded Jean

Monnet, who had been named planning commissioner after the war, and presented by René Pleven, president of the Council of Ministers at the time (September 1950): the European Defense Community (EDC). So that there would be no German army and no German general staff per se, this scheme envisaged a European army, created among the partners of the European Coal and Steel Community (ECSC). The ECSC was an idea that had been put forward four months earlier by Monnet and the then prime minister, Robert Schuman. The six partners were France, West Germany, Italy, Belgium, the Netherlands, and Luxembourg.[65]

De Gaulle (as well as the French Communists) attacked the new EDC plan with vigor. In a memorable statement on June 6, 1952, de Gaulle observed:

> They pretend to establish a "European Defense Community" and create an army called "European" under American command. Pell-mell, along with conquered Germany and Italy, France must pour its men, its arms, and its money into a stateless mélange. This abasement is inflicted on her, in the name of equal rights, in order that Germany supposedly will not have an army while at the same time reestablishing military forces.
>
> Of course France, among all the great nations who today have an army, is the only one that loses hers.[66]

In the end, mainly because of the combined opposition of the Gaullists and the Communists, this originally "French" plan was killed in the National Assembly on August 30, 1954. A substitute plan was quickly put together through the accords of London and Paris in the fall of 1954: West Germany was admitted into NATO, the former anti-German Brussels Pact of 1948 (Britain, France, and the Benelux countries) was modified to include West Germany and Italy, and the "supranational" EDC was abandoned. De Gaulle registered his satisfaction that these accords, "while offering a solid base for the defense of the free nations of Europe, including Great Britain and Germany, in principle leave France the possibility of having an army, a countenance, and an action external to itself."[67]

The modified Brussels Pact of 1954, known as the Western European Union (WEU), did not develop in the face of an ever strengthening NATO military organization. After his return to power, de Gaulle tried to reverse NATO's ascendancy with the vain attempt (described earlier) at creating a tridominium of the United States, Britain, and France. De Gaulle then began taking actions to undercut NATO.

On October 29, 1958, de Gaulle informed the secretary-general of NATO, Paul-Henri Spaak, that he did not accept the idea of creating a new group of defense studies representatives. He cited the need for a general reform of NATO; pending reform, its existing committees would be sufficient.[68] In February 1959, de Gaulle removed French forces from the NATO Mediterranean command, and four months later he refused to stockpile NATO atomic weapons in France.

De Gaulle also became increasingly outspoken in his critique of NATO. Speaking on the origins of the Atlantic Alliance, on September 5, 1960, de Gaulle observed that when it was created, only the United States had the means for defending continental Western Europe, whose states had "postponed the revival of their personality in the international sphere until a much later date, if they did not renounce it altogether." Therefore the alliance was an "integrated" one: "a system whereby the defense of each of the countries of Continental Europe, of Western Europe—not counting England—does not have a national character; a system in which, in fact, everything is under the command of the Americans and in which the Americans decide on the use of the principal weapons, in other words, the atomic weapons."[69]

Soon after this speech, de Gaulle was to confront another complicated scheme—a sort of EDC elevated to the nuclear level—only this time it was not the invention of French supranationalists grouped around Jean Monnet but of a friend of Monnet in the United States: Robert Bowie, a Harvard professor who had been head of the State Department's Policy Planning Staff earlier in the Eisenhower administration. The objective of this Multilateral Force (MLF), which was a nuclear one, was to give Europeans, especially the Germans, a feeling of participation in the use of nuclear weapons while maintaining American control over these weapons—all the while preventing "national" nuclear forces from emerging.

The dictum against "national" nuclear forces was essentially aimed at the French since the British already had nuclear weapons. Thus, although both the British and the French could theoretically pull their forces out of the MLF in a national emergency, this stipulation was meaningless for the French, who had no nuclear weapons at the time.

That the French would not support the MLF was expected; what was not expected was that they fought it tooth and nail and finally destroyed it. Besides being an impediment to France's acquiring nuclear weapons on its own, the MLF would bring the Germans closer to nuclear weapons, which was anathema to de Gaulle's plan for French nuclear hegemony in Western (continental) Europe.

Unlike the British, who benefited from American help, the French were developing nuclear weapons on their own, and in February 1960, French technicians exploded an atomic bomb in the Sahara. In a famous speech three months earlier, before the classes of the French military schools, de Gaulle gave his rationale for French defense policy in general and for French nuclear weapons in particular: France would create an independent nuclear strike force (*force de frappe*) capable of reaching targets anywhere on earth.[70]

De Gaulle saw the French nuclear strike force as serving the cause of equilibrium, not only between the two superpowers—an announced Gaullist policy since the immediate aftermath of the war[71]—but more broadly. Since one could not deny the possibility that someday the United States and the Soviet Union might reconcile, "France, by equipping herself with nuclear armaments, is rendering a service to the equilibrium of the world."[72]

De Gaulle's central objective was that "no State [could] contemplate killing [France] without itself risking death."[73] He remarked in his famous press conference of January 14, 1963,[74] that the nuclear strike force would constitute this deterrent. France would be able to "destroy . . . in a few seconds millions and millions of people. This fact cannot fail to have at least some bearing on the intentions of any possible aggressor."[75]

In the same press conference, de Gaulle, while noting that American nuclear weapons remained "the essential guarantee of world peace" and hailing the "determination" of President Kennedy in the recently concluded Cuban missile affair, emphasized that "American nuclear power does not necessarily and immediately meet all the eventualities concerning Europe and France." Citing the Cuban missile case, in which "[American] means had been set aside for something other than the defense of Europe, even if Europe had been attacked in its turn," de Gaulle evoked a general uncertainty as to "if, where, when, how, and to what extent the American nuclear weapons would be employed to defend Europe."[76]

As de Gaulle recorded in his *Memoirs of Hope,* President Kennedy (in their May 1961 talks in Paris) assured him that the United States would resort to nuclear weapons rather than let Western Europe fall into the hands of the Soviets, but he was not more precise than that. Noted de Gaulle:

> In answer to the specific questions I put to him, he was unable to tell me at what point and against what targets, far or near, strategic or tactical, inside or outside Russia itself, the missiles would in fact be launched. "I am not surprised," I told him. "General Norstad, the Allied Commander-in-Chief, whom I hold in the highest esteem and who has shown me every confidence, has never been able to enlighten me on these points, which are vital to my country."[77]

At another point in his *Memoirs of Hope,* de Gaulle went one step further in his argument against reliance on the American nuclear umbrella:

In May 1961, on his first state visit to Paris, John F. Kennedy is received by General de Gaulle. Unfortunately, the magic of this visit could not obscure the marked increase in problems between the two governments during the thousand days of Kennedy's presidency.

What if America and Russia destroyed Europe while refraining from destroying themselves? "For Russia and America, the deterrent is real. But it does not exist for their respective allies. What, after all, is to prevent Russia and America from wiping out what lies between their own vitals, in other words the European battlefield? Is this not, in fact, what NATO is preparing for?"[78]

This fear was not a totally empty one for Europeans, and it revolved around the concept of "flexible response," introduced by the Kennedy administration as a way of coping with U.S.-Soviet strategic parity coupled with Soviet conventional weapons superiority in the European theater. Flexible response called for gradual escalation on the battlefield before resorting to nuclear weapons.

Meantime, by the mid-1960s, the French nuclear force was nearer to being operational and, more important, the Multilateral Force (MLF) had died before it ever became a reality because of French obstructions. An MLF in which the Americans held a veto on the use of nuclear weapons and, more significant, in which the British also insisted on a veto, had no real value for the Germans. And the Germans were the ones the MLF was supposed to benefit most.

De Gaulle now no longer needed to remain in NATO and fight the MLF from within. He had seen in the Cuban missile crisis, with its unfavorable outcome for the Russians, that America's own nuclear forces remained "the essential guarantee of world peace."[79] It was time for de Gaulle to get out from under a situation he had described earlier, in 1961: "It is intolerable for a great State to leave its destiny up to the decisions and action of another State, however friendly it may be." Furthermore, he claimed, NATO's integrated defense structure actually weakened Europe's defense: "In integration . . . the integrated country loses interest in its national defense, since it is not responsible for it."[80]

Although he had signaled his intent to revise his relationship with NATO at the time the Washington Treaty came up for renewal in 1969,[81] de Gaulle struck earlier. On March 7, 1966, after the MLF had died in the middle of the previous year, de Gaulle took France out of the integrated command of NATO, while retaining, as an ultimate insurance, France's membership in the Atlantic Alliance.

On August 10, 1967, in his usual trenchant, near-brutal style, de Gaulle described the new situation of France, in words that implied France was a member of the Atlantic Alliance in name only:

> France has retaken possession of its forces and has undertaken to give itself the means of dissuasion. . . . in the hypothesis of a war between the two giants, a war which, without striking one another, they could come to wage through an interposed Europe, France would not be automatically the humble auxiliary of one of them and would arrange for itself the chance to be other than a battlefield for their expeditionary corps and a target for their alternating bombs. . . . France, in leaving the system of blocs, has perhaps given the signal of a general evolution toward international détente.[82]

Although de Gaulle expressed satisfaction that France had broken the "stifling rigidity" whereby the two superstates "paralyze[d] and sterilize[d] the rest of the universe, in placing it at times under the thumb of a crushing competition, at times under the yoke of an agreed hegemony between the two rivals,"[83] NATO nevertheless survived. It continued despite de Gaulle's earlier assertion (in 1959) that "the Atlantic Alliance is not imaginable except with France as a part of it."[84]

Of course, de Gaulle had remained "within the alliance" while leaving the NATO military organization on his own terms. NATO, however, made its own adjustments. The Nuclear Planning Group was formed, despite French objections, to fulfill what was perceived as Germany's need to participate in nuclear strategy. And the relationship of French forces to NATO forces in time of war was worked out in the Lemnitzer-Ailleret Accords of 1967 and subsequent agreements. Finally, in 1969, de Gaulle without fanfare renewed France's membership in the Atlantic Alliance. According to a U.S. State Department document of the period, "the France-NATO question constituted the most acute test of the Johnson administration's European and Atlantic policies."[85] However, other issues soured relations between France and the United States in the 1960s, specifically de Gaulle's attempt at monetary independence from the United States while he was moving away from NATO.

De Gaulle's attack on the dollar in 1965 was, together with his withdrawal from the military structure of NATO in early 1966, the most deeply resented of all his actions directed at the United States during the decade. As biographer Jean Lacouture put it, these two crises brought to "red-hot" the anger not only of U.S. policy makers but of the media and public opinion as well.[86] Because the monetary crisis ended even more inconclusively than the NATO issue, thus calling to mind de Gaulle's apparent admiration for the formula "audacity in words, prudence in actions,"[87] it is largely forgotten.

In the early 1960s, France's economic recovery set in as the country moved from protectionism toward the expansion of trade following the economic reforms of 1958, which were aimed at bringing France into line with the provisions of the Treaty of Rome of the previous year. In the process of this trade expansion, stimulated also by a significant devaluation of the franc (by 17.5 percent), the Bank of France began to accumulate dollar reserves. De Gaulle, doubtless conscious of the difficulty postwar French governments had had in recovering the gold that was taken out of the country during the fall of France,[88] wanted to keep as large a portion of these reserves as possible—first 80 percent, then as the accumulation mounted, 90 percent—in gold.[89]

De Gaulle's wishes ran up against U.S. efforts to maintain the parity of the dollar vis-à-vis gold—clearly a fiction since the price of gold had remained fixed at thirty-five dollars an ounce since 1933. The U.S. argument held that it was necessary to maintain the gold exchange standard, whereby reserves held in dollars (or pounds sterling) would be on a par with their theoretical equivalent in gold. This system, which replaced the earlier gold standard, was set in motion at the Bretton Woods Conference in 1944, when the United States held most of the world's gold reserves. This situation had drastically changed by the 1960s.

With the dollar as the currency of reserve under the gold exchange standard, the United States was able more easily to finance its military buildup during the cold war and its military and economic support to those countries resisting Communism. Furthermore, from the U.S. point of view, revaluating the price of gold would not be helpful. John F. Kennedy explained to the French ambassador in Washington, Hervé Alphand, that it would only play into the hands of two inimical regimes who held the world's principal gold-mining deposits—the USSR and the Union of South Africa.[90]

The Gaullists came at the argument from the opposite side. As they saw it, the United States was using the device of the gold exchange standard for political purposes at home—the financing of social programs—while at the same time continuing its military buildup overseas: Not having to balance its budget because the dollar was the reserve currency, the United States did not have to restrict American investment abroad. In other words, the United States was financing its budget deficit at home and American investments abroad by its ability to create dollars.

Furthermore, in this absence of an international mechanism to restrict the creation of dollars, the United States was exporting inflation to other countries. In de Gaulle's words, the United States paid other countries "at least in part with dollars that it is only up to the United States to issue instead of paying them totally in gold, which has real value."[91]

Any foreign holders of dollars could theoretically exchange them for gold, which would have created an impossible situation for the United States had there been a worldwide demand for gold in exchange for dollars. By the mid-1960s, France's hard currency reserves had accumulated sharply, and de Gaulle sought to stimulate such a demand for gold as a way to expose what he saw as the privileged position of the United States. He announced his new policy at a press conference on February 4, 1965. He proposed a return to the gold standard, though he acknowledged that transitional steps would have to be worked out by the major economic powers.[92] Accompanying this rhetoric, France exchanged 977 million dollars for U.S. gold in 1965, in contrast to an average of between 400 to 500 million dollars a year for the previous seven years. However, this trend reversed itself in the late 1960s as the French balance of payments surplus decreased sharply.

In the meantime, the United States and Britain sought ways to avoid pressure on the dollar and the pound from foreign creditors because this pressure would bring on a scarcity of liquidities and impede trade and economic growth. With some success and support from other leading trading nations, the United States and Britain sought to create parallel credit instruments through the International Monetary Fund (IMF)—first referred to as the gold pool and then as special drawing rights (SDRs). A separate French proposition suggested Collective Reserve Units (CRUs), which would be tied to the amount of gold each country had rather than the proportion of its contribution to the IMF. In the end, the latter principle was adopted as the basis of the SDRs.

According to one French expert,[93] one reason for the overall failure of the French campaign was de Gaulle's emphasis on a return to the gold standard, as advocated by his adviser Jacques Rueff, who had been the main catalyst for the economic reforms of 1958: In reality, the pre-1914 gold standard had worked out not as an automatic mechanism but under the hegemonic direction of Great Britain. De Gaulle would have done better, in this view, to have concentrated his efforts on negotiations for alternate credit instruments.

As an operational tactic, de Gaulle's attack on the dollar was a failure. As an element of prophecy, what de Gaulle had foreseen as inevitable came to pass: The United States put an end to the myth of dollar convertibility in 1971, when Richard Nixon unilaterally declared that the dollar would float against other currencies. But this did not mean an end to the privileged position of the United States, as de Gaulle would have hoped. Pierre Mélandri observed:

> From the American point of view, the advantages of the past system were retained. The U.S. currency continued to benefit from being the standard of money, whereas the foundation of this position, the commitment made by the end of 1947 by its Secretary of the Treasury to exchange gold for all dollars presented, was abrogated.[94]

The years of the Johnson administration represented the nadir in French-American relations since Franklin Roosevelt's obstinate snubbing of the Free French movement in World War II. This fact was only partly due to the virtually nonexistent relationship between Lyndon Johnson and Charles de Gaulle. Jean Lacouture has pointed out, "It would be absurd to attribute the multiplication of Gaullist-American disagreements starting at the end of 1963 to the noncommunicability between the French General and the former senator from Texas."[95]

The fact was that de Gaulle had never had a good working relationship with an American president. At the start, he had no illusions about Franklin Roosevelt ("Beneath his patrician mask of courtesy, Roosevelt regarded me without benevolence"),[96] but he recognized the "great man" quality in

Roosevelt and refrained from personal attacks on him. His anger and puzzlement were directed at American foreign policy. In a letter of February 1, 1942, de Gaulle wrote, "Can one explain why the United States government, alone among all the Allies, refrains from establishing with the [French] National Committee the relations necessary for [the] French effort to be combined with the American effort?"[97] Three months later, de Gaulle could sense the growing influence of American policy following the U.S. entry into the war, and he expressed his reservations. On May 26, 1942, de Gaulle wrote, "The imperialism of the United States, which grows with its warlike spirit, definitely has the pretension of resolving questions of the [Middle] East, like all the others."[98]

The period when both de Gaulle and Truman were at the head of their respective countries, April 1945–January 1946, was too short for a strong relationship to develop. As for Eisenhower, although unstinting in his praise for Ike personally, de Gaulle recognized in him an unquestioning representative of American policy: "No doubt he shared the somewhat elementary conviction which inspired the American people as to the primordial mission which had devolved upon the United States, as though by a decree of providence and gave them the right to dominance."[99]

Moreover, with Eisenhower, a dyarchy occurred at the top in foreign relations—John Foster Dulles (secretary of state from 1953 to 1959) had to be dealt with, and de Gaulle's relationship with Dulles was contentious. When Dulles threatened an "agonizing reappraisal" if France did not approve the EDC, which meant an American fallback to a "peripheral defense" of Europe (Great Britain, the Iberian Peninsula, Turkey), de Gaulle declared publicly and with amused deprecation that, "when M. Foster Dulles evoked at Paris the specter of a dramatic revision of American policy toward France, its friend and ally, I am persuaded that he couldn't repress a smile. With the same smile, I reply to him today, 'Don't worry about it, my friend.' "[100]

During the presidency of John F. Kennedy, contentious issues between France and the United States grew when France became a more outspoken player on the world stage with the end of the Algerian War. Kennedy, however, determinedly avoided getting into quarrels with de Gaulle.[101] This was de Gaulle's verdict on Kennedy:

> Entering the scene in a world in which American power had spread far and wide, but whose every wound was suppurating and in which a hostile and monolithic bloc stood opposed to America; enjoying the advantages of youth but suffering the drawbacks of a novice—in spite of many obstacles, the new President was determined to devote himself to the cause of freedom, justice, and progress. It is true that, persuaded it was

the duty of the United States and himself to redress wrongs, he was to be drawn into ill-advised interventions. But the experience of the statesman would no doubt have restrained the impulsiveness of the idealist. John Kennedy had the ability, and had it not been for the crime which killed him, might have had the time to leave his mark on our age.[102]

De Gaulle's correspondence with Kennedy became voluminous, but after the assassination of the president in November 1963, the General's letters to Lyndon Johnson were infrequent and perfunctory. Indeed, the only moment when de Gaulle demonstrated some feeling was when he praised Johnson's "political courage" for having declared a unilateral halt to the bombing of North Vietnam in 1968.[103]

Curiously, the one U.S. president with whom de Gaulle might have established an effective relationship was Richard Nixon, an avowed admirer of de Gaulle. Nixon paid a visit to the General two months after his inauguration, but that was, alas, only one month before de Gaulle self-destructed politically in the referendum of April 1969. (Nevertheless, Nixon and Henry Kissinger labored to improve relations with France, and largely due to their efforts, the French [and British] national nuclear forces were recognized by NATO in 1974 as contributing to Europe's defense.)

De Gaulle's attitude toward the United States had shifted since the period of the late 1940s and early 1950s, when the Soviet threat was at its uppermost. On October 5, 1947, when the French Communist party, in the wake of the creation of the Kominform,[104] was preparing a series of insurrectional strikes in France, de Gaulle observed that "the United States has placed its power, intact, as a counterweight to the worldwide ambitions of the Soviets. Nowhere in the world is there a free man who does not view this American will as salutary."[105]

Similarly, de Gaulle endorsed early on (July 10, 1950) the American intervention in Korea: "For the first time, the world on both sides of the Iron Curtain has realized that the United States is capable of committing itself abroad against Communist domination, not only [in terms of] its money and propaganda but also its force and its blood."[106]

Later, de Gaulle was to modify this judgment on the grounds that American manipulation of the United Nations had cut into the authority of the Security Council, where France's role was of the first rank: "Misunderstanding the functions of the Security Council, the General Assembly arrogated to itself in 1950 the right of decision on the employment of force, which made of it an area of disagreement between the two rivals."[107]

Most fundamentally, apart from the bitter memories of World War II, de Gaulle's political offensive against the United States in the 1960s stemmed from the failure of the tridominium and the American imposition of an "indivisible defense" of Europe. The latter meant that for efficiency's sake, Europe's defense had to be under American command.

In a press conference on July 29, 1963,[108] de Gaulle, after listing his differences with the United States (St. Pierre–Miquelon, delayed recognition of the provisional government of the French Republic; Yalta; Stuttgart; the EDC; the French nuclear strike force; the Franco-German Alliance), nevertheless insisted on the friendship and the alliance between the two countries. "Of all the powers of the world, France is the only one — outside of Russia, I must say — with whom the United States has never exchanged a cannon shot."[109] Also, France was the only country alongside which the United States had fought in three wars: the Revolutionary War, World War I, and World War II.[110] Further, in case of world war, France would be on the side of the United States, which should refute the argument of those who "depict each bruise [in the relationship] as an incurable wound."[111]

In an interview with the journalist Michel Droit in December 1965, just prior to his runoff ballot with François Mitterrand, de Gaulle evoked the theme of the immutability of the French-American relationship in a more backhanded way:

> I do not say that the Americans are anti-French . . . because . . . they have not always accompanied us. In 1914, we were at war against [Kaiser] Wilhelm II, [and] the Americans were not there. They arrived in 1917. In 1940 they were not there, and we were submerged by Hitler; and it was in 1941, because the Japanese sank part of the American fleet at Pearl Harbor, that the United States entered the war. Far be it from me not to recognize the immense service they rendered. . . . I am not anti-American because I do not, at present, always agree with them, . . . for example, regarding the policy they are conducting in Asia. . . . to say I am anti-American [is something] I cannot prevent, but there is, after all, the fundamental essence of things.[112]

THE ATTEMPT TO "DE-ATLANTICIZE" THE EEC

The European Economic Community (EEC) was almost as much a bête noire to de Gaulle as NATO because France would be "dissolved in a federation called 'European' . . . that would in fact be 'Atlantic.' "[113] This "stateless ensemble," said de Gaulle, "would not have a policy other than that of the protector from across the ocean."[114]

The connection made between a "federal" Europe and an "Atlantic" — in other words, American — system lay in the denationalized or "supranational" structures of the EEC: its executive (the EEC Commission at Brussels)[115] and its legislature (the European Parliament at Strasbourg). De Gaulle described the EEC as being incapable of having an independent policy because it was attached, in the political domain, "as in that of defense and the economy, to an Atlantic system—that is to say American—and subordinated, as a consequence, to what the Americans call their leadership." The EEC, organized into a federal structure, "would have as its foundation an Areopagus of competences withdrawn from the States and baptized 'Executive' but also a Parliament without national qualifications, which would be called 'Legislative.' "[116]

Nevertheless, de Gaulle did not attempt to overturn the previous government's decision in March 1957 to join the EEC. He did, however, seek to transform the structure from a federal one to a "Europe of States." The underlying basis for the Gaullist assertion that the EEC was "Atlanticized" appeared to be that it robbed France of its natural advantage as a large state in Europe acting as fully sovereign. At the inception of the supranational (or federal) idea, it was a question, from the Gaullist viewpoint, of a victorious France being deprived of Germany's coal and steel resources through the European Coal and Steel Community (ECSC), a pooling arrangement composed of France, West Germany, Italy, and the Benelux countries, the so-called Six. This was the first of the European "communities" that Jean Monnet and his allies had helped set up. The second, the European Defense Community (EDC), died aborning. Next came the EEC, or Common Market.[117]

De Gaulle readily drew a relationship between the European communities that were being created and NATO: "The one, in the name of European unity, liquidating the advantages which victory had gained us; the other, on the pretext of Atlantic solidarity, subjecting France to the hegemony of the Anglo-Saxons."[118]

In a negative sense, European integration via the route of supranationality (as opposed to state-to-state cooperation) was a threat to de Gaulle's vision of Europe because nothing in such a structure [European integration] could interfere with the protective hegemony of Washington."[119]

The state was important to de Gaulle in the European context, as opposed to a supranational organization, largely because France, when de Gaulle was at the helm of affairs, was the most powerful state of the Six. Throughout, de Gaulle insisted on the central role of the state: "In order to achieve the unification of Europe, individual states are the only valid elements, and when their national interests are at stake, nothing and nobody must be allowed to force their hands."[120]

There were two alternate routes to the construction of Europe, and de Gaulle analyzed them:

Was its objective . . . the harmonization of the practical interests of the six states, their economic solidarity in face of the outside world, and, if possible, their cooperation in foreign policy? Or did it aim to achieve the total fusion of their respective economies and policies in a single entity with its own government, parliament, and laws. . . . Needless to say, having no taste for make-believe, I adopted the former conception. But the latter carried all the hopes and illusions of the supra-national school.[121]

From the outset, then, a clash of views occurred between the supranational vision of Europe, exemplified by Jean Monnet and Robert Schuman, founders of the ECSC, and de Gaulle's view of a Europe of states, which would be led by France and Germany. In a note he wrote at the presidential château at Rambouillet on July 30, 1960, de Gaulle laid out his strategy for a Europe of states as a way of undercutting both the EEC and NATO. Through the mechanism of the European Council, an intergovernmental body of state leaders, the states would achieve primacy over the other EEC institutions, and as a consequence, American dominance through NATO would wither away.[122]

This program was not one that de Gaulle would, or could, carry out all at once. It was not a plan that was to be crowned with success—far from it—but it was something that de Gaulle pursued with a characteristic inner consistency and tenacity of purpose. In a letter to his son, Philippe, early in July 1960, the General explained why it was necessary to play for time: "Our internal and external recovery is proceeding. Overall, if things continue to go for us as they are now, in about five years we will really have become again a great power. Between now and then, it will obviously be necessary that Algeria cease to more or less tie our hands."[123]

By early 1961 de Gaulle was ready to attempt his transformation of the EEC. He would trump the growth of communities (the "communitarian" idea) by placing the most important domain, the political, in the hands of a grouping of the governments of the Six (France, West Germany, Italy, and the Benelux countries).[124] A conference was held in Paris on February 10–11, 1961, and according to the communiqué that was seen and worked over by de Gaulle, the meeting "had as [its] object the search for appropriate means of organizing political cooperation among the six states . . . laying the basis for a political construction that could later develop into the formation of a European Confederation."[125] A study commission was set up under the chairmanship of Christian Fouchet, de Gaulle's ambassador to

Denmark and a former cabinet minister. This was the beginning of the "Fouchet Plan," which was eventually included in a treaty but which de Gaulle ultimately failed to sell to the Six. No doubt de Gaulle's intention was to cut down to size "communitarian" mechanisms that had been set up before he returned to power. "What I proposed at Paris," de Gaulle wrote in April 1961, was the

> institution of an organic and periodic concert of the chiefs of state or of government, the institution of a secretariat for this Areopagus, not only distinct from the "commissions" (Common Market, ECSC, and Euratom), but which would still be above them and would ultimately have overall responsibility over them.[126]

A higher purpose remained beyond mere nationalism in de Gaulle's attempt to trump the communities. It was

> to build Western Europe into an organized union of States so that there can be established little by little, on both sides of the Rhine, the Alps, and perhaps the Channel, a political, economic, cultural, and military entity that is the most powerful, the most prosperous, and the most influential in the world.[127]

De Gaulle maintained that all economic measures were really political acts, and therefore "the economic development of Europe cannot be assured without its political union."[128] Lacking political clout, the communities were ineffective when something really important was at stake. They were only "technical" organs: "As soon as a tragic situation appears, [or there is] a major problem to be solved, it can then be seen that one 'high authority' or another has no authority over the various national categories and that only the States have it."[129] The fundamental Gaullist argument in favor of an umbrella European political authority over the communities was that it would enable Europe to be truly independent.

The initial conference on the Fouchet Plan at Paris in February 1961 had been followed by another successful conference at Bonn in July 1961. The Germans were on board with the French plan, but the Italians hesitated and refused to convene the third, and what was to be the decisive, conference at Rome. Their objections, to which the Dutch and the Belgians adhered, ended the French initiative. According to de Gaulle, their objections were twofold: The French plan, which maintained the sovereignty of states, did not conform to their idea of a European executive (the Commission) and a European legislature (the European Parliament); second, the three would not enter any political organization of which Britain was not a part.[130] Another reason, not stated by de Gaulle, was that Belgium and the Netherlands, as smaller countries in the Six, feared domination by France and Germany in a "Europe of states." On April 17, 1962, Belgium, the Netherlands, and Italy formally put an end to the Fouchet Plan by vetoing it at a meeting in Paris.[131]

Where was Britain in all this? In de Gaulle's press conference of September 5, 1960, by which time France had begun preliminary consultations with the Six on the idea of European political cooperation, he hinted that the British might be included in such an arrangement.[132] Then in July 1961, in the midst of negotiations over the Fouchet Plan, the British applied for membership in the EEC. The British application cast a shadow of uncertainty over what the future makeup of the EEC would be, and by April 1962, de Gaulle's vision of Europe as expressed in the Fouchet Plan was rejected.[133]

The Treaty of Rome, which had created the EEC in March 1957 before de Gaulle returned to power, had one great advantage from the Gaullist point of view: Like the other communities created in the 1950s, it did not include Great Britain, suiting de Gaulle perfectly:

> The Treaty of Rome was concluded between six continental States that are, in short, economically of the same nature. . . . There are many more similarities than differences between them. Moreover, they are adjacent, they interpenetrate, they are extensions of each other through communications. . . . There is a feeling of solidarity between them, firstly owing to the awareness they have of together possessing an important part of the origins of our civilization, and also, with regard to their security, because they are continental countries and they are confronted by the same single threat from one end of their territorial grouping to the other. Finally they have a feeling of solidarity because not one of them is linked on the outside by any special political or military agreement.[134]

The last sentence was not wholly accurate; all these states belonged to NATO, but de Gaulle appeared to be making a contrast between the Six and Great Britain, with its ties to the Commonwealth (and to the United States). Further, to de Gaulle, NATO was only a temporary arrangement.

De Gaulle made these statements in his famous press conference of January 14, 1963,[135] when in one fell swoop he rejected Britain's candidacy for the Common Market (he was to repeat the rejection in 1967) and turned down an American offer of Polaris missiles for France, which would have entailed France's participation in the Multilateral Force (MLF).

De Gaulle's feelings toward the British, to whom the Gaullist movement owed its very inception, were, to say the least, ambivalent. "The British," de Gaulle had written in January 1941, "are valiant and solid allies but really tiresome."[136] De Gaulle's writings stressed the harmoniousness of the British political system and the steadfast qualities of the people. He never failed to express praise for the British performance in the war and he spoke of "our respect for the British people, the admiration for the way they had borne themselves during a crisis in which they had suddenly found themselves alone. . . ."[137] The possibility of Britain and France ever going to war against one another again was unthinkable. In a speech during a visit to London in April 1960, he observed that "Englishmen and Frenchmen, assured of their worth, but in no danger of losing their heads as giants sometimes do, are destined to act together in building world peace."[138]

Yet as de Gaulle put it to Alain Peyrefitte, "Our greatest hereditary enemy was not Germany, it was England."[139] Further, it was inconvenient in the Gaullist scheme of things for Britain to be attached to Europe. At a time when de Gaulle was trying to achieve the unity of Europe (albeit on Gaullist terms), Britain stood as a historical reminder of its constant attempts to prevent European unity: "By virtue of her geography and therefore her policy, she has never been willing to see the Continent united or to merge with it herself. In a sense it might almost be said that therein lay the whole history of Europe for the past eight hundred years."[140]

In rejecting the British application for EEC membership, de Gaulle was dealing with a far different person than his wartime colleague and antagonist, Winston Churchill. At the outset of their relationship, Churchill held de Gaulle in a sort of tutelage. Later, in their many squalls during World War II, de Gaulle in his writings never evinced any lack of respect for Churchill. The same could not be said for Harold Macmillan, whom de Gaulle had also known during the war—Macmillan was the British government's representative in Algiers following the North African landings. De Gaulle's comments on the failure of the summit conference in May 1960, following the U-2 incident, show a faint deprecation of Macmillan: "There was a solemn dirge from Macmillan about 'the collapse of two years of peace-making efforts' and 'the worst crisis his country had experienced since the war.'"[141]

What de Gaulle probably failed to see in Macmillan was a risk-taker of his own proportions (or Winston Churchill's). As Jean Lacouture, de Gaulle's great biographer, said of de Gaulle, "Temerity is in his nature."[142] The puzzlement that observers have noted in the contrasting behavior of de Gaulle—steadfastness in a crisis, cantankerousness at other times—is in part a reflection of this very temerity. De Gaulle was exhilarated by risks.

That Macmillan had failed to tell de Gaulle in the previous month (December 1962) the full details of his plan to negotiate for Polaris missiles with the Americans[143] had little bearing on de Gaulle's decision in January 1963 to reject Britain's application to the EEC. Macmillan's failure did add, however, a further zest of justification for refusing Britain. According to Jean Lacouture, de Gaulle had made known his intentions regarding British membership in a meeting of the French cabinet on December 19. In the meeting, and again with a faint touch of deprecation, de Gaulle quoted a line from an Edith Piaf song and applied it to Macmillan: *"Ne pleurez pas Milord"* (Do not cry milord).[144]

THE FRENCH-GERMAN ALLIANCE AND ITS LIMITATIONS

Jean Lacouture has described the characteristics of de Gaulle's actions in crucial times of his life as composed of five parts: a taste for secrecy, a sense of timing, a concern for consultation, suddenness in decision, and the art of dramatization.[145] Nowhere were these qualities more evident than in de Gaulle's actions in January 1963, nine months after the vetoing of the Fouchet Plan. In his press conference of January 14, 1963, he shocked the Western alliance by turning down Britain's membership in the EEC (without forewarning Macmillan in their meeting at Rambouillet the month before) and, to a lesser extent, by categorically refusing to subscribe to the Nassau Accords and thus enter the MLF. Eight days later he turned around and signed a treaty of alliance with West Germany. In the January 14 press conference, he hinted at what was to come. The German-French relationship was

> a kind of mutual discovery of two neighbors, each noticing the extent to which the other is valid, worthy, and attractive. . . . For the first time in many generations, the Germans and Gauls realize their solidarity. . . . The French-German meeting that will shortly be held here will permit us . . . to organize our cooperation better than it is organized already. . . . there is nothing there that . . . tends toward the building up between Germany and France of some kind of exclusive community. The two countries . . . are committed to be an integral part of Europe . . . on the basis of the Rome Treaty. . . . But it is true that by tightening their

cooperation, Germany and France are setting an example which may be useful to the cooperation of everyone.[146]

In a later press conference on July 23, 1964, de Gaulle traced the thread of developments that led from the attempt to "de-Atlanticize" the EEC through the Fouchet Plan to the Treaty of Cooperation with West Germany. In the following terms, he reviewed his attempts to establish a political concert among the states of Western Europe:

> Since the French plan for the organization of Europe [the Fouchet Plan] had not been adopted by Italy and by the Benelux; . . . and the integration [of Europe] had not been able to lead to other than an American protectorate; and finally, since Great Britain had shown . . . that it was not in a position to accept the common economic rules, and by the Nassau Agreement, that its defense force, and particularly the nuclear part, would not be European for lack of autonomy in relation to the United States, it appeared to [the governments of Germany and France] that their bilateral cooperation could have some usefulness. It was then that, on the proposal of the German government, the treaty of January 22, 1963, was concluded which I had the honor to sign here [at the Elysée] along with Chancellor Adenauer.[147]

Two events intervened to undermine the import of the French-German treaty. One was the preamble added to the treaty in West Germany by the Bundestag (lower house) and the Bundesrat (upper house) on April 16, 1963, which stated in effect that the treaty would not take precedence over West Germany's commitment to the Atlantic Alliance and NATO. De Gaulle later remarked, "The preferential links, contracted outside of us and constantly tightened by Bonn with Washington, took away the inspiration and the substance of this French-German Accord."[148]

The second event was the resignation of the aging Konrad Adenauer in November 1963 and his replacement as German chancellor by Ludwig Erhard, a man almost wholly disposed to go along with American foreign policy. By the middle of the following year, de Gaulle already had a long list of grievances against the German performance in the matter of cooperation. In the same press conference of July 23, 1964,[149] he noted that these complaints had to do with French-German defense cooperation; the necessity for a new orientation for the Atlantic Alliance; the attitude toward the East, specifically the borders in central and eastern Europe; the recognition of China; peace in Indochina and Indonesia; development aid in Africa, Asia, and Latin America; and the agricultural policy of the EEC. On these questions, said de Gaulle, "one cannot say that Germany and France have yet agreed to conduct together a policy, and it cannot be disputed that this is because Bonn has not believed, up till now, that this policy should be European and independent."[150]

Even more striking than de Gaulle's admiration for British institutions and the qualities of the British people is the respect he held for the German fighting spirit. Touring the Stalingrad battlefield in 1944, de Gaulle mused to his Russian hosts, "What a great people," and made plain he was talking about the Germans, not the Russians.[151]

It was almost as though de Gaulle unconsciously desired a less unruly and more steadfast people over whom he could exercise power. However, his writings never expressed any doubt as to the fighting qualities of the French soldier. Referring to the defeat in the Franco-Prussian War, de Gaulle observed that the French soldier had never withheld effort or sacrifice and had not lacked courage:

> But these wonderful troops, this glorious army, saw their qualities reduced to nothing because at their head were leaders unprepared for their role. It took only a few years of intellectual laziness and détente to make of a victorious army a conquered one, and [to make] the leading power of Europe a nation soon crushed under blows, outraged and dismembered.[152]

Alternatively, the problem was a matter of organization; it was not a question of the quality of the human material. In a history lecture he gave at St. Cyr in 1921 on the Franco-Prussian War, de Gaulle contrasted the different conceptions of the two armies. In the French army, "Everyone gives the subordinate echelons detailed orders, which remove their freedom of action and destroy in advance their initiative—things that are all the more important because they don't know the intentions of the command."[153] In contrast, "from top to bottom, the enemy has a will and a doctrine. His will translates into decisions and initiatives." The enemy's orders were clear, concentrated, and articulate. The subordinates "are only waiting for the occasion to exercise their initiative, and this initiative will stem from a common doctrine."[154]

The following is an excerpt from an interview with the writer Georges Duhamel in October 1954, after the publication of the first volume of de Gaulle's *War Memoirs:*

> *Duhamel:* [With regard to] your concepts of the primordial necessity of the offensive . . . you put things in an illuminating way and with a minimum of explanations and technical terms. . . . You are able to see matters of war with a fresh eye. A rare quality, even among the great leaders.
> *De Gaulle:* Not [a rare quality] with the Germans.[155]

Analyzing the North African situation on January 11, 1943, de Gaulle noted that Roosevelt and Churchill had failed to take into account two factors that were at the base of the war from the military point of view. "First factor, the Germans' capacity for speed and audacity; they set foot in Tunisia earlier than the Allies thought [they would]." The second factor was the "mediocrity of the Anglo-Saxon command, aggravated in this instance by the inexperience of the American staffs."[156]

In his earlier writings, de Gaulle—more impetuous and less mature—was unsparing in his views on the German character and on "German furies and ambitions."[157] At one point he wrote: "Our troops tremble with anticipation at the idea of finding themselves, again, face to face with the enemy, the eternal enemy of France. In all hearts beats the same flame."[158] In a letter to his mother in June 1919, de Gaulle, ardent and harsh at the war's end, wrote:

> The peace has been signed. It remains to be executed by the enemy, because such as we know him, he will do nothing, cede nothing, pay nothing, unless he is constrained . . . [to do so], and not only by means of force but by extreme brutality. It is the only method to use with him. His agreements are a smokescreen, his signature a bad joke.[159]

In a similar vein, de Gaulle used the following language to describe the Germans' behavior toward the Poles in the zone of Poland that they occupied after the partition: ". . . using all the majestic brutality and the underhanded obstinateness of which they are capable."[160]

In 1921, de Gaulle wrote that many thought the state of mind of the Germans and the French to be irreconcilable.[161] And to his mother, in August 1919, he wrote, "I follow German opinion closely enough to be able to state that in the soul of the enemy there lies a formidable hatred, not against the Entente in general, and especially not England or America, whom they have already forgiven, but indeed against us."[162]

De Gaulle's attitude toward the Germans began to improve with his visit to the French occupation zone in West Germany in early October 1945. Addressing the German authorities in dignified and even noble tones, de Gaulle said that a mutual comprehension could be achieved because "we are Europeans and Westerners."[163] De Gaulle could see that Germany was utterly crushed and could no longer threaten France. Gradually, de Gaulle decided that Germany, together with France, could play a formidable role on the European and world stage. He proceeded to put this idea into reality immediately after his return to power, inviting Konrad Adenauer to his home at Colombey-les-Deux-Eglises on September 15, 1958.

A EUROPE FROM THE ATLANTIC TO THE URALS

The "Russian temptation" has never been far from the French consciousness, dating back precisely to 1893, when the French government formed a "reverse alliance" with Czar Nicholas II against Kaiser Wilhelm and Germany. The exaggerated hopes of what this alliance would produce were to bring disappointment, among other disappointments, to France in World War I. In 1927, de Gaulle wrote that before World War I, the French were full of illusions about Russian military power, and they retained this confidence for a long time after the war broke out. Then, passing from one extreme to another, the French were full of contempt for the supposed Russian "bulldozer." Similarly, the same shift from one to the other extreme could be seen with "the British army, the Italian intervention on the side of the Entente, and American help [in the war]. . . . In France these errors of appreciation were much less the effect of a too-impulsive national character than a lack of precise information."[164]

In World War II, on the other hand, the Russian contribution was on a totally different scale. Though the Russian "participation in our struggle only took place starting in 1941," de Gaulle observed, "the Communists played their game. It so happened that this game coincided with ours for a certain time, that's all. But let us recognize that during this period of time, they broke the back of the Wehrmacht."[165]

Throughout his public career, de Gaulle made a distinction between Russia as the traditional friend of France, with whom France had never had any fundamental disputes,[166] and the "totalitarian and threatening ideology"[167] of Moscow. In a press conference on April 11, 1961, de Gaulle referred to "the greatest imperialism that the world has ever known—the imperialism of the Soviet Union."[168]

Charles de Gaulle wasted no time, as soon as hostilities began between Germany and Soviet Russia in June 1941, to establish contact with the Soviet ambassador in London. Already, on September 26, 1941, the Soviet government recognized the General as chief of the Free French and delegated Ambassador A. E. Bogomolov as the Soviet representative to the Free French.[169]

The Russian card was something de Gaulle was to play, on and off, for the rest of his public career, from the friendship treaty with Moscow in December 1944 to his disillusionment over the Soviets' crushing of the "Prague Spring" in August 1968. At this moment, when other disappointments began to flood in on the aging General, he began what Jean Lacouture was to call "a fascinating descent toward a nocturnal rendezvous."[170] De Gaulle was to resign the presidency within eight months, and a year and a half after that he would be dead.

With his continental viewpoint, de Gaulle announced after the signing of the French-Soviet Friendship Treaty in December 1944 that it constituted "the act of union signed between the two great powers of the Continent, not only to conduct the war until total victory but also to arrange that Germany, once conquered, remains incapable of doing damage."[171]

The implication here was that, once Germany was defeated, only two "continental" powers would count, France and Russia. But things did not work out quite as de Gaulle had hoped. He was excluded from Yalta, and according to him, it was on the explicit demand of Franklin Roosevelt alone;[172] and he was excluded from the Potsdam Conference of July 1945 concerning the settlement of the German question. But though France was not at Yalta or at Potsdam, as a result of these conferences and the intervening San Francisco conference it nevertheless became a party to the occupation of Germany as well as a permanent member of the United Nations Security Council.

With his sense of history and also, it must be said, with his vast presumption, de Gaulle had another purpose in mind regarding the French-Soviet treaty of alliance and mutual assistance of 1944: "It was a great attempt . . . that I wanted, according to our means, which were weak at the time, to offer to Russia . . . a way really to return to the international community."[173]

The idea of returning Russia to the international community—the Gaullist formula of "the Atlantic to the Urals"—appears to have been first enunciated at the General's press conference of March 25, 1959: "We who live between the Atlantic and the Urals; we who are Europe, possess [along] with its daughter, America, the principal sources and resources of civilization."[174]

In time, de Gaulle was to give "the Atlantic to the Urals" concept a more political and operational tone. The concept would become the symbol of his effort to expand Europe, to cut it loose from America, and to constrain Germany. This came about in the wake of the disappointment over the outcome of the French-German Treaty and the coming to power of Ludwig Erhard. It represented de Gaulle's new European initiative, an attempt to create "a new equilibrium of our continent":[175]

> Certainly the success of so vast and so difficult an enterprise implies many conditions. It is a question of whether Russia can evolve in such a way that she sees her future no longer in the totalitarian constraint imposed on her and on others. It is a question of whether the nations that she has made satellites can play their role in a renewed Europe. It is

a question of whether it can be recognized above all by Germany that the settlement of which she could be the object would imply necessarily [the issue of] her frontiers and that of her armaments, through an accord with all of her neighbors, those of the East and those of the West.[176]

This was another way of saying (and in fact de Gaulle had taken this position soon after his return to power)[177] that Germany would have to accept irrevocably the Oder-Neisse line as its eastern frontier. It was also another way of saying that Germany would have to do without nuclear weapons in perpetuity, in a settlement guaranteed by Russia's and Germany's neighbors, east and west.

And after these "vast and difficult" conditions were fulfilled, a new vision would appear: The six states of the EEC, having established an economic community and having organized themselves in the political and defense areas, would be able to create a "new equilibrium of our continent." Though de Gaulle did not specify what arrangements would be made between Western and Eastern Europe, he described it as "a matter of whether Europe, mother of modern civilization, can establish itself from the Atlantic to the Urals in concord and cooperation. . . ."[178]

This far-reaching vision turned the famous dictum of Lord Ismay, Winston Churchill's military adviser, on its head: NATO served, according to Ismay, to keep "the Americans in, the Russians out, and the Germans down"; de Gaulle's vision of a Europe from the Atlantic to the Urals seemed aimed at bringing the Russians in and putting the Anglo-Americans out, all the while keeping the Germans in check.

De Gaulle's proposal for an "entente from the Atlantic to the Urals" involved first and foremost an approach to Russia. In June 1966, having broken with the NATO military organization three months earlier, de Gaulle embarked on a state visit to Russia. In his response to a toast by Nikolai Podgorny, president of the Presidium of the Supreme Soviet, de Gaulle said that although France remained a country of liberty and a Western nation, it had wanted to break the "unhealthy charm" of the confrontation between the two power blocs and to create with the countries of Eastern Europe a new relationship aimed at "détente, entente, and cooperation." In speaking to the East, Paris had first to address itself to Moscow. De Gaulle noted as the first condition "the reestablishment of Europe in a fruitful ensemble, instead of one paralyzed by a sterile division." And he emphasized that "an entente between states that have been until now antagonists is above all, according to the French, a European problem."[179]

As we noted earlier, de Gaulle's attempt to expand Europe to the East through a sequential policy of "détente, entente, and cooperation" with Russia came to naught two years later with the invasion of Czechoslovakia in August 1968. But de Gaulle had visualized the main contours of what was later to come: a reunited Germany with the Oder-Neisse line as its eastern frontier and still constrained from nuclear weapons production, and a Russia shorn of its ideological carapace, Communism. That the Europe of de Gaulle's vision had less to do with the outcome than the actions of the superpowers themselves (as well as those of the Germans) scarcely detracts from the essential Gaullist thesis of the triumph of nations over ideologies.

THIRD WORLD GAULLISM: THE PULL OF NEUTRALITY

On September 1, 1966, before a crowd of eighty thousand at the National Sports Stadium in Phnom Penh, Charles de Gaulle, in a remark that made clear how important casting off the Algerian incubus had been for the future of French foreign policy, spoke of that war as having engaged neither France's well-being nor its independence. The prestige of France had not suffered from withdrawing from Algeria, and de Gaulle exhorted the United States to do the same in Vietnam.[180] It was a far cry from what the younger (and more expansionist) de Gaulle had written on May 2, 1915, at the start of the Dardanelles expedition: "Our success will be above all a Christian success, and the destruction of the Turkish Empire will be a terrible blow delivered to Islamism [which will be] to the advantage of Christianity."[181]

It was also a far cry from de Gaulle's dispatching of Admiral Thierry d'Argenlieu and General Leclerc to Indochina immediately after World War II in an effort to save Indochina for France. But by the middle to late 1950s General de Gaulle had "married his epoch." He accepted the 1954 Geneva Accords for the neutralization of Vietnam, signed by the government of the previous Fourth Republic. And he was formulating in his mind a solution in Algeria.

In the early 1960s, as he became free to act more boldly after the settlement in Algeria and as the American intervention in Vietnam began to set in, de Gaulle pushed vigorously for a settlement in Southeast Asia on the basis of the 1954 accords. On August 29, 1963, it was announced at the end of a Council of Ministers meeting, presided over by General de Gaulle, that France was ready to help establish a neutral Vietnam that would live in peace and be free of foreign influences.[182]

This was the beginning of de Gaulle's effort to promote an international conference on Southeast Asia with the aim of neutralizing Vietnam along the lines of the 1954 Geneva agreement. It was part of an overall Gaullist thrust, now that France had been restored to the status of a major power, aimed at reducing "the tension provoked by the opposition of two camps around two giants." Since France had broken the "stifling rigidity" of bipolar confrontation, said de Gaulle in 1966, "one is going to see—one sees already—the fading of the constantly and gravely dangerous game known as the cold war."[183]

The centerpiece of this effort to break the "stifling rigidity" of bipolar confrontation was an overture to China, begun in the fall of 1963. It was part and parcel of the effort to bring peace to Southeast Asia, as no international conference on this issue would be possible without including China. In fact, China had been present at the 1954 conference, along with the USSR, the United States, Great Britain, and France—all five—as it turned out a decade later, when de Gaulle took up his Southeast Asia neutralization proposal—being permanent members of the Security Council *and* nuclear powers.

Although the China initiative was begun by de Gaulle in the fall of 1963, the question of relations between France and China went back much further: It had first been raised with the General himself by Marshal Chen Yi during the Geneva Conference on Laos in 1962.[184] In October 1963, de Gaulle sent former prime minister Edgar Faure, who had made a private visit to China in 1962, to Beijing to conduct exploratory talks. Things moved rapidly thereafter. On January 27, 1964, in a joint communiqué published in Beijing and Paris, France and China announced they would establish diplomatic relations within three months' time.

Four days later, on January 31, 1964, in one of his biennial press conferences, General de Gaulle explained the background of his recognition of Beijing. China, he said, was "a sovereign and independent power,"[185] and therefore implicitly like France. Then he spelled out the link to Southeast Asia:

> In fact, there is in Asia no political reality . . . which does not concern or affect China. . . . Thus it would be absolutely impossible to envision, without China, a possible neutrality agreement relating to the Southeast Asian States, in which States for so many reasons, we French feel a very particular and cordial interest—a neutrality which, by definition, must be accepted by all, guaranteed on the international level, and which would exclude both armed agitations supported by any one among them in one or another of the States, and the various forms of external intervention.[186]

A major aim of de Gaulle's China initiative was to include Beijing in a new international conference on Vietnam. However, another major player, the United States, was turning a deaf ear to the General's proposals. De Gaulle's call for the neutralization of Vietnam was causing unease in Saigon, and on January 30, 1964, General Nguyen Khanh led a preemptive coup against supposed "neutralist" (pro-French) elements in the military. Washington was more concerned in this period with the instability in Saigon caused by the General's proposals than it was disposed to consider their merit.

Finally, on June 5, 1964, George Ball, the under secretary of state and a personal emissary of President Johnson, met with de Gaulle in Paris. According to the American account of this meeting, the French president said to Ball, "I do not believe that you can win in this situation [in Vietnam] even though you have more aircraft, cannons, and arms of various kinds." The problem, elaborated the General, was primarily a political and psychological problem. "I do not mean that all of the Vietnamese are against you, but they regard the United States as a foreign power and as a very big foreign power."[187] The General added that the more the United States became involved in the actual conduct of military operations, the more the Vietnamese would turn against the United States, as would others in Southeast Asia.

The General laid out to Ball his proposal for an international conference on Southeast Asia with the participation, besides the United States, of several world powers. The effort could not be led by the Americans alone, said the General, because it would not succeed. A large conference had been attempted in 1954, and though the talks had taken a very long time, this in itself was not a bad thing. If a world conference of the type de Gaulle described could be put into operation, it would change the state of mind of the Vietnamese people and produce a détente.[188]

The account of the meeting ended with a comment by Mr. Ball, with which Ambassador Charles Bohlen associated himself, to the effect that the General probably envisaged that at some time in the not-too-distant future the United States would begin to think seriously about his suggestion of a conference. "He quite likely assumes that we will then ask the French to take soundings with the Chinese and the North Vietnamese."

But the United States never did come back to de Gaulle on this issue, and as the war in Vietnam intensified, the General became more outspoken in his criticism. In the course of a press conference on November 30, 1965, he stated that "an absurd war is being waged"[189] in Southeast Asia. In a press conference three months later, on February 21, 1966, de Gaulle hinted that the Vietnam War had made it untenable for France to remain in NATO: "The conflicts in which America is engaged, as the day before yesterday in Korea, yesterday in Cuba, and today in Vietnam, risk . . . expanding into what could become a general conflagration." Europe could thus be drawn into a general war. As for France, it would be directly implicated "if the involvement of its territory . . . under American command were to last much longer."[190]

Less than a month later, de Gaulle left the military organization of NATO. At the end of 1966, in what was probably his sharpest criticism of American action in Vietnam, he called it

> [an] unjust war because it results, in fact, from the armed intervention of the United States on the territory of Vietnam. [A] detestable war because it [has led] a great nation to ravage a small one.[191]

In its impact on world public opinion, de Gaulle's Phnom Penh speech, referred to earlier,[192] was the apogee of the General's critique of America's Vietnam policy and of his concern with the Third World.[193] De Gaulle's forays into issues outside Europe (largely concerning Vietnam but also Latin America, Mexico, and Quebec) consisted of a large part of conviction and perhaps a small part of revenge. He repeatedly tried to give lessons to the United States (namely, that the United States should apply to Vietnam the principle that each people should be allowed to run its own affairs);[194] he held that France, having gone through a similar experience, had in 1954 subscribed to the neutrality of Vietnam in withdrawing its troops and was the better off for it[195] (as it was better off for having gotten out of Algeria). But particularly regarding Vietnam, his statements were not exempt from a tinge of rancor at the United States' having displaced France as a power in that part of the world. It was the Americans' "certitude of responding to a certain vocation, the aversion that they had toward any colonial regime that was not their own, and finally the natural desire of a people so powerful to ensure new positions for themselves, [that] led them to take our place in Indochina."[196]

As de Gaulle's positions became increasingly aligned with those of the Third World, he began to lose old friends but also to make new ones: in Southeast Asia and the Far East, in Latin America, and in the Arab world. De Gaulle's actions in the Six Day War of June 1967—his embargo on French arms to Israel and his insistent call on the Israelis to leave the captured territories—came as a shock to many in the West.

In a press conference on November 27, 1967, de Gaulle's famous remark that the Jews were an "elite people, sure of themselves and domineering," reinforced the impression that the Gaullist position had become anti-Israeli. Such an expression from the mouth of de Gaulle could be taken as a compliment: These characteristics were his own hallmarks. However, in this instance de Gaulle's words came across as gratuitous and insensitive, despite the fact that he had chosen carefully his extended remarks and had emphasized the "abominable persecutions" that the Jews had suffered during World War II.

De Gaulle's actions in the Arab-Israeli War of 1967 and its aftermath can rather be viewed as part of the General's desire that France conduct an active and effective foreign policy independent of the superpowers. He thought, with some justification, that he had a role to play in the crisis. France was a major supplier of arms to Israel, and an order of fifty French-made Mirage III aircraft for Israel was pending when the crisis broke out in May.

De Gaulle could not have made it plainer, in a meeting with Israeli foreign minister Abba Eban on May 24 as well as in his public statements at the time, that France would not look kindly on the side that fired the first shot. Israel's position, however, was that Egyptian president Gamal Abdel Nasser had already initiated the crisis by announcing the closing of the Straits of Tiran, which led to the Israeli port of Eilat. On the morning of June 5, Israel attacked without warning, crippling the Egyptian air force on the ground in a matter of minutes and setting the stage for a decisive victory in six days' time.

Before the crisis, de Gaulle was certainly interested in bringing France closer to the Arab world; the Algerian issue no longer blocked good relations. But there is no indication that he was waiting for an opportunity to distance France from Israel nor that he was intent on diminishing France's aid to Israel.

That de Gaulle was so insistent on keeping the peace can probably be ascribed to his desire to prevent the two superpowers from increasing their influence in the area through support of their respective clients in a war. The outbreak of the war and the ensuing absence of a settlement demonstrated the limited influence of France in a part of the world where it had exercised leadership until World War II.

De Gaulle correctly foresaw the Israeli expansion of 1967 as a watershed event that would compromise for a very long time what chances there were for Israel to live in peace with its Arab neighbors. In visits to France prior to that time, David Ben Gurion, the founder of the Israeli state, had been told by de Gaulle, "You have brought off a remarkable achievement. Do not overdo it now." As recounted in his *Memoirs of Hope,* de Gaulle warned Ben Gurion against pursuing "ambitions which would plunge the East into terrible upheavals and would gradually lose you international sympathy."[197]

NOTES

[1] Charles de Gaulle, "Renewal, 1958–1962," pt. 1 of *Memoirs of Hope*, trans. Terence Kilmartin (New York: Simon and Schuster, 1970), 721 (hereafter cited as *MH*).

[2] Charles de Gaulle, *Lettres, notes, et carnets*, vol. 6 (Paris: Plon, 1982), 47 (all volumes hereafter cited as *LNC*).

[3] Ibid.

[4] *MH*, pt. 1, 171.

[5] Charles de Gaulle, *Discours et messages*, vol. 4, *Pour l'effort, Août 1962–Décembre 1965* (Paris: Omnibus/Plon, 1993), 967. (In this study, the abbreviation *DM-OP* will indicate when the Omnibus/Plon edition is used. *DM* signifies the earlier Plon edition.)

[6] Raymond Aron, *Sur Clausewitz* (Paris: Historiques, Editions Complexe, 1987), 95.

[7] *LNC*, vol. 4 (1982), 170.

[8] *LNC*, vol. 2 (1980), 311.

[9] *LNC*, vol. 7 (1980), 531.

[10] *LNC*, vol. 3 (1981), 437.

[11] *MH*, pt. 1, 258.

[12] Ibid., 229–30.

[13] Charles de Gaulle, *Discours et messages*, vol. 1, *Pendant la guerre, Juin 1940–Janvier 1944* (Paris: Plon, 1970), 139 (all volumes hereafter cited as *DM*).

[14] See p. 111.

[15] *DM*, vol. 1, 397.

[16] *DM-OP*, vol. 4, 884.

[17] *Major Addresses, Statements, and Press Conferences of General Charles de Gaulle, May 19, 1958–January 31, 1964* (New York: French Embassy Press and Information Bureau, 1964), 59 (hereafter cited as *MASPC*).

[18] *MH*, pt. 1, 202.

[19] *LNC*, vol. 4, 411.

[20] *MH*, pt. 1, 242.

[21] *MH*, pt. 1, 41.

[22] *DM*, vol. 3, *Avec le renouveau, Mai 1958–Juillet 1962*, 5.

[23] Jean Lacouture, *De Gaulle*, vol. 2, *Le politique* (Paris: Seuil, 1985), 431 (all volumes hereafter cited as *JLDG*).

[24] *DM-OP*, vol. 3, *Avec le renouveau, Mai 1958–Juillet 1962*, 615.

[25] Ibid., 616.

[26] Press conference of Oct. 23, 1958. *MASPC*, 25–26.

[27] *MASPC*, 54–55.

[28] *DM*, vol. 3, 40.

[29] Ibid., 33.

[30] Press conference of Oct. 23, 1958. *MASPC*, 26.

[31] Ibid., 55.

[32] *MH*, pt. 1, 96.

[33] *MASPC*, 89.

[34] Press conference of Apr. 11, 1961. Ibid., 114.

[35] See also p. 116.

[36] See p. 115.

[37] Alain Peyrefitte, *C'était de Gaulle* (Paris: Fayard, 1994), 59 (hereafter cited as *APCG*).
[38] *DM-OP*, vol. 3, 705.
[39] *JLDG*, vol. 2, 480–81.
[40] *MASPC*, 73.
[41] Ibid., 127. For the full text of de Gaulle's speech on this occasion, see Part Two, The Documents.
[42] *APCG*, 125.
[43] Ibid., 257.
[44] Press conference of May 15, 1962. *MASPC*, 172.
[45] Press conference of Jan. 31, 1964. Ibid., 245. For excerpts from this press conference, see Part Two, The Documents.
[46] For the full text of this document, see Part Two, The Documents.
[47] Charles de Gaulle, *The Complete War Memoirs of Charles de Gaulle*, vol. 2, *Unity, 1942–1944*, trans. Richard Howard (New York: Simon and Schuster, 1964), 307 (all volumes hereafter cited as *WM*).
[48] *LNC*, vol. 8 (1985), 83.
[49] *MASPC*, 96.
[50] *MH*, pt. 1, 202.
[51] Ibid., 202–3.
[52] Ibid., 203.
[53] *APCG*, 352.
[54] Michel Debré, *Entretiens avec le général de Gaulle, 1961–1969* (Paris: Albin Michel, 1993), 26.
[55] Eisenhower to de Gaulle, Oct. 20, 1958; *Documents of DDE-President*, Dwight D. Eisenhower Presidential Library.
[56] *LNC*, vol. 8, 147–48.
[57] On Aug. 2, 1958, the United States in effect restored its wartime cooperation with Great Britain in atomic weaponry through an amendment of the McMahon Act, which, however, did not apply to France or other countries, under the reasoning that a country had to be already in an advanced state of nuclear development to cooperate thus. It is not known whether there was a link between this legislation and de Gaulle's call the following month for a "tridominium" in nuclear development and other matters.
[58] Address by de Gaulle on May 31, 1960, concerning the failure of the Paris Summit Conference. *MASPC*, 77.
[59] Press conference of Sept. 5, 1960. Ibid., 87.
[60] The United States intervened in the Congo in 1960, when the postindependence government of Patrice Lumumba seemed to be leading the country toward the Soviet bloc. Ibid., 87–88.
[61] See pp. 114–15 for de Gaulle's recapitulation of his foreign policy aims in *Memoirs of Hope*.
[62] *DM-OP*, vol. 5, *Vers le terme, Janvier 1966–Avril 1969*, 998–99.
[63] *MH*, pt. 1, 196.
[64] *DM*, vol. 2, *Dans l'attente, Février 1946–Avril 1958*, 282.
[65] The last three are known together as the Benelux countries.
[66] *DM*, vol. 2, 524.
[67] Ibid., 624–25.
[68] *LNC*, vol. 8, 125.
[69] *MASPC*, 95.
[70] *DM*, vol. 3, 126–27. For a significant excerpt from this speech, see Part Two, The Documents.
[71] In a radio broadcast on Nov. 17, 1945, de Gaulle referred to "the French policy of equilibrium between two very great powers" (meaning the United States and the USSR). *DM*, vol. 1, 650.
[72] Press conference of Nov. 10, 1959. *MASPC*, 61.
[73] Speech of Feb. 5, 1962. Ibid., 159.

[74] For large extracts from this press conference, see Part Two, The Documents.

[75] Press conference of Jan. 14, 1963. *MASPC*, 218.

[76] Ibid., 217.

[77] *MH*, pt. 1, 257–58.

[78] Ibid., 214.

[79] Press conference of Jan. 14, 1963. *MASPC*, 127, 217.

[80] Press conference of Apr. 11, 1961. Ibid., 124.

[81] In a meeting with Secretary of State Dean Rusk on Dec. 16, 1964, de Gaulle told him that when France had created a real nuclear force by 1968 or 1969, and "if by then we were still allies, as he hoped," coordination between the American and French forces should be carried out. Two days earlier, he had told Rusk that discussions on coordination could begin in 1967 or 1968, at which time the French would be ready to take up changes in the alliance. National Security File, Country File France, Dec. 15, 1964, and Dec. 16, 1964, Lyndon Baines Johnson Presidential Library.

[82] *DM-OP*, vol. 5, 1056.

[83] Ibid., 1019.

[84] *DM-OP*, vol. 3, 634.

[85] *Administrative History of the Department of State*, Chapter III, Part B, Section 5 (French Withdrawal and NATO Countermeasures), 14, Lyndon Baines Johnson Presidential Library.

[86] *JLDG*, vol. 3, 372–73.

[87] *WM*, vol. 2, 330.

[88] Alain Prate, *Les batailles économiques du général de Gaulle* (Paris: Plon, 1978), 211.

[89] Ibid.

[90] *JLDG*, vol. 3, *Le souverain*, 373.

[91] Press conference of Feb. 4, 1965. *DM-OP*, vol. 5, 911. For excerpts from this press conference, see Part Two, The Documents.

[92] For excerpts from this press conference on this subject, see Part Two, The Documents.

[93] Henri Bourguinat, "Le rétablissement de la balance des paiements, les relations monétaires extérieures, et la réforme du système monétaire international," in *De Gaulle en son siècle*, vol. 3 (Paris: Plon, 1992), 122–24.

[94] Pierre Mélandri, *Une incertaine alliance: Les Etats-Unis et l'Europe, 1973–1983* (Paris: Publications de la Sorbonne, 1988), 68.

[95] *JLDG*, vol. 3, 370.

[96] *WM*, vol. 2, 393.

[97] *LNC*, vol. 4, 195–96.

[98] Ibid., 276.

[99] *MH*, pt. 1, 209.

[100] Press conference of Apr. 7, 1954. *DM-OP*, vol. 2, 581.

[101] Interview of Charles E. Bohlen with Prof. Arthur M. Schlesinger, Jr., on May 21, 1964; Oral History series, John F. Kennedy Library.

[102] *MH*, pt. 1, 254.

[103] *LNC*, vol. 12, 429.

[104] The Kominform, or Communist Information Bureau, an organization of all Communist parties, was in fact a vehicle for the expansion of Communism worldwide.

[105] *DM-OP*, vol. 2, 373.

[106] *DM*, vol. 2, 375.

[107] During the summer of 1950, the United States, in the absence of the Soviet representative, used the Security Council to approve the action in Korea. Later in the fall, when the Soviet delegate had returned, the United States worked through the General Assembly, which on Oct. 7, 1950, passed a resolution calling for the unification and pacification of all of Korea. *DM-OP*, vol. 4, 915.

[108] For extracts from this press conference, see Part Two, The Documents.

[109] *DM*, vol. 4, 119. Although the United States never had fought a war against either France or Russia, there were naval exchanges between U.S. and French ships in the

post–Revolutionary War period; and U.S. troops were engaged in Russia during its civil war, in 1918–21.

[110] Ibid.

[111] Ibid., 120.

[112] *DM-OP*, vol. 4, 968–69.

[113] *DM-OP*, vol. 4, 934.

[114] Press conference of Sept. 9, 1968. *DM-OP*, vol. 5, 1111.

[115] The Commission is headed by a president assisted by twenty commissioners of various European nations, each with different competences or portfolios assigned to them. The commissioners are independent and not representatives of the countries from which they come.

[116] Press conference of July 23, 1964. *DM-OP*, vol. 4, 885.

[117] There was another "community" set up at the same time as the EEC, known as "Euratom," or the European Atomic Community. This idea of pooling Europe's nuclear resources did not progress, in part because of French obstructions.

[118] *MH*, pt. 1, 10.

[119] Ibid., 192.

[120] Ibid., 189.

[121] Ibid., 183.

[122] For an excerpt from this note, see Part Two, The Documents. Whether meeting as chiefs of state or governments, or as ministerial counterparts, the European Council is the expression of the sovereign states, in contrast to the supranational institutions of the community, such as the Commission.

[123] *LNC*, vol. 8, 379.

[124] In the early 1950s, Jean Monnet had also formed the idea of a European Political Community (EPC), but this was dropped after the failure of the EDC.

[125] *LNC*, vol. 9 (1986), 39–40.

[126] On Sept. 1, 1965, the three communities (the Common Market or European Economic Community, the Coal and Steel Community, and Euratom) were merged into a single community, the European Community, with a single commission, known as the European Commission. Ibid., 76.

[127] Speech of Feb. 5, 1962. The reference to the Channel reflects the fact that Great Britain had posed its candidacy for the EEC in July 1961. *DM-OP*, vol. 2, 777.

[128] Press conference of May 15, 1962. *MASPC*, 176.

[129] "High Authority" was the original name for the executive branch in the three communities. When they were merged, the executive branch became the Commission. Ibid., 93.

[130] *DM-OP*, vol. 4, 886.

[131] *DM-OP*, vol. 5, 1001.

[132] *DM-OP*, vol. 3, 697.

[133] For de Gaulle's summation of this plan, see the extract from his May 15, 1962, press conference in Part Two, The Documents.

[134] Press conference of Jan. 14, 1963. *MASPC*, 212.

[135] For large extracts from this press conference, see Part Two, The Documents.

[136] *LNC*, vol. 3 (1981), 219.

[137] *MH*, pt. 1, 234.

[138] Ibid., 236.

[139] *APCG*, 153.

[140] *MH*, pt. 1, 187.

[141] Ibid., 252.

[142] *JLDG*, vol. 3, 754.

[143] Macmillan met with de Gaulle at Rambouillet on Dec. 15–16, 1962, and with President Kennedy at Nassau on Dec. 18–21, at which time Kennedy acceded to Macmillan's request for the Polaris. A similar offer was made at the same time to de Gaulle, but since the French

had at the time neither the submarines nor the warheads to go with the missiles, the offer was of little meaning.

[144] *JLDG*, vol. 3, 335.

[145] Ibid., 439.

[146] *MASPC*, 220–21.

[147] *DM-OP*, vol. 4, 886. For extracts from the treaty of Jan. 22, 1963, see Part Two, The Documents.

[148] *DM-OP*, vol. 5, 1016.

[149] See p. 142.

[150] France, the largest agricultural producer in the EEC, did not obtain a satisfactory Common Agricultural Policy (CAP) for the EEC until May 1966. A year earlier, France had withdrawn its participation in EEC institutions, pending resolution of this issue. See p. 161. *DM-OP*, vol. 4, 887.

[151] N.B. The interpreter did not add the clarification. *APCG*, 63.

[152] *LNC*, vol. 2, 169–70.

[153] Ibid., 161.

[154] Ibid., 161–62.

[155] *LNC*, vol. 7 (1985), 218.

[156] *LNC*, vol. 4, 491.

[157] *LNC*, vol. 2, 374.

[158] *LNC*, vol. 5 (1983), 70.

[159] *LNC*, vol. 2, 32.

[160] From a lecture on Polish history given to members of the French military mission in Poland, end of 1919. *LNC*, vol. 2, 56.

[161] Ibid., 106.

[162] Ibid., 42.

[163] *LNC*, vol. 6, 92.

[164] *LNC*, vol. 2, 312.

[165] *LNC*, vol. 7, 220.

[166] Speech by de Gaulle in Moscow, June 20, 1966. This assertion, de Gaulle emphasized, was not gainsaid either by the Napoleonic or the Crimean wars. *DM-OP*, vol. 5, 1010.

[167] Press conference of July 29, 1963. *DM*, vol. 4, 122.

[168] *MASPC*, 116.

[169] *DM*, vol. 1, 169.

[170] *JLDG*, vol. 3, 751.

[171] *DM*, vol. 1, 487.

[172] *WM*, vol. 3, *Salvation, 1944–1946*, 759.

[173] Press conference of Mar. 29, 1949. *DM-OP*, vol. 2, 463.

[174] Ibid., 636.

[175] Press conference of Feb. 4, 1965. *DM-OP*, vol. 4, 919.

[176] Ibid.

[177] "The reunification of the two fractions in a single Germany, which would be entirely free, would appear to us the normal destiny of the German people, provided that the latter not call into question their current frontiers." Press conference of Mar. 25, 1959. *DM-OP*, vol. 3, 634.

[178] *DM-OP*, vol. 4, 919–20.

[179] *DM-OP*, vol. 5, 1010.

[180] *DM*, vol. 5, 76. For excerpts from this speech, see Part Two, The Documents.

[181] *LNC*, vol. 1, 180.

[182] *American Foreign Policy: Current Documents, 1963*, Department of State Publication 811 (Washington, D.C.: Government Printing Office, 1967), 869.

[183] Press conference of Oct. 28, 1966. *DM-OP*, vol. 5, 1019–20.

[184] The 1962 conference endorsed the neutrality of Laos. *LNC*, vol. 10 (1987), 30.

[185] *MASPC*, 257. For excerpts from this press conference, see Part Two, The Documents.

[186] Ibid.

[187] *Foreign Relations of the United States, 1964–1968*, vol. 1, *Vietnam 1964* (Washington, D.C.: Government Printing Office, 1992), 467.

[188] Ibid., 469.

[189] *DM-OP*, vol. 4, 947.

[190] *DM-OP*, vol. 5, 999.

[191] Ibid., 1031–32 (Radio-television address, Dec. 31, 1966).

[192] See p. 148.

[193] For excerpts from this speech, see Part Two, The Documents.

[194] Press conference of Oct. 28, 1966. *DM-OP*, vol. 5, 1014.

[195] Press conference of Feb. 21, 1966. Ibid., 1003.

[196] Press conference of July 23, 1964. *DM-OP*, vol. 4, 892.

[197] *MH*, pt. 2, 266.

5

Epilogue: The Legacy

When one discusses the legacy of Charles de Gaulle, it is useful to distinguish between the visionary and the practical, the tangible and the intangible, the long range and the short range. As Professor Stanley Hoffmann has put it, de Gaulle's long-range perspective was extraordinary; his short-range view was more questionable.[1] Nowhere was this polarity more evident than in the withdrawal from the military structure of NATO—seemingly pointless and abrupt at the time, useful and justified, from the French point of view, in the long run.

A de Gaulle was necessary for postwar France—necessary to restore the French sense of worth after a dubious performance on the murderous terrain of 1940, and necessary to preserve the French sense of national identity and purpose in the midst of the crushing requirements for solidarity imposed by the U.S. defense of the free world during the cold war. But through it all, through the forty-odd years of the cold war, France was able to reestablish its national identity and its national purpose in a way that could only have been set in motion by de Gaulle.

Had de Gaulle not been there to enunciate the strident message of the restitution of France, first during the war and then during the turmoil over Algeria, the France of the latter half of the twentieth century would not have turned out in the same way. France would have been more or less categorized as one of a "club of defeated nations of the Continent."[2]

De Gaulle not only restored the image and standing of France through his leadership, he also brought a sense of coherence and command to the French political system with his constitutional reforms, which were effected in two phases, in 1958 and 1962. In taking away Parliament's sole right to make constitutional changes in France—a sacrosanct parliamentary function since the French Revolution—de Gaulle was able to put together a system based on a strong presidency and thus stamp France with the authority of a modern state.

In the first phase, in 1958, the National Assembly gave de Gaulle what he wanted: the power to draft a constitution and submit it to a referendum by the people. De Gaulle then removed the most backward feature of the constitutions of the Third Republic (1875–1940) and the Fourth Republic (1946–58): the power of the National Assembly to vote a government out of office while the president had no power to dismiss the assembly and call for new elections. As Jean Monnet had written, "The permanent danger of being outvoted by an assembly that ran no risk of dissolution had made governmental instability a political way of life."[3]

Governmental instability had also made France the political sick man among the leading nations of Europe, but the French people as a whole had yet to absorb de Gaulle's notion that the defeat of 1940 was in part a systemic failure in France. Only through twelve more unsatisfactory years (1946–58) would the French political class come to fully apprehend what Winston Churchill referred to as the "tyrannical weakness"[4] of the French parliamentary system.

To bring about the second major constitutional reform, in 1962, de Gaulle did not gain the consent of Parliament; he did not even seek it. It is unlikely that he would have gotten consent at that or any other time for the election of a president by universal suffrage—since a president mandated by the people as a whole and with the power to dismiss the assembly and call for new elections would have sounded the death knell of parliamentary supremacy in France. So de Gaulle kept Parliament away from the constitutional revision process in 1962 and initiated his own amendment on a technicality that was questionable—and characterized by Georges Pompidou as "at the limit of legality"[5]—but he got the people to approve it in a referendum.

Ever since the Revolution had opened up a great left-right fissure in French society, the country had oscillated between a disorderly parliamentarianism and a repressive authoritarianism. France had staggered through a dozen constitutions since the end of the ancien régime. De Gaulle put an end to this oscillation. His influence was so commanding (and his stature has increased in the quarter-century since his death) that he was able to put a permanent stamp on *his* constitution. This constitution may be retouched in the future, but it is hard to imagine something really different, different enough to be called the Sixth Republic.

In foreign affairs, the de Gaulle legacy is less tangible. Here de Gaulle was more of a battler *against* than a battler *for*. Here too he was dealing with people who were not French and therefore less able to understand what biographer Jean Lacouture has described as the "tragic character" of the way he handled crises involving French interests—reflecting, in Lacouture's view, a "conflict between a dominating temperament which had been fed on a history of conquest, and an intelligent awareness of contemporary realities."[6]

In the dialectic represented by the figures of Charles de Gaulle and Jean Monnet, the latter saw salvation for France in the postwar period only through merging, together with Germany, into a larger unit called Western Europe; the former saw France's salvation in a Europe of sovereign states led by Germany and most especially France. This Europe would be an independent and competing "third force" between the two superpowers. Neither Monnet's nor de Gaulle's vision has been fully realized: The future of Europe remains uncertain.

De Gaulle did not succeed either in "de-Atlanticizing" the Common Market nor in pointing the way for other countries to leave the military structure of NATO. He did not really try to transform NATO, partly because for him NATO was only a temporary arrangement.

De Gaulle did, however, try mightily to transform the Common Market, and in some respects his dominant personality did bend the EEC to his will. In May 1966, he finally succeeded in incorporating agriculture into the Common Market in addition to the free flow of manufactured goods. Since France is the second largest agricultural exporter after the United States, the policy of EEC subsidies to agriculture (the Common Agricultural Policy—CAP) has been of benefit primarily to French farmers but also to German farmers.

Tied in with the dispute over agriculture, de Gaulle put a check on the European Council's move from unanimous voting to qualified majority voting—a transition that was supposed to have been effected, according to the Treaty of Rome, on January 1, 1966.[7] De Gaulle's boycott of the EEC over the agricultural dispute—the so-called empty chair policy— resulted in the Luxembourg Compromise of January 29, 1966, which allowed for a member state of the European Council to invoke the need for a unanimous vote if its vital interests were at stake. Four months later, the Common Agricultural Policy was agreed on, and France ended its eight-month "empty chair" boycott of the EEC.

Although of questionable legal validity because it is not part of the EEC's treaty structure, the Luxembourg Compromise cast what legal scholar Joseph Weiler has termed the "shadow of the veto" over EEC negotiations. It impeded the integration of the EEC for nearly twenty years, until the passage of the Single European Act (SEA) in December 1985. This act—which had the stated objective of creating by January 1, 1993, a single European market for the exchange of goods, persons, services, and capital—provided that harmonization measures to bring this about would essentially be decided upon by qualified majority voting.[8]

Even today, the Luxembourg Compromise can be invoked implicitly, as France did during the GATT negotiations in 1994.[9] But as Joseph Weiler has pointed out, to invoke the Luxembourg Compromise now, a member state must persuade at least half of the other member states of "the 'vitality' of the national interest claimed."[10]

The principal Gaullist innovation in European policy, indeed in foreign policy in general, was the French-German Alliance, which in the end disappointed de Gaulle because the Germans would not tear themselves loose from America. This alliance has weathered the initial shock of the German Parliament's action in watering it down, and more recently, the profound shock of German reunification, which has made France at last aware that it can no longer hope to direct what has become a reunified Germany.

De Gaulle did not ignore the possibility of eventual German reunification. In fact, he had a blueprint for it, as laid out in his press conference on February 4, 1965, on the twentieth anniversary of Yalta:[11] The problem would not be solved in a day, he said; it would not be solved while the superpowers were in a state of ideological confrontation; the European people were the ones primarily interested in the German question, and they would have to be in agreement; the East European satellites would have to become free; and the Germans would have to accept the Oder-Neisse line as their eastern border and would have to do without nuclear weapons.

De Gaulle seemed to visualize the changes in the Soviet Union as being brought about by a gradual blunting of the force of communist ideology and a gradual loosening of control over its satellites. He did not foresee (nor did virtually anyone else) the relatively sudden implosion of Soviet society and the collapse of the Russian Empire as it had existed for centuries.

De Gaulle added one other condition to German reunification: that the Six of the European Community (EC) be welded into an independent political and defense entity positioned to "make possible a new equilibrium of our continent."[12] Though how this would take place was not spelled out, it would result in Europe as a whole living in peace and cooperation "from the Atlantic to the Urals."

This condition has obviously not been fulfilled. The Fouchet Plan for a political concert among the EC governments was never implemented, and what was incorporated into the Maastricht Treaty of December 1991 under the Common Foreign and Security Policy (CFSP) is only a pale shadow of it. The CFSP, under the treaty's Chapter II, contains a number of caveats, notably that those members of the European Union who are also members of NATO retain their obligations to NATO and also that the CFSP remains outside the system of qualified majority voting under which many of the measures of economic integration have been put into effect. In other words, the progress of a political structure for Europe depends on the unanimity of its members.

Thus, paradoxically, economic integration (though not yet monetary union) is progressing through the medium of the European Community (now called the European Union, under the Treaty of Maastricht), while the political "cooperation among States" dear to de Gaulle remains stunted. Only the French-German Alliance, to which de Gaulle turned after the failure of the Fouchet Plan aimed at bringing about this cooperation, provides any cement for a political structure for Europe. This alliance has become institutionally strengthened through the years: The many French-German interrelationships at the governmental and industrial levels, the biennial summit meetings of the two countries' leaders, and the French-German Defense Council that spawned the Euro-Corps[13] have all contributed to this. The French-German Alliance has become the enduring constant of French foreign policy, and upon this tie the future shape of Europe largely depends. Its future is by no means certain, however, and will require much will (or what the French call voluntarism) to make it successful and lasting.

De Gaulle expressed a powerful current of thought in French history: Independence, lost during World War II, was never to be given up easily again; no foreign power would dominate France in the future; and France would lead in the resurgence of a Europe independent of and eventually in competition with the superpowers.

The General's successors in the Gaullist movement, and indeed most of the political class in France, have largely subscribed to these master themes. Certain powerful Gaullist taboos in the name of independence remain, notably the bar on reentering the integrated military command of NATO. Independence has become the touchstone of the Gaullist legacy in foreign affairs.

But de Gaulle's successors, starting with Georges Pompidou and continuing with Valéry Giscard d'Estaing and François Mitterrand, have expressed these master themes in a more modulated way, giving a markedly more reasonable—and less activist—tone to French policy. France during de Gaulle's tenure, especially from 1962 onward, was a hothouse of provocations and preemptive actions. Gaullist policies could not last for long, and they could not have been carried on by successors. The French people found themselves in a sort of foreign-policy free fall, not knowing what was going to happen next. Many of de Gaulle's visions—Israel's "colonial war" launched in 1967, the need for the French Canadians to rise from their two-hundred-year slumber[14]—prophetic as they were, came across with such force and brutality in the mouth of a statesman that France's isolation only increased. Describing the period during the height of these pronouncements—in 1967—Jean Lacouture observed that "de Gaulle acted in those months as though France had no other rules and obeyed no other laws than those of its solitary salvation, and as though he were invested with a sort of annunciatory mission."[15]

Journalist André Fontaine of *Le Monde* wrote on the day after de Gaulle left office for the last time:

This too-military style, what harm didn't it do to Gaullist diplomacy! It is as easy to defend a government as it is to offend an individual. General de Gaulle did not deprive himself of this. Showing France a love whose sincerity could hardly be doubted, he persuaded himself once and for all that, in the international jungle, you have to refrain from counting on the friendship of others, especially insofar as the great powers are concerned. Rather, you should set yourself to the task of forcing them to respect you. Without question, de Gaulle had earned this respect. On the other hand, he had succeeded in turning away a whole group of people who would have been ready to recognize, in reality, our country's supremacy in Europe—provided he didn't appear to demand this by right.[16]

And yet, was it not this "too-military style," this insensate boldness, that led de Gaulle not to let France accept the surrender of 1940? And did not his continued insistence on France's grandeur and world role mean that, at the approach of the twenty-first century, France remains a major military power and a country whose combination of global interests and global reach remains second only to the United States among the "world powers of the West"?

NOTES

[1] Conversation with the author, Jan. 12, 1995.

[2] This expression is derived from George Ball, *The Past Has Another Pattern: Memoirs* (New York: W. W. Norton, 1982), 81. "Britain, with America's help, had won the war, while the other members of the group [the Organization of European Economic Cooperation—OEEC] were, as one of my Dutch friends put it, 'a club of defeated nations.' "

[3] Jean Monnett, *Memoirs* (Garden City, N.Y.: Doubleday, 1978), 429.

[4] Churchill to Eisenhower, Dec. 7, 1954; *Documents of DDE-President,* Dwight D. Eisenhower Presidential Library.

[5] Alain Peyrefitte, *C'était de Gaulle* (Paris: Fayard, 1994), 248.

[6] Jean Lacouture, *De Gaulle,* vol. 2, *Le politique* (Paris: Seuil, 1985), 155 (all volumes hereafter cited as *JLDG*).

[7] Qualified majority voting in the European Council, which is made up of representatives of the member governments, means that different countries are given varying blocs of votes depending on the size of their populations.

[8] However, political and security matters, and by extension defense, do not come under the qualified majority rubric and remain subject to unanimity of voting.

[9] The latest round in these tariff negotiations, the so-called Uruguay Round, was completed after difficult negotiations, particularly involving the United States and France and mainly concerning access of American agricultural products to Europe. (GATT stands for General Agreement on Tariffs and Trade.)

[10] Joseph Weiler, "The Transformation of Europe," *The Yale Law Journal* 100, no. 8 (June 1991): 2461.

[11] For excerpts from this press conference dealing with this subject, see Part Two, The Documents.

[12] Charles de Gaulle, *Discours et messages,* vol. 4, *Pour l'effort, Août 1962–Décembre 1965* (Paris: Omnibus/Plon, 1933), 419.

[13] This European-only intervention force, with French and German units at its nucleus, now includes the Spanish, the Belgians, and the Luxembourgeois as well.

[14] On July 24, 1967, while on an official visit to Canada, de Gaulle launched the cry "Long live free Quebec" to a crowd in Montreal.

[15] *JLDG,* vol. 3, *Le souverain,* 487.

[16] *Le Monde,* Apr. 29, 1969, 1.

PART TWO

The Documents

6

The Saving of the French Nation

CHARLES DE GAULLE

Radio Broadcast from London

June 18, 1940

On June 18, 1940, one day after his arrival in London from France, Charles de Gaulle made a broadcast to the French nation over the BBC. The event was hastily arranged, the broadcast was not even recorded, and only scattered persons in France happened to hear it. The "appeal of June 18" received very little response at the time but was to acquire enormous significance later on. It marked de Gaulle's break with the new French government of Philippe Pétain as well as the beginning of de Gaulle's setting himself up as an alternative supreme authority to Pétain. He elevated himself to this authority with the words "Moi, le général de Gaulle," in spite of the fact that he was not well known and had only the temporary grade of brigadier general. The genius of the "appeal of June 18" was not only that it recognized that the world war was far from over but that it promised the French, shattered by the German blitzkrieg, a way to continue their lives with honor, albeit under conditions of extraordinary sacrifice. Because of these circumstances and because the appeal lacked authority vis-à-vis Pétain's call for peace, the response to the Free French movement in the beginning was very slow.

The leaders who, for many years past, have been at the head of the French armed forces, have set up a government.

Speeches of General de Gaulle, vol. 1, *1940–1941* (London: Oxford University Press, 1942), 1–2.

Alleging the defeat of our armies, this government has entered into negotiations with the enemy with a view to bringing about a cessation of hostilities. It is quite true that we were, and still are, overwhelmed by enemy mechanized forces, both on the ground and in the air. It was the tanks, the planes, and the tactics of the Germans, far more than the fact that we were outnumbered, that forced our armies to retreat. It was the German tanks, planes, and tactics that provided the element of surprise which brought our leaders to their present plight.

But has the last word been said? Must we abandon all hope? Is our defeat final and irremediable? To those questions I answer—No!

Speaking in full knowledge of the facts, I ask you to believe me when I say that the cause of France is not lost. The very factors that brought about our defeat may one day lead us to victory.

For, remember this, France does not stand alone. She is not isolated. Behind her is a vast Empire, and she can make common cause with the British Empire, which commands the seas and is continuing the struggle. Like England, she can draw unreservedly on the immense industrial resources of the United States.

This war is not limited to our unfortunate country. The outcome of this struggle has not been decided by the Battle of France. This is a world war. Mistakes have been made, there have been delays and untold suffering, but the fact remains that there still exists in the world everything we need to crush our enemies some day. Today we are crushed by the sheer weight of mechanized forces hurled against us, but we can still look to a future in which even greater mechanized force will bring us victory. The destiny of the world is at stake.

I, General de Gaulle, now in London, call on all French officers and men who are present on British soil, or may be in the future, with or without their arms; I call on all engineers and skilled workmen from the armaments factories who are at present on British soil, or may be in the future, to get in touch with me.

Whatever happens, the flame of French resistance must not and shall not die.

Tomorrow, I shall broadcast again from London.

Constitutional Law and Initial Vichy Acts
July 10–12, 1940

On July 10, 1940, the existing French Parliament, by a vote of 549–80 gave full powers to Marshal Philippe Pétain, who then proceeded to issue a series of decrees that in effect abolished the French parliamentary system, notably by prohibiting the Parliament from meeting except on his convocation.

Constitutional Law of July 10, 1940

The President of the Republic promulgates the Constitutional Law whose tenor is as follows:

SOLE ARTICLE. The National Assembly gives complete power to the government of the Republic, under the authority and the signature of Marshal Pétain, for the purpose of promulgating through one or several acts a new Constitution of the French State. This Constitution must guarantee the rights of Work, of the Family, and of the Nation.

It will be ratified by the Assemblies created by it.

The present Constitutional Law deliberated and adopted by the National Assembly will be executed as a law of the State.

Executed at Vichy, July 10, 1940.

Albert Lebrun.

By the President of the Republic: the Marshal of France, President of the Council, Philippe Pétain.

Constitutional Act No. 1 of July 11, 1940

We, Philippe Pétain, Marshal of France, in view of the Constitutional Law of July 10, 1940, declare to assume the functions of the French Chief of State.

As a result, we decree:

Article 2 of the Constitutional Law of February 25, 1875, is abrogated.[1]

Executed at Vichy, July 11, 1940.

Philippe Pétain.

Léon Duguit, Henry Monnier, and Roger Bonnard, *Les constitutions et les principales lois politiques de la France depuis 1789* (Paris: Librairie générale de droit et de jurisprudence, 1952), 358–61.

Constitutional Act No. 2 of July 11, 1940

We, Marshal of France, Chief of the French State, in view of the Constitutional Law of July 10, 1940, decree:

Article 1.1. The Chief of the French State has the plenitude of governmental power; he names and revokes ministers and secretaries of state, who are responsible only before him.

2. He exercises legislative power in the council of Ministers:

1. Until the formation of new assemblies.

2. After this formation, in case of external tension or of a grave internal crisis, on his decision alone, and in the same form. In the same circumstances, he can issue edicts on all provisions of a budgetary and fiscal nature.

3. He promulgates the laws and ensures their execution.

4. He makes all civilian and military nominations for which the law has not provided another mode of designation.

5. He disposes of the armed forces.

6. He has the right of pardon and of amnesty.

7. Envoys and ambassadors of foreign powers are accredited to him. He negotiates and ratifies treaties.

8. He can declare a state of siege in one or several parts of the territory.

9. He cannot declare war without the prior agreement of the legislative assemblies.

Article 2. All provisions of the Constitutional Laws of February 24 and 25, 1875, and July 11, 1875, incompatible with the present law are abrogated.

Executed at Vichy, July 11, 1940.

Philippe Pétain.

Constitutional Act No. 3 of July 11, 1940

We, Marshal of France, Chief of the French State, in view of the Constitutional Law of July 10, 1940, decree:

Article 1. The Senate and the Chamber of Deputies will remain in existence until the formation of the assemblies provided for by the Constitutional Law of July 10, 1940, are formed.

2. The Senate and the Chamber of Deputies are adjourned until further notice.

They cannot meet henceforth unless convoked by the Chief of State.

3. Article 1 of the Constitutional Law of July 16, 1875, is abrogated.[2]

Executed at Vichy, July 11, 1940.

Philippe Pétain.

Constitutional Act No. 4 of July 12, 1940

We, Marshal of France, Chief of the French State, in view of the Constitutional Law of July 10, 1940, decree:

Article 1. If, for whatever reason, before the ratification by the nation of the new constitution, we are prevented from exercising the functions of Chief of State, M. Pierre Laval, vice president of the council of ministers, will assume it in full right.

2. In the case that M. Pierre Laval might be prevented, for whatever reason, he would in turn be replaced by a person whom the council of ministers would designate by a majority of seven votes. Until the investiture of the latter, the functions would be exercised by the council of ministers.

Executed at Vichy, July 12, 1940.

Philippe Pétain.

CHARLES DE GAULLE

From a Speech to the Oxford French Club
November 25, 1941

In this speech, de Gaulle spoke of the problem of the individual's becoming ground down by mass industrial society. De Gaulle was gradually to form a socioeconomic doctrine around this theme, first called "association" and then "participation." He visualized this as a compromise between communism and capitalism, a scheme in which owners and workers would coexist harmoniously, with the workers participating in the decisions and profits of the enterprise. De Gaulle was not able to realize this idea in practical terms.

It must be admitted that in recent times, the change in our mode of life due to machinery, the growing aggregation of humanity, and the widespread uniformity imposed on society have all combined to strike hard at individual liberty. In a world where human beings are herded together for work and

Speeches of General de Gaulle, vol. 1, *1940–1941* (London: Oxford University Press, 1942), 108.

pleasure, and where even their thoughts and interests are determined for them; in a world where housing conditions, clothing, and food are gradually standardized; where everyone reads the same thing in the same papers at the same time; where, from one end of the earth to the other, they see the same films and hear the same news, ideas, and music broadcast; in a world where, at the same hours, similar means of transport take people to the same workshops and offices, restaurants and canteens, sports-grounds and theaters, to the same buildings, blocks, or courts for work, food, recreation, and rest; where men and women are similarly educated and informed, and all lead the same busy life and share the same worries, it is only too obvious that freedom of choice tends to disappear, and individuality—the "essential I"—finds it increasingly difficult to survive. The result is a kind of general mechanization in which only a tremendous effort can preserve the individual as such. This is all the more true since the masses, far from reacting against such standardization, are actually developing a taste for it and encouraging the process.

CHARLES DE GAULLE

From a Speech to the National Defense Public Interest Committee in London

April 1, 1942

On April 1, 1942, General de Gaulle made a speech before the National Defense Public Interest Committee at London in which he explained the reasons behind his rebellion against the French government of the armistice and also described the Gaullist movement as an "elite begun from nothing," whose goal was to create a revolution in French society after the war.

. . . We must not imagine, Gentlemen, that the kind of miracle which is Fighting France can endure forever. We must not imagine that the instinctive and somewhat legendary mysticism which sustains in their ordeal those Frenchmen who, without laws, rights, or government, face death on

Sheila Mathieu and W. G. Corp, trans., *Speeches of General de Gaulle*, vol. 2, *1942* (London: Oxford University Press, 1943), 20.

the battlefield and execution-grounds, exposing their families to reprisals and giving up everything they possess, can go on indefinitely without reward. It all comes down to this: Fighting France means to stand by her Allies, but on the express condition that her Allies stand by her. She maintains that, by fighting at their side, she will regain her independence, her sovereignty, and her greatness, provided that the Allies respect these attributes in her. . . . During the past fifteen hundred years she has acquired the habit of being a great Power, and demands that nobody, her friends least of all, should lose sight of this. In short, Fighting France has but one reason, one justification, for her presence in the camp of freedom: that of being France herself and treated as such by her co-belligerents. . . . How could anyone believe that by keeping in with the regime established in Vichy for Hitler's benefit it would be possible to prevent it from going to the utmost limits in its collaboration with the enemy? Who could seriously imagine that in such a matter Hitler's wishes and dictates could be countered by anything other than the resistance of the French nation, galvanized by Fighting France? . . .

Next, how could we attach any weight to certain suggestions that the democracies should recognize France in the men of Vichy, rather than in the leaders of Fighting France, on the pretext that the latter did not make a definite enough stand in favor of liberty? Such allegations are a flagrant insult to the democracies themselves, ascribing to them the intention of interfering in matters which solely concern the sovereignty of the French people, and likewise implying a ludicrous blindness on their part. For [this means leaning] towards men who have destroyed all freedom in France, and who seek to model their regime on fascism or a caricature of it.

Finally, how could anyone suppose that, in their attitude towards Fighting France, the democracies would give way to an absurd snobbery, letting themselves be influenced by regret at the absence of many once-famous names? . . . Above all, it would mean a grave failure to recognize one thing which dominates the whole French question today—the fact of revolution. For France, betrayed by her ruling and privileged classes, has embarked on the greatest revolution in all her history. . . . I must add that people in the outside world who imagine that when the last shot has been fired they will be able to find a France politically, socially, and morally identical with the land they once knew, are making a signal mistake. At this very moment, in the secrecy of her suffering, an entirely new France is rising, and she will be guided by new men. . . .

CHARLES DE GAULLE

From a Letter to Franklin Delano Roosevelt

October 26, 1942

On October 26, 1942, General de Gaulle wrote a lengthy letter to President Roosevelt, explaining the raison d'être of the Free French movement and giving the reasons why the U.S. government should support it rather than temporize with the pro-Nazi regime of Vichy. The letter was entrusted to André Philip of the French National Committee in London, and its effect may have been diminished by the fact that Philip's interview with Roosevelt consisted in part of a diatribe against American policy in North Africa in the wake of the invasion there. Though Roosevelt said that he might have had a different outlook on de Gaulle if he had seen the letter two years earlier,[3] he never replied to it and maintained to the end a rancorous attitude toward de Gaulle.

Mr. President,

Mr. André Philip will deliver this letter to you. It will explain to you the situation in France at the time he left. To the information he is bringing you on the development and the cohesion of the French resistance groups and, more generally, on the state of mind of the country, I would like to add the following:

You have followed the moral and political evolution of France since 1918. You know that, having carried the main weight of the last war, she emerged from it exhausted. She felt profoundly that the state of relative inferiority that resulted from it exposed her to a grave peril. She believed in the necessity of allied cooperation in order to compensate for this inferiority and bring about a balance of forces.

You are not unaware of the respects in which this cooperation failed her. Indeed it was mainly France's doubt that she would receive real support against the former and future adversary that was the basis for the undulating policy and bad strategy that resulted in our defeat. Our domestic errors and the divisions and abuses that hampered the actions of our institutions were only accessory causes alongside this main fact.

France, therefore, feels keenly the humiliation that has been inflicted on

Charles de Gaulle, *Memoires de guerre*, vol. 2, *L'unité, 1942–1944* (Paris: Plon Presses Pocket, 1959), 399–406.

her, and the injustice of the fate to which she has been subjected. This is why it is necessary, before the end of the war, that France resume her place in the fighting and that, in the meantime, she not have the impression that she ever completely abandoned it. She must be conscious of being one of the countries whose effort brought about victory. This is important for the war and essential for the postwar period.

If France, in the case that it were liberated by the democracies, had an image of itself as a conquered country, there would be a strong reason to fear that its bitterness, its humiliation, and its internal divisions, far from turning it toward the democracies, would cause it to open itself to other influences. You know which ones. This is not an imaginary peril, because the social structure of our country is going to find itself more or less weakened by hardships and despoilments. I would add that then, hatred of the German, which is today very violent because the German is present and the conqueror, will fade out vis-à-vis the German absent and beaten. We saw that before, after 1918. In any case, whatever inspiration France would embrace, having been thrown into a revolutionary situation, the reconstruction of Europe and even the international organization of the peace would be dangerously flawed. It is necessary, therefore, that the victory reconcile France with herself and with her friends, which will not be possible if she does not participate in it.

This is why, if the effort of Fighting France is limited to enlarging by several battalions the forces on the side of freedom, or even to rallying part of the French Empire, this effort would be, in itself, almost negligible in the face of the essential problem: returning France to the war.

You will say to me: Why did you assign to me this goal? And on what basis are you entitled [to do so]?

It is true that I found myself, at the moment of the armistice of Vichy, in a completely unheard-of situation. Belonging to the last regular and independent government of the Third Republic, I strongly proclaimed the wish to maintain France in the war. The government that seized power in the despair and panic of the nation ordered: "Stop the fighting." In France and outside of France, the elected bodies, the representatives of the government, the Presidents of the Assemblies either resigned themselves to the situation or kept silent. If the President of the Republic, if the Parliament and its leaders had called on the country to continue the struggle, I would not have even thought of speaking to the country or in its name. Political leaders and high-ranking military officers were in a position, on various occasions, to speak and to act, for example, in North Africa. They did not show at any moment either the confidence, or the conviction in their mandate, sufficient to make war. That it was a question of the failure of an elite is incontestable. In their minds, the French people have already drawn that conclusion. In any event, I was alone. Should I have kept quiet?

This is why I took the action that seemed to me necessary in order that France not abandon the struggle, and to call on all Frenchmen in France and outside France to continue fighting. Does this mean that my companions and I set ourselves up at any point as the Government of France? In no way. We held ourselves and proclaimed ourselves as an essentially provisional authority responsible before the future national representation and applying the laws of the Third Republic.

I was not a political personality. All my life I had remained confined to my specialty. When, before the war, I tried to interest political leaders in my ideas, it was in order to induce them to achieve a military objective for the country. By the same token, at the time of the armistice of Vichy, it was initially in a military context that I made an appeal to the country. But from the fact that more and more people replied, that territories joined or were joined to Fighting France, and that we were always the sole ones to act in an organized manner, we saw larger responsibilities come to us. We saw created in France a sort of mystique, of which we were the center, and which united, little by little, all the elements of the resistance. It was thus that we have become, by the force of events, a French moral entity. This reality creates duties that weigh heavily upon us and from which we cannot withdraw without being derelict with respect to the country and without betraying the hopes that the people of France have placed in us.

People say to us that we should not engage in politics. If by that it is understood that it is not up to us to take part in the partisan struggles of old, or to dictate one day the institutions of the country, we do not need any such recommendations, because it is our very principle that we should abstain from such pretensions. But we do not shrink before the word "politics" if it is a matter of reassembling, not just some troops, but indeed the French nation in the war, or if it is a matter of dealing with the Allies concerning the interests of France, at the same time as we defend them, for France, against the enemy. In effect, who but ourselves could represent these interests? Or else should France be silent on what concerns her? Or else should her affairs be handled with the United Nations by the people of Vichy, to the degree and under the form that Mr. Hitler judges suitable? It is not a question of distrust on our part concerning our allies but rather of the three following facts that dominate and command our persons: only the French can be the judge of French interests; the French people are naturally persuaded that, among the Allies, we speak for them, just as we fight for them at [the Allies'] side; in their misfortune, the

French are extremely sensitive as to what happens to their Empire, and any appearance of abuse committed in this regard by an ally is exploited by the enemy and by Vichy in a manner that is dangerous to national feeling. Because unprecedented circumstances in our History have assigned us this task, does this mean that we were thinking of imposing a personal power in France, as some have whispered abroad? If we harbored sentiments so low as to deprive the French people of their future freedom, we would show proof of a singular ignorance of our own people. The French people are by nature the most opposed to personal power. At no time has it been easy to impose such a power on them. But tomorrow, after Pétain's odious exercise of personal power, thanks to the connivance of the Germans and the internal oppression, and after the long and hard constraints of the invasion, who then would have the absurdity to imagine that one could establish and maintain a personal power in France? Whatever services that he was able to do [for the country] in the past, the dreamer who would try that [to establish one-man rule] would find everyone against him.

It is remarkable, moreover, that we are not taxed by anyone in France with aspirations to dictatorship. . . . [Though some] reproach us as being mercenaries in the pay of the democracies, they have never accused us of wanting to establish in France a personal and antidemocratic power. . . . Wisdom and justice require that Fighting France be really and substantially assisted. Apart from the material and moral support that the Allies can give us, and without in any way asking that we be recognized as the Government of France, we think it necessary that we be approached each time that it is a question of the general interests of France, whether with regard to French participation in the war or with regard to the administration of French territories that the development of the war gradually puts in the position of resuming the fighting and that have not been able to rally spontaneously to us.

Your name and your person have an immense and uncontested prestige in France. France knows that she can count on your friendship. But ultimately, in your dialogue with her, who can be your interlocutor? Is it the France of yesterday? The men who were the most representative of it have let it be known to me that they merge with us. Is it the France of Vichy? Perhaps you think that one day its leaders could take up arms again at our side. Alas! I do not believe it. But even admitting that that were possible, it is now certain that they are collaborating with Hitler. In your dialogues with them there is always this third [party] present. Is this the France of tomorrow? How can one know where France truly is as long as she has not designated her leaders by a freely constituted assembly? In the meantime, however, is it not necessary that the French nation have proof that she has not deserted the camp of the Allies and that she is politically present, as she is, in spite of everything, and by us—militarily and politically?

I have been told that people in your entourage fear that in recognizing our existence you would compromise the possibility that certain elements, notably military, who depend at present on the Vichy Government, would soon reenter the war. But do you think that, in ignoring the French who are fighting, you will be able to draw the others into combat? Besides, the danger implied for France exists in the fact that the Allies would provoke divisions within it by favoring the formation of several rival groups, some neutralized with the agreement of the Allies themselves, others fighting in a dispersed manner for the same nation! Finally, have not two years of cruel experiences shown that each element that has separated from Vichy has been led either to join Fighting France or to play an individual role that is isolated and not important? The French people, in their terrible situation, naturally see things very simply. For them there is only the choice between fighting and capitulation. For them, combat is represented by Fighting France, and their instinct demands a concentration around those whom they see as the very symbol of their effort. Moreover, therein lies the fundamental reason why, despite the incredible difficulties in which Fighting France has been existing and struggling for more than two years, [it] has maintained and increased its cohesion.

In spite of the capitulation and the armistice, France retains in the world a power that is impossible to ignore. It is important to know how it will return to the fighting in the camp of the United Nations while safeguarding both its sensibility and its unity. Among the problems of the war, the latter is one of the most important. This is why I ask you to accept the idea of a general and direct examination of relations between the United States and Fighting France. Whatever the form of a general examination might be, I do not believe there is another way of approaching frankly a problem that I profoundly feel must be resolved, in the interest of the sacred cause for which we are fighting.

I ask you to accept, Mr. President, the assurances of my high esteem.

From the Ordinance on the Reestablishment of Republican Legality on Continental [French] Territory

August 9, 1944

In the midst of the Normandy campaign and shortly before the taking of Paris, de Gaulle's provisional government took up the problem of the restoration of "republican legality" in France. The ordinance of August 9, 1944, reaffirmed France's status as a Republic and declared null and void all constitutional laws of the Vichy regime as well as numerous other specific laws, including those discriminating against Jews. Other laws of the Vichy regime that were not specified in the ordinance were to remain in place.

The liberation of the continental territory should be [done] immediately, accompanied by the reestablishment of the republican legality that was in force before the installation of the regime imposed owing to the presence of the enemy. . . .

Article 1. The form of Government of France is and remains the Republic. In law, the latter has never ceased to exist.

Article 2. Consequently, the following are declared null and void: all the legislative or statutory constitutional laws, as well as the decrees issued for their execution . . . [that were] promulgated on the continental territory subsequent to June 16, 1940, and until the establishment of the Provisional Government of the French Republic.

Article 3. The nullity of the following laws is expressly determined:

The law called the "constitutional law of July 10, 1940."

All laws called "constitutional laws."

All laws that established special tribunals.

All laws that established forced labor on behalf of the enemy.

All laws relative to associations called secret.

All laws that establish or apply any discrimination whatsoever based on Jewishness. . . .

Léon Duguit, Henry Monnier, and Roger Bonnard, *Les constitutions et les principales lois politiques de la France depuis 1789* (Paris: Librairie générale de droit et de jurisprudence, 1952), 451, 453–54.

NOTES

[1] The article referred to specified that the president is elected by a majority of the Chamber of Deputies and the Senate.

[2] The abrogated article had to do with the obligatory timing and duration (five months per year) of the sessions of the two chambers.

[3] Jean Lacouture, *De Gaulle,* vol. 1, *Le rebelle* (Paris: Seuil, 1984), 546.

7

The Reordering of the French State

CHARLES DE GAULLE

From the Speech at Bayeux
June 16, 1946

On June 16, 1946, in Bayeux, Charles de Gaulle, out of power for six months, spelled out for his audience his program for constitutional change in France. In this speech are all the elements of the Gaullist constitutional program except one: election of a president by universal suffrage. De Gaulle explained later that he did not want to shock his audience by enunciating this proposal as well . . . a proposal that has had a controversial history in France, stemming from the fact that the first election of this kind brought Louis-Napoléon Bonaparte to power in 1848, and that four years later he then staged a coup. All the other elements of the Gaullist program appear: a strong executive with the right to dissolve Parliament and the right to invoke special emergency powers; a two-house legislature confined to legislative functions and separated from the executive, albeit with the right to a vote of no confidence in the government; and an independent judiciary.

It was here on the soil of the ancestors that the State reappeared;[1] the legitimate State because it rested on the interest and the sentiment of the nation; the State whose real sovereignty had become transported to the side of war, freedom, and victory, while servitude only retained the

Charles de Gaulle, *Discours et messages,* vol. 2, *Dans l'attente, Février 1946–Avril 1958* (Paris: Omnibus/Plon, 1970), 309–14.

appearances; the State safeguarded in its rights, its dignity, its authority, in the midst of the vicissitudes, of its being stripped bare, and of intrigues; the State preserved from foreign interference; the State capable of reestablishing around itself all the forces of the nation and the French Union, to achieve final victory in common with the Allies, of dealing on an equal basis with the other great nations of the world, of preserving public order, of making sure that justice is rendered, and of beginning our reconstruction.

If this great work was achieved outside the previous framework of our institutions, it was because they had not responded to national necessities and had themselves abdicated in the turmoil. Salvation had to come from elsewhere.

It came, first of all from an elite, spontaneously springing up from the depths of the nation and which, above all preoccupation with party or class, devoted itself to combat for the liberation, the grandeur, and the renovation of France. The psychology of this elite, which started from nothing and which, despite heavy losses, was to draw behind it all of the Empire and all of France, was comprised of a feeling of moral superiority; of an awareness of exercising a kind of priestly function based on sacrifice and example; of a passion for risk and enterprise; of a scorn for agitations, pretensions, and jockeying; of an unlimited confidence in the strength and the guile of its powerful conspiracy, as well as in the victory and the future of the nation.

It could not have succeeded, however, without the assent of the great masses of France. The latter, indeed, in their instinctive will to survive and to triumph, had never seen in the disaster of 1940 anything but an incident in a world war in which France served as an advanced outpost. If many gave way, by force, to the circumstances, the number of those who accepted them in their minds and hearts was literally infinitesimal. Never did France believe that the enemy was not the enemy, nor that salvation lay elsewhere than on the side of the arms of freedom. Gradually, as the veils were lifted, the deep feelings of the country appeared in their reality. Everywhere that the Cross of Lorraine appeared there crumbled the structure of an authority that was only fictitious, although in appearance it was constitutionally based. . . .

. . . Once the salvation of the State was assured . . . the task above all that was most urgent and essential was the establishment of new French institutions. As soon as it was possible, therefore, the French people were invited to elect their constituents, at the same time limiting their mandates and reserving for themselves the definitive decision. . . .

However, the nation and the French Union are still waiting for a

Constitution. . . . Although it is regrettable that the edifice remains to be built, everyone can agree that a success that has been somewhat postponed is worth more than a rapid but unfortunate outcome.

During a period no longer than two generations, France was invaded seven times and went through thirteen regimes. Indeed the misfortunes of a people tell everything. From these numerous disturbances in our public life have accumulated the poisons fed by our ancient Gallic propensity for divisions and quarrels. The incredible trials that we have just experienced have naturally aggravated this propensity. The present world situation, in which the Powers between whom we are placed confront each other behind opposing ideologies, adds a disturbingly passionate factor to our political struggles. In brief, the rivalry of the parties in our country is of a fundamental nature that calls into question, and too often pushes into the background, the higher interests of the country. That is a patent fact, which has to do with the national temperament, the accidents of History, and the disturbances of the present; but it is indispensable for the future of the country and of democracy that our institutions take this tendency into account and beware, so that the credibility of the laws, the cohesion of government, the efficiency of the administration, and the prestige and authority of the State can be preserved.

In effect, trouble in the State has an ineluctable consequence: the disaffection of the citizens toward institutions. It just takes one event, then, for the threat of dictatorship to appear. All the more so because the mechanical organization of modern society daily makes a sense of order more necessary and more desired with regard to the direction and the functioning of the [state] apparatus. How, and why, did the First, Second, and Third Republics come to an end? How, and why, did the Italian democracy, the German Weimar Republic, and the Spanish Republic give way to the regimes that followed? And yet, what is dictatorship, if not a great adventure? Its beginnings no doubt seem advantageous. In the midst of the enthusiasm of one side and the resignation of the other, in the rigorous order that it imposes—replete with stunning decor and one-sided propaganda—at the outset it takes a dynamic direction that sharply contrasts with the anarchy that preceded it. But it is the fate of dictatorship to exaggerate what it undertakes. As the citizens become impatient with its constraints and nostalgic for their lost freedom, the dictatorship must, whatever the cost, be able to compensate with broader and broader accomplishments. The nation becomes a machine on which the master imposes a regime of unchecked acceleration. In the end something has to give way. The grandiose edifice collapses in blood and misfortune. The nation is left broken and worse off than when the adventure began.

It suffices to evoke this in order to understand to what extent it is necessary that our new democratic institutions compensate by themselves the effects of our perpetual political tumult. . . . Certainly, it is the very essence of democracy that public opinion is expressed and that it attempts, through the ballot, to orient public action according to its thinking. But also all principles and experiences demand that the powers of government— legislative, executive, and judicial—be clearly separated and well balanced and that above the political contingencies there be established a means of national arbitration that stands for the values of continuity in the midst of [political] combinations.

It is clear and understood that the definitive vote on laws and budgets is cast by an Assembly elected by direct and universal suffrage. But the first move of such an Assembly is not made with complete clairvoyance and clarity. It is therefore necessary to delegate to a second Assembly, which is elected and composed in another way, the role of publicly examining what the first Assembly has considered, of formulating amendments, and of proposing bills. If the mainstream of the nation's politics is naturally represented within the Chamber of Deputies, individual localities have their own inclinations and their own rights—in the Métropole and, first and foremost, in the overseas territories, which are attached to the French Union by very diverse links. . . . The future of 100 million men and women who live under our flag is in a federated type of organization. . . .

Everything, then, leads us to create a second Chamber whose members basically would be elected by our general and municipal councils. . . . It will be a matter of normal practice to include representatives from economic, familial, and intellectual organizations in order to make the voice of the major activities of the country heard within the State itself. Together with the local assemblies of the overseas territories, the members of this Assembly will form the Grand Council of the French Union. . . .

It is quite evident that executive power cannot stem from the Parliament, which is composed of the two Chambers, and which exercises legislative power, without ending in a confusion of powers in which the Government would soon be nothing more than an assemblage of delegations. Of course it was necessary, during the present transitional period, to have the National Constituent Assembly elect the President of the Transitional Government, because, given the tabula rasa, there was no other acceptable way of designating [him]. . . . [But] how can unity, cohesion, and discipline be maintained over the long term if the source of executive power is within the Parliament, which it is supposed to balance, and if each of the members of the Government—which is collectively

responsible to the whole national electorate—is no more than a party representative? Executive power must therefore proceed from a Head of State who is situated above the parties, who is elected by a college that encompasses Parliament but is also much broader than it and composed in such a way as to make him the President of the French Union as well as of the Republic. It is the task of the Head of State to reconcile the general interest, where appointments are concerned, with the [political] perspective that emerges from the Parliament. It will be his job to appoint ministers and, of course, the Prime Minister, who has to direct the policy and the work of the Government. It is the job of the Head of State to promulgate laws and issue decrees. . . . He presides over the Councils of the Government and exercises therein an influence of continuity that the nation cannot do without. He serves as an arbiter above political contingencies, either normally through the Council or, in moments of serious confusion, in inviting the country to make its sovereign decision known through elections. It is also his duty, if the nation is in danger, to guarantee national independence as well as the treaties concluded by France.
. . . Let us take ourselves as we are. Let us take the century as it is. . . . Let us be lucid enough and strong enough to give ourselves . . . that which will bring us together when, constantly, we tend to be divided against ourselves! All our History is an alternation between the immense pain of a dispersed people and the fertile grandeurs of a free nation grouped under the aegis of a strong State.

CHARLES DE GAULLE

From the Statement against Osservatore Romano

1951

When in 1951, the Vatican newspaper Osservatore Romano *came out prior to the elections with an article favoring the Christian Democratic party in France (the Mouvement Républicain Populaire), General de Gaulle issued a scathing statement in a press conference, which included the following excerpt.*

Charles de Gaulle, *Discours et messages*, vol. 2, *Dans l'attente, Février 1946–Avril 1958* (Paris: Plon, 1970), 447–48.

If it [the Vatican's endorsement of the Christian Democratic party] is a matter of faith and dogma, there wouldn't be any question. I am as Catholic as M. Alessandrini, who wrote this article. I am presuming that he is as Catholic as I am. If it is a matter of politics in general, M. Alessandrini has the perfect right . . . to have the opinions he desires, just as I have the right to have mine. . . . I have often been in agreement with *Osservatore Romano,* but not always, particularly during the recent war.

If it is a question of French politics, M. Alessandrini is not French. It seems to me, who is, that he ought to consider that fact when he deals with French affairs. But I particularly regret that this article has created an equivocal situation whereby people who are not well informed have been unduly led to believe that the religious hierarchy was intervening in the French electoral campaign. Yes, I find that deplorable, and all the more so in that the great respect I have for the hierarchy gives me the assurance that it is false.

CHARLES DE GAULLE

Speech to the National Assembly

June 1, 1958

On June 1, 1958, as France faced a possible civil war over Algeria, de Gaulle told the French National Assembly the conditions under which he would return to power: the right to draft a new constitution that would be submitted to the people for approval in a referendum and power to govern without the Parliament for a period of six months. He was approved by a vote of 329–224.

The rapidly accelerating degradation of the State, the immediate danger to French unity, Algeria in the throes of trials and emotions, Corsica suffering from a feverish contagion, opposing movements in Metropolitan France hourly whipping up their passions and, reinforcing their action, the Army, long tried by sanguinary and praiseworthy tasks but shocked by the lack of any real authority, our international position disparaged even within our

Major Addresses, Statements, and Press Conferences of General Charles de Gaulle, May 19, 1958–January 31, 1964 (New York: French Embassy Press and Information Bureau, 1964), 7–8.

alliances—such is the situation of our country. At this very moment, when so many opportunities, in so many directions, are offered to France, she finds herself threatened by disruption and perhaps even civil war.

It is in these circumstances that I offered my services to try, once again, to lead the country, the State, and the Republic to safety; and that, designated by the Chief of State, I have been led to ask the National Assembly to invest me with a heavy task.

In order to perform this task, means are necessary.

If you invest this Government, it will propose that you give it these means right away. It will ask you for full powers in order to be in a position to act with all the effectiveness, speed, and responsibility demanded by the circumstances. It will ask you for these powers for a period of six months, hoping that at the end of this time—order having been re-established in the State, hope regained in Algeria, unity restored in the nation—it will be possible for the public powers to resume their normal course.

But what good would be a temporary remedy, a remedy of sorts, for a disastrous state of affairs unless we decided to eradicate the deep-seated cause of our troubles? This cause—the Assembly knows and the nation is convinced of it—is the confusion and, by the same token, the helplessness of constituted authority.

The Government which I shall form, provided I obtain your vote of confidence, will submit to you without delay a bill reforming Article 90 of the Constitution, thus enabling the National Assembly to give a mandate to the Government to formulate and then propose to the country, through a referendum, the indispensable changes. In the explanatory statement which will be submitted to you at the same time as the text, the Government will specify the three principles which must be the basis of the republican regime in France and to which it pledges that its bill will conform: universal suffrage is the source of all power; the executive and the legislative branches must be separate and apart so that the Government and the Parliament can, each for its own part and on its own responsibility, assume its full powers; the Government must be responsible to the Parliament.

Through the same constitutional reform, the country will be given a formal opportunity to organize the relations between the French Republic and the peoples associated with it. The Government will pledge itself to promote this new organization in the draft which it will put to the vote of the women and men of France.

Having received this double mandate, conferred on it by the National Assembly, the Government will be able to undertake the immense task which will have thus been defined. If I am to assume this double mandate,

I shall first and foremost need your confidence. Then the Parliament must without delay—for events do not permit of any delay—enact into law the bills which will be submitted to it. These laws once passed, the Assemblies will adjourn until the date set for the opening of their next regular session. Thus the Government of the Republic, having been invested by the elected representatives of the nation and given, with extreme urgency, the means for action, can then be responsible for the unity, integrity, and independence of France.

Constitutional Law
June 3, 1958

In a constitutional law passed by the National Assembly on June 3, 1958, the government formed by Charles de Gaulle was given the power to draft a new constitution and submit it to a referendum by the people.

SOLE ARTICLE. By derogation of the provisions of its article 90, the constitution will be revised by the government invested on June 1, 1958, and this [will be] in the following forms:

The government of the Republic establishes a draft constitutional law, putting into effect the following principles:

1. Only universal suffrage is the source of power. It is by universal suffrage or by its elected authorities that legislative power and executive power are derived.

2. Executive power and legislative power must be effectively separated so that the government and the parliament assume, each one for its part and under its responsibility, their full attributions.

3. The government must be responsible before the parliament.

4. The judicial authority must remain independent to be in a position to ensure the respect of essential liberties such as they are defined by the preamble of the Constitution of 1946 and by the Declaration of the Rights of Man [of 1789] to which it refers.

5. The constitution must permit the organization of the relationship of the Republic with the peoples that are associated with it.

Jean Chatelain, *La nouvelle constitution et le régime politique de la France* (Paris: Editions Berger-Levrault, 1959), 349.

To establish this draft, the government receives the advice of a consultative committee, on which will sit in particular members of parliament designated by the competent commissions of the National Assembly and the Council of the Republic. The number of members of the consultative committee designated by each of the commissions is at least equal to a third of the number of the members of these commissions; the total number of members of the consultative committee designated by the commissions is equal to two-thirds of the members of the committee.

The draft law established by the council of ministers, after the opinion of the Council of State, is submitted to a referendum. The constitutional law embodying a revision of the constitution is promulgated by the president of the Republic within eight days of its adoption.

CHARLES DE GAULLE

Memorandum on the Directory

September 17, 1958

On September 17, 1958, President de Gaulle addressed a memorandum to President Eisenhower and Prime Minister Macmillan, proposing a tripartite governance in strategic matters by the United States, Great Britain, and France. In what came to be known as the "Memorandum on the Directory" by its reference to this three-way entity, de Gaulle stressed that nuclear strategy should also be included as a matter for discussion, and he signaled his dissatisfaction with the way NATO was being run—that is, without sufficient consultation by the United States with its principal allies. Finally, he held out the threat of an eventual French withdrawal from NATO.

Dear Mr. President,

When I had the pleasure of meeting with Mr. John Foster Dulles in July, I acquainted him with my views on the subject of the reorganization of the defense of the Free World. The events which have taken place since then

Letter from Charles de Gaulle to Dwight D. Eisenhower (known as the "Memorandum on the Directory"), September 17, 1958. *Documents of Dwight D. Eisenhower* (Ann Whitman File), International Series, Box 13, Folder 1, De Gaulle: June 1958–October 30, 1959 (Dwight D. Eisenhower Presidential Library, DDEL).

have reinforced the conviction of the French Government in this regard. It is this which has determined it to make certain propositions to the American and British Governments.

Because of the importance of this problem, I have charged Mr. Hervé Alphand with bringing it personally to your attention on my behalf. I would hope that the attached memorandum, which I am also sending to Mr. Macmillan, can, without delay, be the subject of an in-depth discussion among the three governments.

I am aware of how much the situation in the Far East can cause you concern, and I am keen to assure you, on this occasion, of my sincere and reliable friendship. I can only hope more fervently that we can work together in better conditions so that our alliance can become more coherent and more efficient. It is in this spirit that I am acquainting you with the conclusions to which I have come and on which I will be happy to know your personal views.

Please accept, dear Mr. President, my faithful sentiments and my very high consideration.

Memorandum

The recent events in the Middle East and in the Formosa Straits have served to demonstrate that the present organization of the Western alliance no longer responds to the necessary conditions of security, as regards the Free World in its entirety. The solidarity in the risks encountered does not correspond to an indispensable cooperation concerning the decisions taken and the responsibilities. The French Government is led to draw conclusions from this and to make certain propositions.

1. The Atlantic alliance was conceived and its implementation was prepared with a view of a zone of possible action which no longer responds to political and strategic realities. The world being what it is, one can no longer consider as adapted to its objective an organization such as NATO, which is limited to the security of the North Atlantic, as if that which takes place, for example, in the Middle East and in Africa, would not immediately and directly interest Europe, and as if the indivisible responsibilities of France did not extend to Africa, the Indian Ocean, and the Pacific, by the same token as those of the United States and Great Britain. Moreover, the radius of action of ships and aircraft, and the range of weapons, renders militarily obsolete that narrow a system. It is true that in the beginning it was admitted that atomic weapons, obviously capital, would for a long time remain the monopoly of the United States, which could

appear to justify that at a world-wide level, decisions concerning defense were in practice delegated to the Government of Washington. But on this point as well, it must be admitted that such a fact, which was admitted at the beginning, is in reality no longer valid.

2. France cannot consider that NATO, under its present form, satisfies the security requirements of the Free World and, particularly, her own. It seems to her necessary that at a world-wide political and strategic level, there should be instituted an organization comprising the United States, Great Britain, and France. This organization would, on the one hand, take common decisions on political questions dealing with world security, and on the other hand, establish and, as the case required, apply strategic action plans, particularly as regards the use of nuclear weapons. It would then be feasible to foresee and organize possible theaters of operations subordinated to the overall organization (such as the Arctic, the Atlantic, the Pacific, [and] the Indian Ocean), which could, if needed, be divided into subtheaters.

3. The French Government considers such an organization of security as indispensable. From now on it subordinates to it all development of its current participation in NATO and proposes, if it appears necessary to arrive at it, to invoke the procedure of the revision of the North Atlantic Treaty in conformity with Article 12.

4. The French Government suggests that the questions raised in this note be as soon as possible the subject of consultations between the United States, Great Britain, and France. It proposes that these consultations take place in Washington, and to begin with, through the Ambassadors and the Standing Group [of NATO].

CHARLES DE GAULLE

From a Speech to the French Military Schools
November 3, 1959

In a speech before the classes of the French military schools, de Gaulle paid tribute to the central role of the military in French history and announced plans for a nuclear strike force (force de frappe).

Charles de Gaulle, *Discours et messages*, vol. 3, *Avec le renouveau, Mai 1958–Juillet 1962* (Paris: Plon, 1970), 126–27.

The defense of France must be French. This is a necessity that was not always recognized over the course of the last several years. . . . . if over the long run it were accepted that the defense of France ceased to exist in a national framework, or was confounded, or melded, with something else, it would not be possible for us to maintain a State. The Government's raison d'être has always been the defense of the independence and integrity of the territory. In France in particular, all our regimes have been based on that. . . . If, therefore, a government lost its essential responsibility, it would lose by the same token its justification.

. . . It is clearly necessary that we be able to acquire, over the course of the coming years, a force capable of acting on our behalf, what can be called a strike force *(force de frappe)*. . . . at the base of this force would be atomic weapons. . . . the force would be [so] fashioned as to strike anywhere on earth.

CHARLES DE GAULLE

From a Memorandum on the EEC and NATO

July 30, 1960

On July 30, 1960, Charles de Gaulle, at the presidential château at Rambouillet, wrote a memorandum concerning his plan to undercut both the EEC and NATO.

"Europe" cannot at present exist except through an organized cooperation of States. Everything dictates that this should come about through an accord between France and Germany, to which would then adhere Italy, Holland, Belgium, and Luxembourg, in a first phase.

To adopt this conception would be to admit that the "supranational" organisms, which were constituted among the Six and which tend, inevitably and abusively, to become irresponsible superstates, would be reformed, subordinated to the governments, and utilized for the normal tasks of the [European] Council and for technical [matters].

Charles de Gaulle, *Lettres, notes, et carnets,* vol. 8 (Paris: Plon, 1985), 382. The European Council is made up of the chiefs of state (or government) of the EEC (now called the European Union [EU] since the Treaty of Maastricht was signed in February 1992).

To adopt this conception is also to put an end to American "integration," which the Atlantic Alliance presently represents and which contradicts the existence of a Europe having, from the international point of view, its own personality and responsibility.

CHARLES DE GAULLE

Speech Denouncing the Algiers Putsch
April 23, 1961

On April 23, 1961, President de Gaulle, in a speech to the nation, denounced a putsch two days earlier by leading French military figures in Algeria. The "pronunciamento" issued by a "quartet of retired generals," as de Gaulle put it, was the culmination of a larval revolt by the professional army in Algeria, growing out of dissatisfaction with de Gaulle's Algerian policy aimed at ending the rule of one million Europeans over nine million Muslims in Algeria. De Gaulle, who made the speech in military uniform, was able in his appeal for unity to gain sway especially over the conscript element in the French army in Algeria, and the revolt was crushed in four days' time.

An insurrectional power has set itself up in Algeria by a military pronunciamento. Those guilty of this usurpation have exploited the passion of officers of certain units, the inflamed support of one part of the population of European origin, misguided by fears and myths, the impotence of authorities overwhelmed by the military conspiracy.

This power has an appearance: a quartet of retired generals. It has a reality: a group of partisan, ambitious, and fanatical officers. This group and this quartet possess a limited and expeditious ability, but they see and know the nation and the world only as deformed by their fanaticism.

Their venture cannot but lead to a national disaster. For the immense effort of recovery in France — begun at the depths of the abyss on June 18, 1940; continued later despite everything until victory was gained, inde-

Major Addresses, Statements, and Press Conferences of General Charles de Gaulle, May 19, 1958–January 31, 1964 (New York: French Embassy Press and Information Bureau, 1964), 127–28.

pendence assured, the Republic restored; resumed three years ago in order to remake the State, maintain the national unity, rebuild our power, restore our position in the world, pursue our task overseas through a necessary decolonization—all these risks being made useless, on the very eve of success, by the odious and stupid adventure in Algeria.

Now the State is flouted, the nation defied, our power degraded, our international prestige lowered, our role and our place in Africa jeopardized. And by whom? Alas! Alas! By men whose duty, honor, and reason for being was to serve and obey.

In the name of France, I order that all means—I say all means—be employed everywhere to bar the route to these men, until they are subjugated. I forbid any Frenchmen, and first of all any soldier, to execute any of their orders. The argument that it might be locally necessary to accept their command under the pretext of operational or administrative obligations can fool no one.

The civil and military leaders who have the right to assume responsibilities are those who have been legally named and precisely those the insurgents prevent from doing so.

The future for the usurpers should only be that provided them by the rigors of the law.

In the face of the misfortune that looms over the country and of the threat that hangs over the Republic, I have decided, having formally consulted the Constitutional Council, the Premier, the President of the Senate, the President of the National Assembly, to put into force Article 16 of our Constitution. As of today, I will take, if necessary directly, the measures that appear to me to be required by the circumstances.

In this way, I confirm myself in the French and republican legality which was conferred upon me by the nation and which I will maintain no matter what happens until the end of my term, or until I lack either force or life; and I will take measures to make sure that this legality remains after me.

Frenchwomen, Frenchmen, see where France risks going, compared with what she was becoming.

Frenchwomen, Frenchmen, help me.

CHARLES DE GAULLE

From a Press Conference—
Excerpt on the Fouchet Plan

May 15, 1962

On May 15, 1962, President de Gaulle presented his view on the Fouchet Plan, named after his minister of education, Christian Fouchet. The plan was essentially an attempt to impose over the "communitarian" institutions of the European Coal and Steel Community (1952), Euratom, and the European Economic Community (1957) an intergovernmental political directory of the Six (France, Germany, Italy, and the Benelux countries). The plan failed to gain acceptance, partly because the others feared a French-German domination, and partly because they were reluctant, considering that Great Britain, whose application for membership in the EEC was pending, would eventually want to be consulted on the matter.

In the French view, this economic construction [of Europe] is not enough. Western Europe—whether it be a matter of its actions vis-à-vis other people, of its own defense, of its contribution to the development of regions that are in need of it, or of its duty to European balance and international détente—Western Europe must form itself politically. Moreover, if it did not succeed in doing so, the European Community itself could not in the long run become stronger or even continue to exist. In other words, Europe must have institutions that will lead it to form a political union, just as it is already a union in the economic sphere.

Thus France took the initiative of proposing such an organization and, as you know, last year in April the six Heads of State or of Government met in Paris to discuss France's project. They did so again in Bonn in July. Then a Political Commission was formed in Paris—the Fouchet Commission—which was given the task of drawing up the final text for a treaty of union. . . . Finally it was agreed that there would be a summit meeting of the Six in Rome in order to conclude matters, should this be possible. You know the reasons why we have not yet succeeded.

What is it that France is proposing to her five partners? I shall repeat it

Major Addresses, Statements, and Press Conferences of General Charles de Gaulle, May 19, 1958–January 31, 1964 (New York: French Embassy Press and Information Bureau, 1964), 174–76.

once again: To organize ourselves politically, let us begin at the beginning. Let us organize our cooperation, let our Heads of State or of Government meet periodically to examine our problems together and to make decisions with regard to these problems which will be the decisions of Europe. Let us set up a political commission, a defense commission, and a cultural commission, just as we have already formed an economic commission in Brussels which studies common questions and prepares the decisions of the six Governments. Naturally, the political commission and the others will proceed, in this regard, in conditions that are appropriate to their particular domains. Moreover, the Ministers in charge of these various fields will meet whenever necessary to implement in concert the decisions that will be taken by the [European] Council. Finally, we have a European parliamentary assembly that meets in Strasbourg and is composed of delegations from our six national Parliaments. Let us enable this assembly to discuss common political questions as it already discusses economic questions. After we have tried it, we shall see, in three years' time, what we can do to strengthen our ties. . . .

I would like, incidentally, since the opportunity has arisen, to point out to you, gentlemen of the press—and you are perhaps going to be very surprised by this—that I have never personally, in any of my statements, spoken of a "Europe of Nations," although it is always being claimed that I have done so. . . .

But it is true that the nation is a human and sentimental element, whereas Europe can be built on the basis of active, authoritative, and responsible elements. What elements? The State, of course; for in this respect, it is only the States that are valid, legitimate, and capable of achievement. I have already said, and I repeat, that at the present time there cannot be any other Europe than a Europe of States, apart, of course, from myths, stories, and parades. What is happening with regard to the [European] Economic Community proves this every day, for it is the States, and only the States, that created this Economic Community . . . and it is the States that give it reality and efficiency.

NOTE

[1] This is a reference to de Gaulle's visit to Bayeux on June 14, 1944—the first time he had been to France since June 1940.

8

The Traditional European Concert

CHARLES DE GAULLE

*From a Press Conference—Excerpts on
Britain's Common Market Application
and the Nassau Agreement*

January 14, 1963

*In a press conference on January 14, 1963, a month after the Nassau
Agreement whereby the United States would supply Polaris missiles to Britain, President de Gaulle refused a similar offer for France, which was
without real meaning, and at the same time vetoed Britain's application for
membership in the European Economic Community. The Polaris agreement
was presented by de Gaulle as the symbol of Britain's infidelity to the creation
of a European identity separate from the United States. And the Polaris
agreement, part of a larger proposal known as the Multilateral Force (MLF),
provided the occasion for de Gaulle to explain why the MLF proposal was not
to the liking of France, which would continue to pursue its own independent
nuclear deterrent.*

Great Britain and the EEC

Then Great Britain applied for membership in the Common Market. It did
so after refusing earlier to participate in the community that was being
built, and after then having created a free trade area with six other States,

*Major Addresses, Statements, and Press Conferences of General Charles de Gaulle, May 19,
1958–January 31, 1964* (New York: French Embassy Press and Information Bureau, 1964),
213–19.

and finally . . . after having put some pressure on the Six in order to prevent the application of the Common Market from really getting started. Britain thus in turn requested membership, but on its own conditions. This undoubtedly raises for each of the six States and for England problems of a very great dimension.

England is, in effect, insular, maritime, linked through its trade, markets, and food supply to very diverse and often very distant countries. Its activities are essentially industrial and commercial, and only slightly agricultural. It has . . . very marked and original customs and traditions. In short, the nature, structure, and economic context of England differ profoundly from those of the other States of the Continent. . . .

One was sometimes led to believe that our British friends, in applying for membership in the Common Market, agreed to change their own ways even to the point of applying all the conditions accepted and practiced by the Six, but the question is to know if Great Britain can at present place itself, with the Continent and like it, within a tariff that is truly common, give up all preference with regard to the Commonwealth, cease to claim that its agriculture be privileged, and even more, consider as null and void the commitments it has made with the countries that are part of its free trade area. That question is the one at issue.

One cannot say that it has now been resolved. Will it be so one day? Obviously, only Britain can answer that.

The question is raised all the more since, following Britain, other States which are, I repeat, linked to it in the Free Trade Area, for the same reasons as Great Britain, would or will want to enter the Common Market.

It must be agreed that the entry first of Great Britain and then of those other States will completely change the series of adjustments, agreements, compensations, and regulations already established between the Six, because all these States, like Britain, have very important traits of their own. We would then have to envisage the construction of another Common Market. But the 11-member, then 13-member, and then perhaps 18-member Common Market that would be built would, without any doubt, hardly resemble the one the Six have built.

Moreover, this Community, growing in that way, would be confronted with all the problems of its economic relations with a crowd of other States, and first of all with the United States.

It is foreseeable that the cohesion of all its members, who would be very numerous and very diverse, would not hold for long and that in the end there would appear a colossal Atlantic Community under American dependence and leadership which would soon completely swallow up the European Community.

This is an assumption that can be perfectly justified in the eyes of some, but it is not at all what France wanted to do and what France is doing, which is a strictly European construction.

Then, it is possible that Britain would one day come round to transforming itself enough to belong to the European Community without restriction and without reservation, and placing it ahead of everything else, and in that case the Six would open the door to it and France would place no obstacle in its path. . . .

The Nassau Agreement

Principles and realities combine to lead France to equip herself with an atomic force of her own. This does not exclude, of course, the combination of the action of this force with the action of the similar forces of its allies. But, for us, in this specific case, integration is something that is unimaginable. Indeed, as you know, we have begun with our own and only means to invent, test, and construct atomic bombs and the vehicles for launching them.

. . . Then, in the Bahamas, America and Britain concluded an agreement and we were asked to subscribe to it ourselves. . . . It is a question of constituting a so-called multilateral atomic force, in which Britain would turn over the weapons it has and will have and in which the Americans would place a few of their own. This multilateral force is assigned to the defense of Europe and is under the American NATO command. It is nevertheless understood that the British retain the possibility of withdrawing their atomic weapons for their own use should supreme national interest seem to them to demand it.

. . . Britain may purchase from America, if it so desires, Polaris missiles, which are, as you know, launched from submarines specially built for that purpose and which carry the thermonuclear warheads adapted to them. . . . To build these submarines, the British receive privileged assistance from the Americans. . . . This assistance was never offered to us and . . . despite what some report . . . we have never asked for it.

France has taken note of the Anglo-American Nassau agreement. As it was conceived, no one will be surprised that we cannot subscribe to it. It truly would not be useful for us to buy Polaris missiles when we have neither the submarines to launch them nor the thermonuclear warheads to arm them. . . .

But also, it does not meet with the principle about which I just spoke and which consists of disposing in our own right of our deterrent force. To turn over our weapons to a multilateral force, under a foreign command, would be to act contrary to that principle of our defense and our policy. It is true that we too can theoretically retain the ability to take back in our hands, in the supreme hypothesis, our atomic weapons incorporated in the multilateral force. But how could we do it in practice in the unheard-of moments of the atomic apocalypse. . . .

In sum, we will adhere to the decision we have made: to construct and, if necessary, to employ our atomic force ourselves.

From the French-German Treaty
January 22, 1963

On January 22, 1963, eight days after rejecting Britain's application for membership in the EEC, de Gaulle signed a treaty of friendship and cooperation with Konrad Adenauer, thus fulfilling the Gaullist dictum that ruse should be among the properties of a chief of state. Called the Elysée Treaty, because it was signed by the two leaders at the Elysée Palace of the French president, the initiative represented a reaction to the failed Fouchet Plan. It essentially sought, through the medium of a French-German alliance, to create the core of a European intergovernmental political directory.

Common Declaration

General Charles de Gaulle, President of the French Republic, and Dr. Konrad Adenauer, Chancellor of the Federal Republic of Germany,

At the close of the conference which was held in Paris on January 21 and 22, 1963, and which was attended, on the French side, by the Premier, the Minister of Foreign Affairs, the Minister of the Armed Forces, and the Minister of National Education and, on the German side, by the Minister of Foreign Affairs, the Minister of Defense, and the Minister of Family and Youth Affairs,

Convinced that the reconciliation of the German people and the French people, bringing an end to the age-old rivalries, constitutes a historic event which profoundly transforms the relations of the two peoples,

Reprinted from an unofficial translation issued by the Press and Information Service, French Embassy, New York, N.Y.

Conscious of the solidarity which unites the two peoples both with respect to their security and with respect to their economic and cultural development,

Observing particularly that young people have become aware of this solidarity and find themselves called upon to play the determinant role in the consolidation of French-German friendship,

Recognizing that a strengthening of the cooperation between the two countries constitutes a vital stage along the road to a united Europe, which is the goal of the two peoples,

Have agreed to the organization and to the principles of the cooperation between the two States as they are stated in the Treaty signed this day.

Done at Paris, on the twenty-second day of January in the year one thousand nine hundred and sixty-three, in both the French and German languages.

The President of   *The Federal Chancellor of*
the French Republic: *the Federal Republic of Germany:*
Charles de Gaulle   Konrad Adenauer

Bundestag Preamble
to the French-German Treaty
April 1963

The April 1963 preamble to the Elysée Treaty placed by the German Bundestag in effect undermined the French-German exclusiveness embodied in the treaty. It did so by invoking a whole range of agreements that would have to remain unaffected by the treaty, including NATO and GATT.

Convinced that the treaty concluded on 22 January 1963 between the Federal Republic of Germany and the French Republic will intensify and

Reproduced from a translation that appeared in *The Bulletin* of May 21, 1963, issued by the Press and Information Office of the German Federal Government. The German act containing this preamble ratifying the French-German treaty of cooperation, signed at Paris, January 22, 1963, was approved by the Bundestag on May 16 and by the Bundesrat on May 31, 1963.

The French National Assembly approved the treaty on June 14, 1963, and the Senate approved the treaty on June 21.

develop the reconciliation and friendship between the German and the French peoples,

Stating that this treaty does not affect the rights and obligations resulting from multilateral treaties concluded by the Federal Republic of Germany,

Resolved to serve by the application of this treaty the great aims to which the Federal Republic of Germany, in concert with the other States allied to her, has aspired for years, and which determine her policy,

To wit, the preservation and consolidation of the unity of the free nations and in particular of a close partnership between Europe and the United States of America, the realization of the right of self-determination for the German people, and the restoration of German unity,

collective defense within the framework of the North Atlantic Alliance, and the integration of the armed forces of the States bound together in that Alliance,

the unification of Europe by following the course adopted by the establishment of the European Communities, with the inclusion of Great Britain and other States wishing to accede, and the further strengthening of those Communities,

the elimination of trade barriers by negotiations between the European Economic Community, Great Britain, and the United States of America as well as other States within the framework of the General Agreement on Tariffs and Trade,

Conscious that a Franco-German cooperation inspired by such aims will benefit all nations and serve the peace of the world and will thereby also promote the welfare of the German and French peoples,

the Bundestag enacts the following Law.

CHARLES DE GAULLE

From a Press Conference—Excerpts on U.S. Relations and Nuclear Testing

July 29, 1963

In a press conference on July 29, 1963, President de Gaulle placed France's relations with the United States in a historical perspective. De Gaulle in effect turned upside down charges of Gaullist ingratitude toward the United States. In de Gaulle's perspective, laced with irony, the United States had not always stood with France. The alliance at the time of the American Revolution had not been renewed until the United States entered World War I tardily in 1917 and World War II, again tardily, in 1941. However, the many differences in postwar French-American relations were only "scratches," not deep wounds: France—apart from Russia—was the only major power with whom the United States had not exchanged a cannon shot.

In the same press conference, de Gaulle gave his rationale for France's pursuing its own national nuclear deterrent, without which France's "own security and her own independence will never belong to her."

Relations with the United States

There has been much agitation, particularly in the American press; over the past several months. I will say to you that the experience I have had personally over the past 25 years with public reactions in the United States has made me less than surprised with the outbursts that pass for opinion. . . .

Some of you will remember. It was the case, for example, in the heroic period, when I was led to occupy the islands of St. Pierre and Miquelon, or when the Government of Liberation was formed in North Africa, or when it happened that I disapproved of Yalta and declined to go to Algiers to meet with Roosevelt after that detestable conference, or also after the Victory, on the occasion of the maintenance of our troops at Stuttgart until a zone of occupation in Germany was recognized for France. It was the case later concerning the famous plan for a "European Defense Commu-

Charles de Gaulle, *Discours et messages*, vol. 4, *Pour l'effort, Août 1962–Décembre 1965* (Paris: Plon, 1970), 119–23.

nity," which consisted of depriving our country not of its defense expenditures but in fact of its army and which, from the depths of my retirement, I categorically opposed. It is the case today with subjects which, by the way, are very important, such as the organization of Europe, the creation of a French atomic force, the French-German treaty, etc. But it seems to me useful to emphasize right away that all this agitation of the press, of the political milieux, and of more or less unofficial organizations which holds sway on the other side of the Atlantic, and which naturally finds a rapid echo among different kinds of oppositionists [in France]—all this agitation . . . cannot alter in France that which is fundamental with respect to America. For us the fundamental bases of French-American relations are friendship and alliance.

Friendship! Here it is almost two hundred years that it exists as an eminent psychological reality responding to the nature of the two countries, developed by all sorts of tendencies, of influences, of relations, of specific and reciprocal links, maintained by the fact that, of all the powers of the world, France is the only one—outside of Russia, I must say—with whom the United States has never exchanged a cannon shot, while at the same time she is the only one who fought alongside [the United States] in three wars: the [Revolutionary] War, and the First and Second World Wars—in conditions that are forever unforgettable.

For such a moral capital to wear down, it would require dissensions infinitely serious and infinitely long. . . . As for the French-American alliance, if, from the time of Washington, Franklin, Lafayette, de Grasse, [and] Rochambeau, it was not renewed until during the First World War in 1917 and 1918, and during the Second World War, from December 1941 onwards, it is a fact that it exists now and that it is incumbent upon the two countries to maintain it. As long as, in effect, the Free World is facing a Soviet Bloc which is capable of overwhelming any country, and which is driven by a dominating and detestable ideology, it is necessary that people on both sides of the Ocean who want to defend themselves are linked together to do so.

. . . The United States . . . possesses nuclear weapons without which the fate of the world would be rapidly settled, and France . . . whatever the current inferiority of its means . . . is politically, geographically, morally, [and] militarily essential to the coalition.

If then . . . there are divergences between Washington and Paris on the functioning and organization of the alliance, the latter itself—that is, the fact is that in case of general war, France, with the means that she has, would be on the side of the United States, which would be, I believe, reciprocal—is unquestioned, except in the wild imaginings of those who make a profession of alarming people in depicting each cut as an incurable wound. . . . But both sides should adapt to the new situation.

In my opinion, the differences of today stem quite simply from the intrinsic changes which have taken place, and are continuing [to do so], in the absolute and relative situation of America and France. . . . The situation in France has profoundly changed. Her new institutions have put her in a position to will and to act. Her internal development has brought her prosperity and has caused her to acquire the means of power. . . . How would the modalities of the relations with the United States not be modified? All the more so in that the United States sees, in view of its problems, great changes which have taken place in the type of hegemonic solidarity which has characterized its relations with France since World War II.

From the political point of view, it is true that the Soviet Bloc retains a totalitarian and threatening ideology, and that even recently . . . the scandal of the Berlin Wall, and the installation of nuclear weapons in Cuba, have shown that, by this fact, peace remains precarious. Meantime, the human evolution in Russia and the satellites, the important economic and social difficulties in the life of these countries, and especially the beginnings of an opposition which is becoming manifest between, on the one hand, a European empire possessing immense Asiatic territories, and which have made it the greatest colonial power of our time, and, on the other, the Empire of China, its neighbor along a distance of 10,000 kilometers, with a population of 700 million, an empire which is indestructible, ambitious, and denuded of everything—all this can, in effect, introduce some new conjunctures in the concerns of the Kremlin and induce it to bring a note of sincerity to the refrain it devotes to peaceful coexistence.

France, in fact, has believed for a long time that there can come a day when a real détente and even a sincere entente would permit a complete change in the relations between East and West in Europe, and she expects when this day comes . . . to make some constructive proposals with regard to peace, equilibrium, and the destiny of Europe. But for the moment she will not subscribe to any scheme arrived at over her head concerning Europe and especially Germany. . . .

Nuclear Testing

Let us move to the Moscow Agreement [the Limited Test Ban Treaty].

That the Soviets and the Anglo-Saxons should decide directly to halt their nuclear testing in space, in the atmosphere, and at sea is itself satisfying, and we sympathize with the pleasure that President Kennedy expressed the day before yesterday on the subject of this event. . . . However, the category of underground testing remains outside this agreement.

. . . the agreement changes nothing [regarding] the terrible threat that the nuclear weapons of the two rivals weighs on the world and, above all, on the peoples who do not have any. In these conditions . . . it is completely natural that a country like France, which is beginning to have the means of freeing itself from this permanent terror, should continue on this course. . . .

. . . if one day the Americans and Soviets agreed on disarmament, that is, on the destruction and controlled interdiction of their nuclear weapons, we would wholeheartedly renounce acquiring them.

[France has] propose[d] to the three other atomic powers certain initial measures of effective disarmament, in particular with regard to air and sea cosmic delivery vehicles capable of launching nuclear projectiles. What has taken place in Moscow has only confirmed her in this intention, and she plans, before the end of this year, to invite the States involved to study with her this problem, which may not yet be insoluble. . . . But . . . a simple agreement between the Soviets and the Anglo-Saxons, already invested with an incommensurable power, which continually reinforces and each day confirms their respective hegemonies, will not deter France from one day acquiring means of the same sort, without which, since the others have them, her own security and her own independence will never belong to her.

CHARLES DE GAULLE

From a Press Conference—Excerpts on China, Vietnam, and the Presidency

January 31, 1964

In a press conference on January 31, 1964, President de Gaulle explained the reasoning behind his recognition of the People's Republic of China. In his opening remarks, de Gaulle put China in historical perspective in one of those paragraphs of seminal insight that from time to time appear in his

Major Addresses, Statements, and Press Conferences of General Charles de Gaulle, May 19, 1958–January 31, 1964 (New York: French Embassy Press and Information Bureau, 1969), 246–48, 256–57.

work. De Gaulle tied the recognition of China to a larger purpose of peace in Southeast Asia. De Gaulle hoped to achieve this through a conference of the major interested powers, including China. His reasoning was that even if the conference dragged on for a long time, it would have the effect of bringing about détente in the situation. The Johnson administration, however, disliked the proposal, fearing it would feed neutralist sentiment in the uncertain situation in South Vietnam following the assassination of Ngo Dinh Diem the previous November.

In the same press conference, de Gaulle made a dithyrambic recital of the powers of the presidency.

China and Vietnam

China, a great people, the most numerous on earth, a race in which the capacity for patience, labor, and industry of its individuals has, for thousands of years, arduously compensated for its collective lack of method and cohesion, and has built a very special and profound civilization; a tremendous country, geographically compact though without unity, extending from Asia Minor and the steppes of Europe to the long shoreline of the Pacific, and from the Siberian ice to the tropical regions of India and Tonkin; a State older than history, steadily resolved upon independence, tirelessly striving for centralization, instinctively inward-looking and scornful of foreigners, but conscious and proud of an immutable duration—such is Eternal China.

Her first contact with modern nations was very abrupt and very costly. In one century, many interventions, demands, expeditions, invasions—European, American, Japanese—inflicted as many humiliations and dismemberments. These terrible national shocks, as well as the determination of her leaders to transform their country at any cost, so that she might achieve the same power and the same condition as the nations that had oppressed her, led China to revolution. . . .

It is true that Soviet Russia at first lent China considerable aid. . . . This was the period when the Kremlin, utilizing here as elsewhere its rigorous preponderance within the Communist Church to support the supremacy of Russia over the peoples whom a dictatorship similar to its own had subordinated to it, intended to keep China under its rule and thereby dominate Asia. But the illusion has been dispelled. Doubtless there still remains between the regimes in power in Moscow and in Peking a certain doctrinal solidarity that may be manifested in the world rivalry of ideologies. Yet under a cloak that is torn a little more every day, appears the inevitable difference in national policies. . . .

Given the fact that for fifteen years almost the whole of China has been gathered under a government that imposes its laws, and that externally China has shown herself to be an independent and sovereign power, France has been disposed to enter into regular relations with Peking. . . . Doubtless the force of circumstances had led us, as it had led America, England, the Soviet Union, India, and other States, to negotiate with the Chinese representatives, when in 1954 the Geneva Conference decided the fate of Indochina or when in 1962, under the same form and in the same city, the situation in Laos was somewhat defined. But the weight of evidence and of reason increasing day by day, the French Republic estimated, for its part, that the time had come to place its relations with the People's Republic of China on a normal, in other words a diplomatic, basis. We have met with an identical intention in Peking, and therefore on this point, former Premier Edgar Faure requested to make an unofficial sounding on the spot and returned to Paris with positive indications. It was then that the two States arrived at an unofficial agreement to carry out the measures necessary.

Presidency

[It is] the President . . . in accordance with our Constitution, [who] is the man of the nation, put into position by the nation itself in order to answer for its destiny; the President, who selects the Premier, who also names the other members of the Cabinet, who has the right to change the Premier . . . ; the President who sanctions the decisions taken in the councils, promulgates the laws, negotiates and signs the treaties, enacts into law or not the measures proposed to him, is the chief of the armed forces, appoints the public officials; the President who, in case of danger, should take it upon himself to do all that is necessary—the President is obviously the only one to hold and to delegate the authority of the State.

. . . the spirit of the new Constitution, while retaining a legislative parliament, consists in seeing to it that the power . . . emanates directly from the people, which implies that the Head of State, elected by the nation, is the source and holder of this power. . . . The indivisible authority of the State is entrusted completely to the President by the people who elected him. . . . There is no other authority—either ministerial, civilian, military, or judicial—that is not entrusted to and maintained by him.

CHARLES DE GAULLE

From a Press Conference—Excerpts on Monetary Policy and German Reunification

February 4, 1965

De Gaulle's biennial press conference of February 4, 1965, was notable for at least two points: his attack on the dollar and his enunciation of a long-range plan for German reunification.

De Gaulle had long felt that the myth of dollar convertibility with gold should be challenged because, as the system then stood, the United States could increase the supply of dollars at will, in effect exempting it from balancing its budget and allowing it to increase its investments abroad and, in the process, to export inflation. De Gaulle's call for a return to the gold standard, though not practical at the time, presaged the decision of the Nixon administration in 1971 to end the system of the gold exchange standard and let the dollar float against other currencies.

Of Germany, de Gaulle's vision was essentially accurate. Germany would renounce its former eastern territories on a permanent basis and would not acquire nuclear weapons. However, though the eventual German settlement of 1989–90 came about as a result of an agreement between the Big Four (the United States, Britain, France, and the USSR), the accord was basically between Chancellor Helmut Kohl and President Mikhail Gorbachev.

Monetary Policy

[A] system [of monetary relations] appeared in the aftermath of the First World War and was established following the Second. . . . This system . . . emerging from the Genoa Conference, in 1922, granted to two currencies, the pound and the dollar, the privilege of being honored as gold equivalents for all external payments, whereas the other [currencies] were not. Subsequently, when the pound was devalued in 1931 and the dollar in 1933, this arrangement appeared to have been compromised. But America survived its Depression. After this, the Second World War ruined the European currencies and set inflation in motion there. Since almost all the

Charles de Gaulle, *Discours et messages*, vol. 4, *Pour l'effort, Août 1962–Décembre 1965* (Paris: Omnibus/Plon, 1993), 910–13, 916–20.

world's gold reserves were then held by the United States, which, as supplier to the world, had been able to preserve the value of its own currency, it appeared natural that the other states would bring dollars and gold indistinguishably into their money reserves, and that their foreign exchange balances would reflect American credit instruments and currencies as well as gold. All the more so in that America had no problem settling her debts in gold if this was demanded of her. This international monetary system, this "Gold Exchange Standard," has consequently been accepted virtually since that time.

. . . The conditions that, in earlier times, brought forth the "Gold Exchange Standard" have now been modified. The currencies of the states of Western Europe are today restored, to the point where the total gold reserves of the Six are equal to those of the Americans. They would be even greater if the Six decided to transfer into precious metal all the dollars they are holding. This means that the arrangement that granted to the dollar a transcendent value as an international currency no longer rests on its original basis, that is, the possession by America of most of the world's gold reserves. But beyond this, the acceptance by many states, in principle, of dollars on the same basis as gold in order to offset deficits profitable to them in the American balance of payments enables the United States to incur debts abroad free of charge. What the United States pays, it pays in part at least in dollars, which it alone can issue, instead of paying them completely in gold, which has real value. . . . This unilateral facility that is granted to America contributes to blurring the idea that the dollar is an impartial and international instrument of exchange, whereas [in fact] it is a method of credit appropriated to a [single] state.

Obviously, there are other consequences to this situation. There is in particular the fact that the United States—not having to settle, at least totally, its negative payment balances in gold, according to the former rules that impelled states to take the necessary measures, sometimes rigorous ones, to correct their disequilibrium—undergoes year after year a budget deficit. Not that it has a negative commercial balance. Quite the contrary! Its exports of materials always exceed its imports. But it is also the case for dollars, more of which go abroad than come back. In other words, there is created in America, by means that should be called inflation, capital in the form of loans in dollars to states or private individuals, which is exported abroad. Since the increase in the money supply resulting from this makes investment internally in the United States less profitable, there is a growing American propensity to invest abroad. As a consequence, certain countries undergo a sort of expropriation of a number of their own enterprises.

. . . The circumstances are such today that one could well wonder how much trouble would be caused if all the states holding dollars would sooner or later wish to convert them into gold. . . . For all these reasons, France is advocating that the system be changed. . . . We consider it necessary that all international exchanges be established . . . on an indisputable monetary basis not bearing the stamp of any particular country.

[On] what basis? In truth, one cannot see in this regard that there should be any other criterion, or standard, than gold. . . . Certainly the ending, without rude shocks, of the "Gold Exchange Standard," and the restoration of the gold standard, the complementary measures and transitional steps that would be necessary, particularly the organization of international credit on this new basis, should be a matter of careful coordination among the states, notably those whose economic and financial capability gives them a particular responsibility.

German Reunification

For France, everything comes down to three [action] issues, closely linked: (a) act in such a way that Germany henceforth is an element of progress and peace; (b) under such conditions, help in its reunification; (c) take the path and choose the framework that will bring this about.

. . . It is clear that real peace, and even more so, fruitful relations between West and East, will not be established as long as there are the German anomalies, the worries that they cause, and the trials that they bring. . . . The problem . . . will not be solved out of the confrontation between the ideologies and the forces that oppose each other today in the world. What needs to be done cannot be done, except by the entente and the concerted action of the peoples who have always been, who are, and who will remain principally interested in the fate of the German neighbors—in brief, the European people. The latter should envisage first examining together, then settling together in common, in order to jointly guarantee, the solution to a question that is essentially that of their continent; this is the only way that can bring rebirth; this is the only link that can maintain a Europe in a state of equilibrium, of peace, and of cooperation from one end to the other of the territory that nature has granted it.

Clearly, the success of so vast and so difficult an enterprise implies many conditions. It is a matter of whether Russia can evolve in such a way that it sees its future no longer in the totalitarian constraints imposed upon itself and upon others, but in the progress accomplished in common by free men and free peoples. It is a matter of whether the nations that she has made satellites will be able to play their role in a renewed Europe. It is a matter of whether Germany especially can recognize that a settlement involving it would necessarily include its frontiers and its armaments, as agreed to by all of its neighbors, East and West. It is a matter of whether the six states that, let us hope, are in the process of achieving the economic community of Western Europe, will succeed in organizing themselves in the political area and that of defense, in order to make possible a new equilibrium for our continent. It is a matter of whether Europe, mother of modern civilization, can establish itself from the Atlantic to the Urals in peace and cooperation, with a view to the development of its immense resources and in a way to play, jointly with its daughter America, the role that is incumbent on it with regard to the progress of the two billion men who are terribly in need of it. What a part Germany could play in this world ambition of a rejuvenated Ancient Continent![21]

CHARLES DE GAULLE

From a Speech in Phnom Penh, Cambodia
September 1, 1966

In what was perhaps his most aggressively "Third World" speech, Charles de Gaulle addressed a crowd of some eighty thousand people at the National Sports Stadium in Phnom Penh on September 1, 1966. De Gaulle described how France was better off for having left its former colonial territories and exhorted the United States to follow suit in Vietnam.

The example [France] gave previously in North Africa, in bringing deliberately to an end a sterile combat on a terrain that, however, her forces uncontestedly dominated, that she [had] administered directly for 132 years and where more than a million of her children were settled. But since this combat engaged neither her well-being nor her independence,

Charles de Gaulle, *Discours et messages*, vol. 5, *Vers le terme, Février 1966–Avril 1969* (Paris: Plon, 1970), 76.

and in the epoch in which we live could lead to nothing but ever increasing losses, hatreds, and destruction, she willed and was able to withdraw from it, without—quite the contrary—her prestige, her power, and her prosperity having suffered.

. . . The policy of neutrality, which flowed from the [1954 Geneva] accords, alone could have spared Indochina from becoming a terrain of confrontation between rival dominations and ideologies and a solicitation for American intervention. . . . One saw the political and military authority of the United States become established in South Vietnam and, at the same time, the war resuming under the form of a national resistance. After this, illusions relative to the use of force led to the continued reinforcement of the expeditionary corps and a more and more extended escalation in Asia, closer and closer to China, more and more provocative with regard to the Soviet Union, more and more disapproved by a number of people in Europe, Africa, and Latin America, and, in the final analysis, more and more threatening for the peace of the world.

9

The Legacy

MICHEL DROIT

From an Interview with de Gaulle

June 7, 1968

On June 7, 1968, following a month of uprising in Paris that finally died down at the end of May, President de Gaulle gave an interview to the journalist Michel Droit, whom de Gaulle had used before to get across his point of view. When Droit asked de Gaulle why he had left Paris and gone incommunicado to Baden-Baden for several hours on May 29, the General recounted a number of setbacks in his life that had led him to contemplate, at least temporarily, abandoning his responsibilities. This series of events began with the fall of France in 1940. (At two points in his life, de Gaulle actually did step away from his responsibilities: when he left as head of the provisional government in January 1946, and when he resigned as chief of state in April 1969.)

MICHEL DROIT: France has just gone through an internal crisis, political and social, without precedent since the beginning of the century. . . . I would like . . . to pose to you most of the questions that would burn the lips of most Frenchmen if they found themselves in front of you.

    The first of these questions touches directly on what we have just gone through. I think that all observers are in agreement; the two days

Charles de Gaulle, *Discours et messages*, vol. 5, *Vers le terme, Février 1966–Avril 1969* (Paris: Omnibus/Plon, 1993), 1082.

that have been decisive in the crisis until now are those in which you took the personal initiative of operations, that is, the day of Wednesday, May 29, when you left Paris, and that of the day of Thursday, May 30, when you returned to Paris to address the country. Therefore, what I wanted to ask you is this, General: Why did you leave Paris on May 29? What was on your mind when you said [in your speech of May 30], "I envisaged all eventualities." What exactly did you mean by that, and could it have gone as far as your departure, your definitive retirement? Finally, after what analysis did you arrive at the conclusions that you announced to the French people on the evening of Thursday, May 30?

GENERAL DE GAULLE: Yes! On May 29 I was tempted to withdraw. And at the same time, I thought that, if I left, threatening subversion would descend on and carry away the Republic. So, once again, I resolved [to continue].

You know, in the something like thirty years since I have been identified with History, it has occurred to me sometimes to ask myself if I shouldn't leave it. This was the case, for example, in September 1940, after Dakar, when my companions, after having absorbed the fire of French forces who shot at the Free French, whereas the enemy was at Paris, I doubted whether we could ever turn them against the invader of France. It was the case in London, in March 1942, when, in the face of a dissidence within Free France, a dissidence in which the British Government had been the accomplice if not the instigator, I went out into the English countryside, letting it be known that I would not pursue my enterprise on the side of Great Britain if my conditions were not accepted. It was the case in 1946, when, submerged by the sterile torrent of [political] parties over whom I had no hold, and not being able to act any more in the position that I held, I left it. It was the case in 1954, when I saw the *Rassemblement* that I had formed and which was in the process of coming apart; at that point I left it and returned to my home. It was the case on the evening of the first round of the presidential election [of 1965], when a wave of sadness nearly carried me far away.

And so, on May 29, I put questions to myself and then, on May 30, having said to the country what I had to say to it and having received its response in the form of an immense human sea on [the place de] la Concorde and the Champs-Elysées, and then of all the magnificent parades that took place in so many cities, I understood that my call had given the signal of salvation, and I felt fortified in my resolve by the will of the French [people].

CHARLES DE GAULLE

Description of Greatness

July 1932

Although the referendum of April 27, 1969, did not appear to be on a fundamental issue, de Gaulle saw it as a vote of no confidence. On the day after the vote went against him, he resigned. In an uncanny prefiguration of that scene, de Gaulle had written the following description of greatness nearly forty years before.

Aloofness, character, and the personification of greatness, these qualities . . . surround with prestige those who are prepared to carry a burden which is too heavy for lesser mortals. The price they have to pay for leadership is unceasing self-discipline, the constant taking of risks, and a perpetual inner struggle. The degree of suffering involved varies according to the temperament of the individual; but it is bound to be no less tormenting than the hair shirt of the penitent. This helps to explain those cases of withdrawal which, otherwise, are so hard to understand. It constantly happens that men with an unbroken record of success and public applause suddenly lay the burden down. . . . Contentment and tranquility and the simple joys which go by the name of happiness are denied to those who fill positions of power. The choice must be made, and it is a hard one: whence that vague sense of melancholy which hangs about the skirts of majesty. . . . One day somebody said to Napoléon, as they were looking at an old and noble monument: "How sad it is!" "Yes," came the reply, "as sad as greatness."

Charles de Gaulle, *The Edge of the Sword*, trans. Gerard Hopkins (Westport, Conn.: Greenwood, 1960), 65–66.

CHARLES DE GAULLE

"For My Funeral"

Written Will, January 16, 1952

On January 16, 1952, Charles de Gaulle drafted his last will and testament, an action that was prompted by the pomp associated with the recent funeral of his wartime associate General Jean de Lattre de Tassigny. De Gaulle wanted an extremely simple funeral in the church at Colombey-les-Deux-Eglises, and to be buried in the adjacent cemetery next to his retarded daughter, Anne, who had died in 1948. He wanted no national ceremony; only family members, his wartime "compagnons of the Liberation," and members of the local municipal council were to have reserved places at the funeral. As the years passed, he neither changed the will nor the recipients of the copies: his son Philippe, his daughter Mrs. Alain de Boissieu, and Georges Pompidou (despite the strain that developed between Pompidou and the General after the events of May 1968).

De Gaulle's wishes were respected in the spirit but not in the letter. He died of a sudden abdominal aneurysm on the evening of November 9, 1970, at home in the company of his wife, Yvonne. As specified by his wife, he was dressed in a uniform, and a rosary given to him by Pope Paul VI was placed in his hands. Yvonne de Gaulle burned his bedclothes and assorted garments; she wanted no "relics," though she kept his kepi, his greatcoat, and his decorations, which were given to the Museum of the Liberation.

Very few people were allowed to see the body before the casket was closed. The funeral ceremony was held at the church; de Gaulle's nephew François, bishop of Langres, was one of the presiding clergy.

Meantime, on the same day, November 12, a solemn mass was celebrated at the Cathedral of Notre Dame in Paris. This symbolic event (since there was no catafalque) was attended by President Georges Pompidou, President Richard Nixon, former prime ministers Anthony Eden and Harold Macmillan, and other chiefs of state and prominent persons.

I want my funeral to be held at Colombey-les-Deux-Eglises. If I die elsewhere, my body should be transported to my home, without any public ceremony.

Charles de Gaulle, *Lettres, notes, et carnets*, vol. 7 (Paris: Plon, 1985), 58–59. The headnote is based on Jean Lacouture, *De Gaulle*, vol. 3, *Le souverain* (Paris: Seuil, 1984), 786–97.

My grave will be where my daughter Anne already lies and where one day my wife will lie. Inscription: Charles de Gaulle (1890–   ). Nothing else.

The ceremony will be organized by my son, my daughter, my son-in-law, my daughter-in-law, assisted by my advisers, in such a way that it will be extremely simple. I do not want a national funeral. Neither president, nor ministers, nor committees of the assemblies, nor constituent bodies. Only the armed services will be able to participate as such; but their participation will have to be of a very modest dimension, without music, without fanfares, without bugles.

No speech should be made, either at the Church or elsewhere. No funeral oration in Parliament. No reserved seating during the ceremony, except for my family, for my *Companions,* members of the Order of Liberation, [and] for the municipal council of Colombey. If the men and women of France and other countries wish to honor my memory, they will be able to accompany my body to its last resting place. But I desire that it be taken there in silence.

I am declaring my refusal in advance of all distinction, promotion, dignity, citation, decoration, whether it be French or foreign. If one were conferred on me, this would be in violation of my last wishes.

A de Gaulle Chronology
(1890–1970)

1890

November 22:   Charles de Gaulle is born at Lille, the son of Henri de Gaulle and Jeanne Maillot de Gaulle.

1909

September 30:   De Gaulle enters St. Cyr Military Academy.

1914

August 3:   Britain declares war on Germany.
August 4:   France declares war on Germany.

1916

March 2:   De Gaulle is wounded and taken prisoner at Fort Douaumont, near Verdun.

1918

November 11:   Armistice ends World War I.

1919

September: De Gaulle is assigned to the French military mission in Poland.

1921

February: De Gaulle is named professor of history at St. Cyr.
April 6:   De Gaulle marries Yvonne Vendroux.

1922

De Gaulle's first book, *La discorde chez l'ennemi* (*The Enemy's Dissensions*), is published.

1925

July: De Gaulle is assigned to the staff of Marshal Pétain, vice president of the Supreme War Council.

1929

October: De Gaulle is assigned to the French army of the Levant, in Lebanon.

1931

November: De Gaulle is assigned to the General Secretariat of National Defense.

1932

July: De Gaulle's second book, *Le fil de l'épée (The Edge of the Sword)*, is published.

1933

March: Hitler is named chancellor of Germany.

1934

May 5:   De Gaulle's *Vers l'armée de métier (The Army of the Future)* is published.

1935

October 2:   Mussolini invades Ethiopia.
December 5:   De Gaulle meets Paul Reynaud through a Paris journalist, Jean Auburtin.

1936

March 7:   Hitler sends troops into the Rhineland, which was demilitarized by the Treaty of Versailles.
July 17:   Outbreak of civil war in Spain.

1937

September: De Gaulle is assigned command of the 507th Tank Regiment at Metz.

1938

March 12:   Hitler takes over Austria.
September: De Gaulle's book *La France et son armée (France and Her Army)* is published after a dispute with Marshal Pétain over its authorship. Munich crisis; Sudetenland is ceded to Germany.

1939

March 15:   Hitler invades the rest of Czechoslovakia.

March 31: Britain gives a guarantee to Poland.
September 1: Germany invades Poland.
September 2: De Gaulle is named commander of tanks of the Fifth Army.
September 3: Britain and then France declare war on Germany.

1940

January 21: De Gaulle addresses a memorandum to eighty civilian and military persons in France on the urgency of creating an armored strike force.
March 21: Paul Reynaud becomes French premier.
March 28: Britain and France mutually pledge not to make a separate peace with Germany.
April 9: Hitler invades Denmark and Norway.
April 24: De Gaulle is named commander of the Fourth Armored Division, which is in the process of being formed.
May 10: Hitler invades the Low Countries and France. Rout of French forces in the midst of a few isolated French successes, notably under de Gaulle's command.
June 1: De Gaulle is named temporary brigadier general.
June 5: De Gaulle is named under secretary of state for national defense and war in the cabinet of Paul Reynaud.
June 16: Marshal Pétain is named prime minister.
June 18: De Gaulle appeals from London for a continuation of the struggle.
June 22: France signs armistice with Germany.
June 28: De Gaulle is recognized as chief of the Free French by the British government.
July 3: The French fleet is attacked by British warships at Mers-el-Kebir.
July 10: The French National Assembly turns over full powers to Pétain.
August 4: De Gaulle is condemned to death in absentia by the French court at Clermont-Ferrand.
August 30: The Anglo–Free French attempt to capture Dakar fails.
October: Discriminatory laws against the Jews in France are promulgated by Vichy.
October 24: Hitler and Pétain meet at Montoire.
October 27: The Council of the French Empire is established by de Gaulle.

1941

June 22: Hitler invades USSR.
August 14: Atlantic Charter is signed between the United States and Great Britain.
September 24: The French National Committee is established by de Gaulle in London.
December 7: The Japanese attack the U.S. fleet at Pearl Harbor, bringing the United States into the war.
December 10: Germany and Italy declare war on the United States.

1942

May–June: The Battle of Bir Hakeim constitutes the first significant Free French engagement in the war.
November 8:   The Allies invade North Africa.
November 11:   The Germans occupy the rest of France.
November 27:   The French fleet is scuttled at Toulon.
December 24:   Admiral Darlan is assassinated at Algiers.

1943

January: At Casablanca Conference Generals de Gaulle and Giraud shake hands, stiffly.
February: The Germans are defeated at Stalingrad.
February 21:   Jean Moulin is charged with leading the National Council of the Resistance.
June 3:   The French Committee of National Liberation is formed at Algiers by de Gaulle and Giraud.
June 21:   Jean Moulin is arrested near Lyons and later dies under German torture.
September 17:   The Consultative Assembly of the Resistance is formed in Algiers.

1944

January 30:   De Gaulle opens the Brazzaville Conference and calls for eventual emancipation of Africa.
June 3:   The Provisional Government of the French Republic is formed.
June 6:   D-day begins the invasion of Normandy.
June 14:   De Gaulle arrives in France at Bayeux.
August 25:   The French Second Armored Division takes Paris.
August 26:   De Gaulle leads a parade on the Champs-Elysées.
September 8:   De Gaulle forms a government in France.
December 10:   The French-Soviet friendship treaty is signed.

1945

February 8:   The Yalta Conference opens, without France.
May 7:   V-E Day marks the end of the War in Europe.

1946

January 20:   De Gaulle resigns as head of government.
June 16:   De Gaulle gives speech at Bayeux.
October 13:   Referendum approves new constitution.

1947

April 7:   De Gaulle forms a political movement (Rally for the French People).

1949

April 4: The North Atlantic Treaty is signed.

1954

August 30: The French National Assembly rejects the European Defense Community.

October 22: De Gaulle's *War Memoirs* (vol. 1) is published.

December 30: The National Assembly approves the Paris Accords on German rearmament in NATO.

1958

May 13: The Committee of Public Safety in Algiers calls for de Gaulle's return to power.

June 1: The National Assembly votes de Gaulle into power, 329–224.

September 28: The new constitution receives approval by 80 percent of the votes.

December 21: De Gaulle is elected president.

1960

January: "Revolt of the barricades" occurs in Algiers.

May: The Big Four summit fails after the U-2 incident.

1961

February 8: The referendum on self-determination for Algeria passes with 75 percent in favor.

February 11: Meetings begin on the Fouchet Plan.

April 22: Four ex-generals stage a putsch in Algiers.

May 20: French-Algerian Evian talks open.

August 4: Britain applies to the Common Market.

August 13: The Berlin Wall goes up.

1962

March 18: The Evian Accords on Algeria are signed.

April 8: The Evian Accords pass by referendum.

April 17: The Fouchet Plan is rejected.

August 22: Attack at Petit-Clamart; de Gaulle and his family are unharmed.

October: The Cuban missile crisis occurs.

November 18: A referendum passes on the election of the president by universal suffrage.

1963

January 14: De Gaulle rejects the British EEC entry and the American offer of Polaris missiles.

January 22: The French-German cooperation treaty is signed.
April 16: The German Parliament adds a modifying preamble to the French-German treaty.
August 3: The USSR, the United States, and Britain sign a nuclear test ban treaty.
November 22: John F. Kennedy is assassinated.

1964

January 27: France recognizes the People's Republic of China.

1965

February 4: De Gaulle launches an attack on the dollar.
June 30: France begins its "empty chair" boycott of EEC.
December 19: De Gaulle wins the second round of presidential elections over Mitterrand.

1966

March 7: France withdraws from the integrated military structure of NATO.
May 11: The Common Agricultural Policy agreement ends France's boycott of the EEC.
September 1: De Gaulle attacks U.S. Vietnam policy in a speech at Phnom Penh.
October 26: NATO headquarters move to Brussels.

1967

January: The British again apply to the EEC.
March 12: Legislative elections leave de Gaulle supporters with only a three-seat majority.
June 5: Israel launches the Six Day War; France places embargo on arms to belligerents.

1968

May: Student uprisings are held in Paris.
May 24: De Gaulle announces a referendum on "participation."
May 30: The referendum is discarded in favor of new legislative elections.
June 30: The government wins 365 of 485 seats.
July 10: De Gaulle replaces Pompidou with Couve de Murville as prime minister.

1969

April 4: De Gaulle renews France's membership in the Atlantic Alliance.
April 27: The referendum on regionalization and reform of the Senate is defeated by 53 percent of the voters.

April 28: De Gaulle resigns.

June 15: Georges Pompidou is elected president.

1970

October 23: De Gaulle's *Memoirs of Hope* (vol. 1) is published.

November 9: General de Gaulle dies.

November 12: An official ceremony is held at the Cathedral of Notre Dame; de Gaulle is buried privately at Colombey.

Questions for Consideration

1. Compare and contrast the Gaullist concept of "legitimacy" and the concept of "legality" in the Anglo-American sense.
2. Was de Gaulle justified in claiming to represent the legitimacy of the French state?
3. Do you think that Vichy forfeited its claim to the representation of the French state because of its collaboration with the Germans and its espousal of Nazi policies?
4. Stanley Hoffmann has pointed out that there were many political strands in the Vichy regime. By no means were all participants fascists and pro-Germans. There were notables, there were technocrats, there was corporatism and Catholic social thought represented in Vichy, as well as the bulk of the French military. Many in the Vichy regime were anti-German. Was the regime as a whole compromised because of Vichy's policies toward the Jews?
5. Was the United States justified in invoking the indivisibility of the defense of the West and therefore its command over the integrated military structure of NATO? How much did this doctrine mask a quest for hegemony?
6. Was de Gaulle following a realistic and prudent policy by deciding to equip France with an independent nuclear strike force?
7. Discuss de Gaulle's Algeria policy. Was it correct to cause the expulsion or departure of one million Europeans from a country in which France had been present since 1830?
8. Do you consider de Gaulle to have been basically an autocrat behind a mask of adherence to "republican legality"?
9. Do you believe that the experience of "cohabitation" has fundamentally altered the position of the president as envisaged in the present French constitution?
10. Do you think that de Gaulle's record shows him to have been too difficult a personality for other world leaders to deal with on an effective and systematic basis?
11. Discuss de Gaulle's attack on the dollar in 1965. Was this a fair appraisal of the undue advantage the United States had gained because of the monetary position of the dollar? Or was de Gaulle displaying an insufficient

appreciation of the responsibilities the United States had shouldered for the defense of the free world during the cold war?

12. From the point of view of the future cohesion and unity of Europe, was de Gaulle justified in twice rejecting Britain's application to the Common Market?

13. Assess the motivation behind the policies that de Gaulle adopted before, during, and in the wake of the Arab-Israeli war of 1967.

14. Discuss whether de Gaulle's recognition of China and his call for neutralization of Southeast Asia was harmful to the aims of U.S. policy.

15. What do you consider to have been de Gaulle's most important contribution?

Suggestions for Further Reading

Andrews, William G., and Stanley Hoffmann, eds. *The Impact of the Fifth Republic in France.* Albany, N.Y.: State University of New York Press, 1981.

De Gaulle, Charles. *The Army of the Future.* Philadelphia: Lippincott, 1941.

———. *The Complete War Memoirs of Charles de Gaulle.* 3 vols. Translated by Jonathan Griffin (vol. 1), Richard Howard (vols. 2 and 3). New York: Simon and Schuster, 1964.

———. *The Edge of the Sword.* Translated by Gerard Hopkins. Westport, Conn.: Greenwood, 1960.

———. *Memoirs of Hope: Renewal and Endeavor.* Translated by Terence Kilmartin. New York: Simon and Schuster, 1971.

Gordon, Philip H. *A Certain Idea of France: French Security Policy and the Gaullist Legacy.* Princeton, N.J.: Princeton University Press, 1993.

Grosser, Alfred. *The Western Alliance.* New York: Continuum, 1980.

Hoffmann, Stanley. *Decline or Renewal? France since the 1930s.* New York: Viking, 1974.

———. "The Foreign Policy of Charles de Gaulle." In *The Diplomats, 1939–1979,* edited by Gordon A. Craig and Francis L. Loewenheim. Princeton, N.J.: Princeton University Press, 1994.

———. *In Search of France.* Cambridge: Harvard University Press, 1963.

———. "The Nation, Nationalisms, and After: The Case of France." In *The Tanner Lectures on Human Values,* vol. 15, edited by Grethe B. Peterson. Salt Lake City: University of Utah Press, 1994.

Horne, Alastair. *A Savage War of Peace: Algeria, 1954–1962.* Hong Kong: Elisabeth Sifton Books–Penguin Books, 1977.

Hurstfield, Julian G. *America and the French Nation, 1939–1945.* Chapel Hill, N.C.: University of North Carolina Press, 1986.

Kissinger, Henry A. *The Troubled Partnership: A Reappraisal of the Atlantic Alliance.* New York: McGraw-Hill, 1965.

———. *Years of Upheaval.* Boston: Little, Brown, 1982.

Kuisel, Richard F. *Seducing the French: The Dilemma of Americanization.* Berkeley: University of California Press, 1993.

Lacouture, Jean. *De Gaulle.* 2 vols. Translated by Patrick O'Brian (vol. 1) and Alan Sheridan (vol. 2). New York: Simon and Schuster, 1991, 1992.

Laloy, Jean. *Yalta: Yesterday, Today, Tomorrow.* Translated by William R. Tyler. New York: Harper and Row, 1988.

Langer, William L. *Our Vichy Gamble.* New York: Knopf, 1947.

Marrus, Michael R., and Robert D. Paxton. *Vichy France and the Jews.* New York: Basic Books, 1981.

Monnet, Jean. *Memoirs.* Garden City, N.Y.: Doubleday, 1978.

Paxton, Robert D., and Nicholas Wahl, eds. *De Gaulle and the United States: A Centennial Reappraisal.* Providence, R.I.: Berg, 1993.

Vaïsse, Maurice. "France and the Suez Crisis." In *Suez 1956: The Crisis and Its Consequences,* edited by William Roger Louis and Roger Owen. Oxford: Clarendon Press, 1989.

Wall, Irwin M. *The United States and the Making of Postwar France, 1945–54.* Cambridge: Cambridge University Press, 1991.

The Gaullist Itinerary

Above: 1940: France is overrun by Germany and three-fifths of the country is occupied. Note demarcation line between occupied and free zones (broken line).

Right: 1945: France emerges as one of the victors over Germany and is accorded its own occupation zone, alongside of the U.S. and British zones.

1. GREATER HESSE
2. WUERTTEMBERG-BADEN
3. BAVARIA

France Today

Index

Pages with illustrations are indicated by italics.